Arts Therapies
and Sexual Offending

also edited by Marian Liebmann

Art Therapy with Physical Conditions
Edited by Marian Liebmann and Sally Weston
Foreword by Trevor Thompson
ISBN 978 1 84905 349 5
eISBN 978 0 85700 911 1

Art Therapy with Neurological Conditions
Edited by Marian Liebmann and Sally Weston
Foreword by Jackie Ashley
ISBN 978 1 84905 348 8
eISBN 978 0 85700 912 8

Art Therapy and Anger
Edited by Marian Liebmann
ISBN 978 1 84310 425 4
eISBN 978 1 84642 810 4

Mediation in Context
Edited by Marian Liebmann
ISBN 978 1 85302 618 8
eISBN 978 0 85700 580 9

Art Therapy, Race and Culture
*Edited by Jean Campbell, Marian Liebmann, Frederica
Brooks, Jenny Jones and Cathy Ward*
Foreword by Suman Fernando
ISBN 978 1 85302 578 5
eISBN 978 0 85700 234 1

Arts Approaches to Conflict
Edited by Marian Liebmann
ISBN 978 1 85302 293 7

Art Therapy with Offenders
Edited by Marian Liebmann
ISBN 978 1 85302 171 8
eISBN 978 1 84642 987 3

Art Therapy in Practice
Edited by Marian Liebmann
ISBN 978 1 85302 058 2
eISBN 978 1 84642 985 9

Arts Therapies
and Sexual Offending

Edited by
SIMON HASTILOW
and MARIAN LIEBMANN

Foreword by Stanley Ruszczynski

Jessica Kingsley Publishers
London and Philadelphia

First published in Great Britain in 2021 by Jessica Kingsley Publishers
An Hachette Company

1

Copyright © Jessica Kingsley Publishers 2021
Foreword copyright © Stanley Ruszczynski 2021

Front cover image photographed by Willie Derks Photography

A CIP catalogue record for this title is available from the
British Library and the Library of Congress

ISBN 978 1 78775 064 7
eISBN 978 1 78775 065 4

Printed and bound in Great Britain by CPI Group

Jessica Kingsley Publishers' policy is to use papers that are natural,
renewable and recyclable products and made from wood grown in
sustainable forests. The logging and manufacturing processes are expected
to conform to the environmental regulations of the country of origin.

Jessica Kingsley Publishers
Carmelite House
50 Victoria Embankment
London EC4Y 0DZ

www.jkp.com

Contents

List of Figures

Foreword

It is probably generally agreed that the most difficult patients and clients in the care of the criminal justice system and the forensic services are sex offenders. Because of the nature of their offending they are described as disturbed and difficult, but more accurately we should describe them as disturbing, because their behaviour often arouses difficult feelings in most of us, including in the staff who work with them. Because of these disturbing feelings aroused in us, such offenders are often demonized, marginalized and not considered worthy of care and treatment.

The sexual offence is always an act of aggression, emotional and physical, with the aggression being sexualized into what Robert Stoller called 'an erotic form of hatred' (Stoller 2018, p.4). The sexual offender, by definition, is attacking the most intimate, vulnerable and private part of the victim – the sexual body, which is rooted in early infantile experiences with the parental caregivers. With child victims, the sexual offender is also attacking the child's age-appropriate innocence, and inherent need to trust the dependency on and safe attachment to adults. Such safe dependency and attachment are necessary so as to experience the developmental importance of recognizing the indisputability of our human need to manage dependence and to recognize generational differences. Without these there is likely to develop a narcissistic and antisocial personality structure, with major problems in developing healthy relationships.

It is likely that the sexual offender, especially the child sexual offender, is demonstrating that his/her emotional vulnerability is at the most primitive bodily level where language did not exist and the abuse and neglect remained in the experience of the vulnerable physical body.

We know that most sex offenders were themselves the victims of emotional, sexual and/or physical abuse. This absence of reasonable parental care leaves the infant not only without the experience of having been cared for, but also of having been the victim of the parental difficulties and traumas. As a result, there has been little experience of having difficult emotional states understood and managed and therefore eventually learning to do so for oneself. Hence, unconsciously reversing this interaction through an identification with the aggressor and the neglecter and becoming the aggressor or neglecter and 'creating' a victim in the person they have attacked, is often the unconscious psychological escape from their unbearable experience of having been neglected and abused.

Such evacuative behaviour becomes the only form of communication because the use of language is missing or compromised. The lack of an internal thinking space results in the likelihood that the offender will use surrounding external space, especially other people, to externalize unbearable internal states. In doing so, by emotionally projective processes and actual behaviours, the other becomes the one feeling the unbearable emotional states.

If such patients and offenders enact their internal states, then in the clinical situation the practitioner, in his/her affective response is likely to become the recipient of that projective process. From a clinical perspective, therefore, the clinician needs to have a setting and develop a stance in which this projective and sometimes behavioural emotional evacuation can be experienced, understood, thought about and eventually used to inform comments and understandings offered to the patient/offender.

In the more traditional psychological talking therapies, the transference–countertransference relationship is the arena for that re-emergence of these unconscious unbearable states. The practitioner makes him/herself available to be the recipient of the projection of these internal states and by paying careful attention to the feelings projected into the therapist, the countertransference, some access may eventually be gained to what cannot be spoken. It could be said that such a clinician offers him/herself as the canvas or screen onto which the patient will unconsciously project his/her unbearable emotional states. Coming to understand what is being written or drawn on that canvas becomes the information by which the patient's internal world might come to be understood.

Many of the papers in this collection describe work with art therapy, but also cover dramatherapy, music therapy and dance movement therapy. They describe work in the prison system, in secure psychiatric settings and in the community. In each case offenders are offered a setting in which they can make use of a form of therapeutic engagement through which they can express something of themselves in the use they make of the particular 'arts therapy' experience being offered.

In these settings, the creative process itself has the potential to become the vehicle by which the offender will unconsciously express internal states that cannot be verbalized. The 'artwork', whether that is drawing, painting, movement, making music, role-play acting or writing a story, becomes the vehicle for the behavioural expression of internal states that cannot be verbalized directly. It is relevant to say that these interventions take place in the context of a relationship with the arts therapist, a relationship that creates the boundaried setting for the patient's self-expression.

The skill of the arts therapist is twofold. The therapist has to have a skill and capacity in the particular art form that is being used, and the ability to read, understand, interpret and then be able to facilitate joint exploration of what the patient might be unconsciously feeling and expressing in the art work being done.

The papers in this collection clearly and vividly show this double capacity in action with often very demanding and disturbing offenders. The medium of the art form is repeatedly shown to have that capacity to invite and allow the offender to express that which is considered to be most inexpressible because it is unbearable. The arts therapist's receptivity to this communication enables the beginnings of some understanding to emerge, and begins the very slow and often long process of allowing the offender to believe that unbearable infantile states can be communicated, heard, understood and used to learn from. Thoughtfulness can slowly begin to replace action as a way of being with oneself and with others.

Stanley Ruszczynski, Psychoanalyst, Consultant Adult Psychotherapist (past Clinical Director, 2005–2016), Portman Clinic, Tavistock and Portman NHS Foundation Trust

Reference
Stoller, R.J. (2018) *Perversion: The Erotic Form of Hatred*. London: Routledge.

Acknowledgements

There are numerous people who have contributed to this book coming into being. We are grateful to them all, but there are a few who require a special mention. We would like to thank Jo Beaton for her advice and guidance in relation to supporting our thinking around current sex offender treatment. We would like to thank Emma Allen, Rosy Marshall and Katie Smith, who contributed draft chapters for this book that were unable to be included for various reasons. We thank JKP for their ongoing support and advice. Most importantly we would like to thank all the men and women who generously consented for their therapy work to be written about, and without whose commitment to engaging in therapy there would be no book.

Introduction

MARIAN LIEBMANN

Setting the scene

Sex offenders must be the most reviled group in society. They are seen as the 'lowest of the low', kicked and beaten if discovered, thought of as people who can't change and on whom it is pointless to spend any effort. In prison they have to be segregated for their own safety, and are mostly held in Vulnerable Prisoner Units, or whole prisons allocated to sex offenders. A paediatrician, mistaken for a paedophile by an ignorant person, had excrement and firebrands posted through her letterbox, and had to move to a new house.

And yet sex offending is also part of many cultures. It is not so very long (2003) since forced sex within marriage was designated as rape in England and Wales, after a landmark ruling in the House of Lords in 1991, followed by the Sexual Offences Act 2003 (Law Commission 1992; 'When did marital rape become a crime?' 2018); previously sex was seen as a man's 'conjugal right'. And child abuse of many kinds has proved to be rife across classes and generations. I was shocked to hear from a social worker friend in about 1970, covering a country area of the UK, that it was quite usual for father–daughter incest to take place, with the rationale that 'it's nice if your first child is your dad's'.

Times have changed, and we are now much more aware of the damage done by child sex abuse, rape and other sex offences. Indeed, much mental illness can be traced back to 'adverse childhood experiences' (ACE), much of which is child sex abuse. And many more people are coming forward to tell of their experiences in children's homes, boarding schools and church institutions. It is acknowledged that there is still a long way to go to put right the harm done in these places. This has been given impetus by the 'Me Too' movement highlighting historical sex abuse in media situations, including many famous people and high-ranking institutions.

It is worth noting that the term 'sex offences' covers a wide range of behaviours. At the most serious end, perpetrators include child molesters, rapists and sexual killers, while at the least serious end we may be talking about indecent assaults involving putting an unwanted arm around someone or shouting indecent phrases at people. The word 'paedophile' is usually taken to mean a serious offender, although technically it means someone sexually attracted to children, who may or may not act on this.

There is considerable debate about terminology. The most common term in use is 'sex offender' or 'sexual offender' (both of these are used by contributors to this book), but there is also a move to use less stigmatizing language, to acknowledge the fact that this may be a significant part of someone's life but is not their total identity. This makes a distinction between the person and the offence. A term used in some institutions is 'men who have committed sexual offences' (MCSOs). In line with this we changed the original title of this book, *Arts Therapies with Sex Offenders*, to *Arts Therapies and Sexual Offending*.

Most sex offenders are men, but there are some women who offend sexually, and we have included one chapter about a woman offender.

Literature review: Some common themes

Looking at the literature regarding arts therapists working with sexual offending over the past 30 years, two aspects become apparent. First, as some of the writers themselves comment, there is a paucity of literature from the arts therapies with this client group (Ackerman 1992; McKenzie, Chisholm and Murray 2000). Second, several common themes surface time and again, regardless of the modality.

Kaser (1991) writes about the physical nature of using a drum kit in music therapy sessions, leading to improved coordination, better body awareness, a sense of control and a cathartic experience. This is echoed by Skaggs (1997), commenting on how arts forms generally can involve bodily movement, making a link to the physical aspect of being sexually abused, evoking memories and feelings.

Other writers have highlighted the significance of a non-verbal component in therapy, whether art, music or dance movement, where there has been pre-verbal trauma (Mazloomian and Moon 2007; Skaggs 1997; Watson 2002). Writing as a music therapist, Watson (2002) reflects on common goals in work with sex offenders, such as social interaction, building intimacy skills, listening to others, stress management, tolerance of others, regulating emotions and increasing the ability in turn-taking. Some of these are echoed by Ackerman (1992) writing an individual case study of art therapy with a man convicted of sexual offences against children. He identifies improved self-concept, self-efficacy and body image. The client also reduced his reported somatic complaints and increased his emotional expression.

McKenzie *et al.* (2000) reported the aims and themes in therapy being guided by psychology literature but the method being guided by art therapy. This was useful for participants to become more emotionally articulate. The artwork helped them to access thoughts and feelings. The thought that engaging in arts therapies promotes emotional intelligence is highlighted throughout the literature (Aulich 1994; Hagood 1994; Skaggs 1997). For some, the development of an increased capacity to name and express feelings was a prerequisite to developing empathy, a key aim in much work with sexual offenders (Ackerman 1992; Gerber 1994). Gerber (1994), writing about art therapy with juvenile sex offenders, warns against the risk of focusing on their own victimhood too early, as this can be used to justify their actions or avoid responsibility.

Another key theme permeating the literature is the client's avoidance of engaging in therapy, or the denial or minimization of their offending. Kaser (1991) advocates the use of a drum kit to address control issues, resistance to treatment and denial, and for building trust. He also points out that taping the sessions gives the potential for challenging misperceptions when the client expresses pathological behaviour, such as playing too loudly and dominating the session. In art therapy the image can also function as a means of challenging minimization and denial (Gerber 1994; Hagood 1994). Aulich (1994) recognizes that resistance to therapy may come at a point where the client is beginning to realize the magnitude of what they have done. She posits that they may need to reassert their power and control when they re-engage.

This in turn links to the theme that, for therapists working with people who have committed sexual offences, the work will evoke uncomfortable feelings. It is important for therapists to acknowledge feelings of hate and disgust and to consider why the client may need to evoke them (Aulich 1994). McKenzie *et al.* (2000) also highlight the emotional impact on therapists; forcing them to consider their own attitudes towards sexuality, while also stretching their skills and imagination when faced with the barriers imposed by learning disabilities and resistance to exploring offences.

Clearly, engaging in robust supervision is indispensable (Aulich 1994). The feelings evoked in therapists may link also to the therapist's gender, working with a mostly male client group. Naitove (1988) reflects on the value of an empathic approach, in relation to the issue of female therapists working with male perpetrators, focusing on the perpetrator having been a victim themselves at a vulnerable age. Sometimes working with a male therapist can be preferable, if working with a female therapist is perceived as anti-therapeutic, for instance, when it is too provoking for the client and therefore risky for the therapist (Aulich 1994).

Mazloomian and Moon (2007) consider the significance of male clients having non-abusing male role models. Aulich (1994) suggests that female therapists may be attacked and denigrated in the images and in the clients' attitudes and behaviours. Hagood (1994) questions the use of sexually explicit images appearing in clients' artwork as it could feed deviant sexual fantasies. Sexual imagery can be seen as an attack but can also be thought of as a means for the client to process being abused themselves (Aulich 1994).

Hackett (2016) reports on the efficacy of art therapy in reducing the incidence of disturbing dreams of a sexually deviant nature. The main emphasis in this study is on the distress caused by sexually deviant dreams and their reduction being linked to making drawings of the dreams and exploring these with the therapist. Although the client was male and the therapist female, this did not feature in how the work was reported or reflected upon.

So far, an increase in the wealth of literature has not been forthcoming since Ackerman's comments in the 1990s. It is to be hoped that this book will go some way to redressing the situation.

Recent books on arts therapy work with offenders

Although there have been several recent volumes on arts therapy work with offenders, only a few have contained chapters on sex offenders. These are listed below. Some of the contributors have already been mentioned in the section above highlighting common themes.

Art Therapy with Offenders (1994) (edited by Marian Liebmann)
This book was the first to include art therapy with offenders and includes two chapters on work with adolescent sex offenders, one from the UK, one from the US. Lynn Aulich (UK) describes several individual case studies at an Adolescent Secure Unit, while Maralynn Hagood (US) describes working with a group of boys in the community. She emphasizes the addictive component of sexual offending.

Forensic Arts Therapies: Anthology of Practice and Research (2016) (edited by Kate Rothwell)
A chapter by Simon Hackett charts art psychotherapy in a low-secure unit with an adult with autistic spectrum disorder and sexually deviant dreams. The chapter by Jenny Wood and Rebecca Johns reflects on how to deal with 'feeling repulsed' in the context of work with a sex offender in a low-secure unit.

Forensic Music Therapy: A Treatment for Men and Women in Secure Hospital Settings (2012) (edited by John Adlam, Helen Odell-Miller and Stella Compton-Dickinson)
This book has two chapters that make reference to music therapy work with sex offenders. Rebecca Roberts mentions clients with index offences of a sexual nature in her chapter about death and loss within a forensic music therapy group. Petra Hervey and Helen Odell-Miller, in their chapter on music therapy, personality disorder and the Forensic Mental Health Team, mention the introduction of music therapy to a unit whose clients' offence history includes sexual assault.

Violent States and Creative States: Volume 2 (2018) (edited by John Adlam, Tilman Kluttig and Bandy Lee)
Tamsin Cottis touches on the theme of sexuality and aggression in her chapter relating to integrative arts therapies work with young people with learning disabilities, but does not refer to sexual offending.

In their chapter on working with murderers, Sarita Bose, Martha Ferrito, Alex Maguire, Martina Mindang and Andrew Ware mention the role of fantasy in sexually sadistic killings.

Working with sex offenders

Some people would say, 'Why work with sex offenders? Just lock them up (or kill them – as in some societies) and throw away the key.' However, if we want to help prevent the creation of further victims, we need to offer sex offenders treatment and hope that they can change. And research has shown that many (though sadly not all) sex offenders can change; can gain enough insight to see where they have gone wrong; and can control themselves well enough to pose no threat to the community (Levenson and Macgowan 2004; Olver *et al.* 2007; Rice and Harris 2003).

This can only happen if we treat sex offenders as human beings, with the potential for change, rather than as evil monsters to be cast out of society. Indeed, many sex offenders are otherwise upright citizens, working as teachers, social workers and pastors – but who have abused their positions of power, trust and respect. We also need to remember that a large majority of sex offenders (but not all) have been sexually abused as children and are somehow unconsciously copying behaviour that was done to them. A sex offender I worked with said ruefully, 'I offended against my stepson in exactly the same way – and at the same age – as my father did to me.'

Nevertheless, therapeutic work with sex offenders is challenging. Many sex offenders deny what they have done, because of the sense of shame, and because of the serious consequences of a guilty verdict, usually a long prison sentence. Some deny their offence because they do not see it as an offence – still believing the old myth that when a woman says, 'No', she really means, 'Yes', or that they thought their victim was an adult, when in reality they were a child. Many sex offenders are immature and assume they are on the same level as children, ignoring the fact that they are adults and have adult responsibilities. One sex offender of 23 could not understand why parents were reluctant to let their children 'come out to play' with him; emotionally he was still a child. Many sex offenders have missed developmental milestones and have limited ability to articulate their emotions.

These factors may make it difficult for sex offenders to engage in therapy. As the chapters in this book will demonstrate, it is difficult for many offenders to show their vulnerability. Especially if they have been abused as children, they have struggled to survive emotionally by covering up and burying their terrible experiences; it takes courage to open up after many years of silence. They may also fear the consequences – they may be further prosecuted or detained for admissions of further offences or risky thoughts. In many ways the system penalizes vulnerability.

In mental health secure units, the phrase 'index offence' is often heard; this is the offence that resulted in the arrest and detainment of the perpetrator. But it may not be the first or last offence or tell the whole story – that person's life did not start with the 'index offence', even though it may have been the first event to bring them into custody. The phrase 'index offence' can also be seen as a way of 'sanitizing' the offence by drawing a veil over it, omitting details of what was done, and ignoring multiple offences and previous risky behaviour. It is more constructive to talk about all the offences, and to include patients' lives before they offended – often they start by being victims.

Most sex offenders are in prison, where the main form of treatment until recently was the Sex Offender Treatment Programme (SOTP). This consisted of a suite of programmes designed for people at different levels of risk and need: the Rolling Programme, for men assessed as low risk; the Core Programme for medium-, high- and very high-risk men; the Extended Programme and the Better Lives Booster programme, for those who needed additional treatment following completion of the Core SOTP.

The Core SOTP comprised 84 sessions, and included developing insight into the reasons for offending, looking back across an individual's life as well as at triggers for the offence, developing victim empathy and planning and developing strengths and alternatives for the future.

For many years, it was the mainstay of sex offender treatment; however, recent research (Mews, Di Bella and Purver 2017) has shown that the Core SOTP did not reduce sexual re-offending rates as it intended to. In fact, those who had completed the Core SOTP were found to be more likely to sexually re-offend than the non-treated matched comparison group. Consequently, the programme has become discredited and is no longer used in the UK.

Alternative treatment programmes have since been designed and are being delivered in a number of prisons in the UK for people who have committed sexual offences. The programmes draw strongly on the Good Lives model, which focuses on building strengths in the areas of developing intimate relationships, managing emotions and problems, dealing with unhelpful thoughts and attitudes, and building hope, support and a positive identity for the future.

Arts therapies and sexual offending

It is well known that arts therapies can help with many mental health difficulties, and this will apply to many sex offenders who may be ill at the time of offending. But they also have a special role to play in view of the issues outlined above. Many of these conditions do not respond to medication, and often verbal therapy is too difficult. Sometimes arts therapies are seen as a last resort, especially in psychiatric hospitals and secure units, so arts therapists often work with quite difficult issues, and with patients seen as problematic by other staff.

As the chapters will show, arts therapies can form a bridge for patients and clients (different words are used, depending on the setting), a way in to work on emotions. This book includes all the arts therapies – while the majority of the chapters are about art therapy, there are also chapters on dramatherapy, music therapy and dance movement therapy. Some therapists describe their work as arts therapies, some prefer arts psychotherapies – these describe similar processes. The chapters show the benefits of using arts therapies in a variety of different contexts.

With many people who need help with mental health conditions, there is now a recognition that, rather than seeing them as having a personal deficit, we should see them as suffering the consequences of previous trauma, often as young children. So, we should be asking not 'What is wrong with you?' but 'What happened to you?'. This is often called 'trauma-informed' therapy and applies to sex offenders as much as to others with mental health difficulties.

Risk

Many of the chapters contain fuller discussion of risk than is possible here. But it is worth noting here that risk is a recurrent theme in working with sex offenders – mostly the risk they pose to the public by potential re-offending. Unless their offence is very minor, most sex offenders are sent to prison, either for a finite term or for an indefinite time, depending on the perceived risk if they are released.

A few prisoners may be transferred to mental health secure units at the end of their prison sentences if they are deemed to pose a risk of offending related to their mental health needs. If an individual has complex needs related to a personality disorder or a mental health disorder that cannot be managed in a prison setting, they may be referred to a mental health secure unit. They need to meet the criteria for detention under the Mental Health Act 1983 and present a grave and immediate risk to others if this referral is to a high-secure hospital. To be assessed as suitable for a medium-secure unit the individual will have a diagnosis or be likely to meet the criteria for a personality disorder and for their personality difficulties and offending behaviour to be functionally linked.

In the UK, there are high-secure, medium-secure and low-secure mental health hospitals and units, and sex offenders progress through them as their risk lessens. In a low-secure unit, patients are then allowed out gradually, first supervised, then unsupervised, then released on licence (so that they can be recalled at any time if their risk escalates). Arts therapies can be an integral part of a sentence plan to lower offenders' risk of re-offending.

When sex offenders are released into the community in the UK, there will be ongoing monitoring and risk management. The National Probation Service (NPS) is responsible for the supervision of men assessed as at medium/high risk of reconviction or harm from sexual offences. This process involves in-depth assessment of the individual's risk factors, designing and implementing a risk management plan, having regular meetings to monitor and support the person's reintegration into society. Those convicted of sexual offences are likely to be subject to additional measures, namely: licence conditions, which are restrictions imposed to manage risk of re-offending, police checks, sex offender registration, sexual harm prevention orders and Multi Agency Public Protection Arrangements (MAPPA),[1] a process where multiple agencies coordinate risk management and support

---

1   In Northern Ireland, referred to as Public Protection Arrangements Northern Ireland (PPANI).

services for an individual. A few sex offenders are able to get support from a voluntary agency, Circles UK, providing Circles for Support and Accountability, a group of trained volunteers who meet with a sex offender over a year after being released from prison.[2]

Another aspect of risk is the risk that some institutions feel is incurred by the publication of sensitive material – perhaps fearing bad publicity due to the nature of the work, or challenges from the person's family. This has led to difficulty for some authors of chapters in this book in getting consent from their institutions to publish their work, and two authors have had to drop out. Authors generally use pseudonyms for their case studies, or composite cases that include details taken from several different cases to illustrate the work accurately, but without disclosing confidential personal details. They also aim to get written consent from the subject whose work is being described in their chapter, but occasionally this is not possible because the subject has moved on and is no longer accessible. Sometimes the original manager who approved the project is no longer there, and a new manager is more risk-averse and refuses permission to go ahead.

Supervision

Clearly such high-profile and intensive work requires good supervision. Indeed, it is mentioned specifically in several of the chapters. Supervisors can help therapists to keep their balance in work that can be emotionally draining, turbulent and confusing. They can help discuss theories on which therapists base their work and help with transference and countertransference responses. Most arts therapies use psychodynamic theories to support their work, but they are not the only theories – some therapists use attachment theories, some use narrative approaches, one uses Lacanian theory, another uses 'trauma-informed' therapy; and many use psychosocial arts interventions alongside other therapeutic approaches.

In addition to specific arts therapy supervision, most arts therapists working with sex offenders are part of a multi-disciplinary team, including psychiatrists, psychologists, social workers, nurses and other mental health professionals. Each of these brings their own skills, so that decisions are taken as a team rather than resting on one

---

2   See www.circles-uk.org.uk

professional's shoulders. Supervision includes processing therapists' uncomfortable and disturbing feelings – this usually involves much talking and discussion but can also include working with the arts as a parallel process to that of the clients or patients.

Scope of this book

Although all the work described is concerned with sex offending, this can mean many things, from someone shouting offensive sexual insults to someone committing a serious rape or sexual murder. The settings too vary widely. A few chapters describe work in prisons, although it is worth noting that most sex offenders in prisons have no access to arts therapies. The majority of chapters outline work within mental health secure units, for those who are deemed to be a risk to the public through mental ill health – usually because of offending, often, but not always, sexual offending. They may be transferred from a prison if their mental health deteriorates, or they may be given a hospital order from the court, if their offence was deemed to be due to mental illness.

There are also chapters about sex offending in the community, especially for young people who may not be 'sex offenders' but have engaged in sexually harmful behaviour. Arts therapies can help to prevent further harm and educate young people into healthier ways of responding to problematic situations. So we have one chapter from a school and one from a voluntary organization providing therapies for children and young people.

The age range covers from children to people in their sixties. Almost all the chapters describe sexual offending by men, but there is one chapter about a woman sex offender. There is a diversity of ethnic backgrounds, and race and culture issues make themselves known in many cases. Most of the work described comes from UK institutions, but we also have two contributions from the USA (both from California) and one from the Netherlands.

Chapter summaries

These show the wide variety of work being undertaken in this field. There seemed no easy way of categorizing the chapters or subsuming them under clear subheadings, so they do not follow any particular order.

Chapter 1

Kate Burn – Restorative Hope: Keeping Families Together after Sibling Sexual Abuse

This chapter describes an innovative restorative justice project that aims to keep families together after sibling sexual abuse, in contrast to the usual practice of splitting up siblings to prevent further harm. Family dynamics after abuse are outlined, then the Restore Project is described. A case study of a nine-year-old boy shows the contribution of art therapy to keeping conflicting feelings contained in the same piece of work. The pilot project was so successful that the practices have been adopted as part of the multi-agency team's approach, and interest has been shown from other parts of the UK and Europe.

Chapter 2

Kate Smith – Story, Shadow, Shame and Risk: Dramatherapy with Male Personality-Disordered Sexual Offenders in Medium-Secure Forensic Settings

This chapter looks at the use of imagination and storytelling within long-term dramatherapy work. It includes consideration of risk and how this can be measured, involving patients in the process, through building up trust. It then goes on to look at the way story and particularly fairy tales can be used to help patients tell their full stories, often disclosing early abuse that has led to distortions in their thinking. This can then lead to patients being more able to empathize with their victims and recognize their own risk. There is the hope then that they can use their insights to lower their risk and exist more safely in society.

Chapter 3

Jessica Collier – Behind Closed Doors: Art Psychotherapy with Female Sexual Offenders

This chapter explores the way stereotypes of women's behaviour prevent us being able to comprehend or even see sexual offences committed by them. Because they are mostly victims of sexual abuse and violence, it is difficult to acknowledge that they can also be perpetrators – and sometimes both. A historical perspective on incest, rape and the law shows how women were regarded as male property until recently, and this has influenced how women are seen. These themes are demonstrated in a case study of a female sex offender in prison, who engaged in individual art therapy for a year and could only see herself as the victim, unable to acknowledge any responsibility for the offence.

Chapter 4

Preetha Ramasubramanian and Dawn Batcup – Exploring Maternal and Erotic Transference in Dance Movement Psychotherapy with a Sex Offender

The focus of this chapter is a case study in a forensic unit of dance movement psychotherapy work with a sexual offender with schizophrenia. It shows in detail some of the interactions that can take place through using body movements and the metaphors arising from this. The case study is supported by a wide range of psychoanalytical texts shedding light on the thoughts and feelings evoked by the dance movement psychotherapy process.

Chapter 5

Amy Pfenning and Marian Husted – The Use of Art Therapy to Address Dynamic Risk Factors in Sex Offender Treatment

This chapter describes the different forms of art therapy at a 1200-place mental health facility for male sex offenders in California. It describes their risk-need-responsivity model, which offers a Sex Offender Treatment Program alongside a variety of art therapy approaches, including targeted art therapy groups on particular aspects of risk and need, such as building empathy, working on intimacy issues, and dealing with anger and frustration. Alongside these groups are studio groups focusing on building self-esteem through art projects, such as ceramics, painting and leather-work. They can be offered to patients as a way in for those not yet ready for in-depth work, or to accompany the personal work. The chapter includes four case studies, showing encouraging results from long-term work.

Chapter 6
Eva Marie Chadwick – Beauty and the Beast: Trauma-Informed Dramatherapy with a Male Patient in a Forensic Setting

This chapter introduces the development of a trauma-informed dramatherapy intervention. It describes a case study of a man with gender dysphoria who developed several female personas, and presented with unprocessed traumas. The dramatherapy intervention integrated trauma-informed methods, including Lifespan Integration into the therapeutic process. Creative and reflective work included the author's own visual images post-session and supervision. These methods combined to help the patient reduce anxiety and complex coping mechanisms, and achieve a sense of safety and peace.

Chapter 7
Simon Hastilow – Development of Self-Perception: Art Therapy with Sex Offenders in a Therapeutic Community Prison

This chapter concerns an art therapy group on a prison wing for sexual offenders run on therapeutic community lines. There is discussion of the way beliefs can influence the commission of sexual offences, and the way that low self-esteem can also be involved. A case study shows how one man's artwork changed to reflect a growing sense of self-esteem, and how this made it possible for the man to contemplate a change in behaviour and relationships.

Chapter 8
Alice Myles – Diagnosis, Ethics and the Sexual Offender Subject: A Lacanian Psychoanalytic Perspective

In this chapter the author suggests that Lacanian psychoanalytic theory can make a specific contribution to art psychotherapy with sexual offenders. After laying out some of the basic Lacanian theoretical concepts, the author shows their application in her discussion of the artwork of a man who had murdered and attempted a sexual assault on a 12-year-old girl from a minority ethnic group, picking up on metaphors used in the artwork that echoed the offence. The chapter shows how a Lacanian framework can be helpful in viewing sexual offenders' artwork in a different way and how this opens up new possibilities for clinical engagement.

Chapter 9
Steve Cobbett – Music Therapy with Juvenile Sex Offenders with Social, Emotional and Mental Health Needs

This chapter starts with a summary of the increasing prevalence and needs of this group of clients. It goes on to consider the evidence of the efficacy of different therapeutic treatments. Although there is as yet little hard evidence for arts therapies, there is considerable evidence for different therapeutic approaches working on the risk factors for juvenile sex offenders (e.g. work on self-esteem). A case study of individual work with a 14-year-old boy illustrates the range of approaches and methods that can be included in music therapy. These approaches are summarized at the end of the chapter.

Chapter 10
Ronald P.M.H Lay – Beads, Bees, Glitter and Perversion: Forensic Art Therapy with Older Adults

This chapter provides an overview of working in art therapy in a secure inpatient setting in Northern California over a period of 12 years. It is divided into three sections: Naivety to nuanced; Beleaguered to boundaried; and Restraints to recovery. There is an emphasis on the crucial role of trust in developing relationships. The clients were able to be involved in a variety of art activities, including individual and group projects, fostering a shift away from offenders seeing themselves as solely identified by their offences to becoming more rounded human beings. The chapter includes several short vignettes illustrating the potential of this approach.

Chapter 11
Themis Kyriakidou – Attachment, Trauma and Art Therapy in the Treatment of Sexual Offending

This chapter draws attention to the recently researched links between early trauma, insecure attachment and sexual offending. This research is then applied to a case study in a secure unit of a young man with a mild learning disability and a history of indecent assaults and sexualized behaviour. After undertaking the Sex Offender Treatment Programme (SOTP), the young man requested art therapy to look at family relationships, and significant work was undertaken in the three months before his discharge from hospital. The case study shows how work on the trauma he suffered helped to clear the way for working on his sexual offences.

Chapter 12

Katie Greenwood – Finding Paul: Dramatherapy with a Man Whose Denial Rendered Him 'Stuck' in the Criminal Justice System

This chapter is unusual in that it describes work with a patient who consistently denied his offence. This meant that he could not engage in offence-related treatment, which might have led to a reduction of risk in the eyes of the Ministry of Justice. The patient and the multi-disciplinary team seemed totally stuck. The introduction of dramatherapy was a 'last hope'. The work was focused around helping the patient find some other identities apart from that of 'sex offender', using the medium of stories. Through this, the patient arrived at a place where he was able to make a tentative change, and this was eventually mirrored by the multi-disciplinary team. This then led to the patient being considered for home leave for the first time.

Chapter 13

Thijs de Moor – Expressing the Crime for a Young Sex Offender Using Art Therapy in a Forensic Psychiatric Hospital in the Netherlands

This chapter outlines the role of treatment for sexual offenders in a forensic psychiatric hospital in the Netherlands, and the specific role of art therapy within that setting. The treatment is targeted at sexual offenders who cannot benefit from verbal therapies and is tailored to individual patients. The chapter includes a long case study of 58 individual sessions with a patient who needed to work through several stages before being able to work on his offence. These stages included establishing trust, working with art assignments to keep centred, developing emotional expression, learning to control aggressive behaviour, playing, and finally working on his offence.

Chapter 14
Kate Snowden – Knowing Me, Knowing You: Bodies in Relationship, Working with Adolescents with Learning Disabilities and Harmful Sexual Behaviours

The subject of learning-disabled young people and sex is one that most people prefer to avoid. This chapter considers this reluctance in the context of harmful sexual behaviours. The author shows how the bodily nature of dance movement psychotherapy can help with these issues in the community – both with the young people and in clinical supervision of the work. The chapter also includes consideration of case management issues and links with other organizations, essential in community provision.

Chapter 15
Lucy Gibson-Hill – Art Therapy with Long-Term Patients at Risk of Sexual Offending

This chapter describes work with two long-term patients who have spent a large portion of their adult lives incarcerated in mental health secure wards, being deemed at risk of committing sexual offences. The men whose work is described had been transferred from medium- to low-secure units and received art therapy on a long-term basis, as well as therapeutic visits to art galleries. The chapter concludes with some visible results from the work done, in terms of improved and less risky behaviour.

Chapter 16
Maxine Daniels – Role-Play as a Therapeutic Tool: A Research Study of Sexual Offenders' Experiences of Victim Empathy Role-Play

This chapter describes research into the use of role-play to develop victim empathy with sexual offenders in prison, with a focus on sexual offenders' experiences during the role-plays. Semi-structured interviews were conducted with 11 sex offenders, and their responses gave rise to seven themes. These themes were then correlated with the stages in the Assimilation of a Problematic Experience (APE) scale. The conclusion drawn is that victim empathy role-play can be used as a therapeutic tool for offenders to gain insight into their 'abusing part of self', leading to their seeing victims as people rather than objects.

Chapter 17
Anna Green – Group and Individual Art Therapy with a Sexually Inappropriate Patient in an NHS Low-Secure Unit

This chapter compares group art therapy and individual art therapy with a patient displaying inappropriate behaviour, namely, commenting on the art therapist's clothes, jewellery and personal behaviour. In the group art therapy, the patient continued to make remarks, also commenting on the art therapist's artwork, and was distracted by other members of the group. A switch to individual art therapy enabled the art therapist to encourage the patient to focus on his own work, and this led to his gaining more independence and a better sense of self. He was also able to develop a more appropriate relationship with the art therapist. Throughout the chapter the role of supervision is highlighted.

The importance of hope
Many of the patients and clients described in this book have spent many years in custodial settings. It is easy to take the view that they are hopeless cases, and too risky to ever release – although this is true for some people. But the work being done using arts psychotherapies described here shows its potential in reaching offenders who do not respond well to other treatments, and this gives them hope that they can change and take their place in society without being a risk to others. It is to be hoped that the success of the work described in this book will encourage more use of arts therapies with sex offending.

Note: Names in case studies have been changed or fictionalized to preserve confidentiality.

References

Ackerman, J. (1992) 'Art-therapy intervention designed to increase self-esteem of an incarcerated pedophile.' *American Journal of Art Therapy 30*, 4, 143–149.

Adlam, J., Kluttig, T. and Lee, B. (eds) (2018) *Violent States and Creative States: Volume 2*. London: Jessica Kingsley Publishers.

Adlam, J., Odell-Miller, H. and Compton-Dickinson, S. (eds) (2012) *Forensic Music Therapy: A Treatment for Men and Women in Secure Hospital Settings*. London: Jessica Kingsley Publishers.

Aulich, L. (1994) 'Fear and Loathing: Art Therapy, Sex Offenders, and Gender.' In M. Liebmann (ed.) *Art Therapy with Offenders*. London: Jessica Kingsley Publishers.

Gerber, J. (1994) 'The use of art therapy in juvenile sex offender specific treatment.' *The Arts in Psychotherapy 21*, 367–374.

Hackett, S. (2016) 'Art Psychotherapy with an Adult with Autistic Spectrum Disorder and Sexually Deviant Dreams: A Single-case Study Including the Client's Responses to Treatment.' In K. Rothwell (ed.) *Forensic Arts Therapies: Anthology of Practice and Research*. London: Free Association Books.

Hagood, M. (1994) 'Group Art Therapy with Adolescent Sex Offenders: An American Experience.' In M. Liebmann (ed.) *Art Therapy with Offenders*. London: Jessica Kingsley Publishers.

Kaser, V.A. (1991) 'Music therapy treatment of pedophilia using the drum set.' *The Arts in Psychotherapy 18*, 7–15.

Law Commission (1992) *Criminal Law: Rape Within Marriage*. Accessed on 8/1/2020 at www.gov.uk/government/publications/criminal-law-rape-within-marriage

Levenson, J.S. and Macgowan, M.J. (2004) 'Engagement, denial, and treatment progress among sex offenders in group therapy.' *Sexual Abuse: A Journal of Research and Treatment 16*, 1, 49–63.

Liebmann, M. (ed.) (1994) *Art Therapy with Offenders*. London: Jessica Kingsley Publishers.

Mazloomian, H. and Moon, B.L. (2007) 'Images from purgatory: Art therapy with male adolescent sexual abusers.' *Art Therapy 24*, 1, 16–21.

McKenzie, K., Chisholm, D. and Murray, G. (2000) 'Working with sex offenders who have a learning disability.' *International Journal of Art Therapy: Inscape 5*, 2, 62–69.

Mews, A., Di Bella, L. and Purver, M. (2017) *Impact Evaluation of the Prison-based Core Sex Offender Treatment Programme. Ministry of Justice Analytical Series*. London: Ministry of Justice.

Naitove, C.E. (1988) 'Arts therapy with child molesters: An historical perspective on the act and an approach to treatment.' *The Arts in Psychotherapy 15*, 151–160.

Olver, M.E., Wong, S.C., Nicholaichuk, T. and Gordon, A. (2007) 'The validity and reliability of the Violence Risk Scale-Sexual Offender version: Assessing sex offender risk and evaluating therapeutic change.' *Psychological Assessment 19*, 3, 318.

Rice, M.E. and Harris, G.T. (2003) 'The size and sign of treatment effects in sex offender therapy.' *Annals of the New York Academy of Sciences 989*, 1, 428–440.

Rothwell, K. (ed.) (2016) *Forensic Arts Therapies: Anthology of Practice and Research*. London: Free Association Books.

Skaggs, R. (1997) 'Music-centered creative arts in a sex offender treatment program for male juveniles.' *Music Therapy Perspectives 15*, 2, 73–78.

Watson, D.M. (2002) 'Drumming and improvisation with adult male sexual offenders.' *Music Therapy Perspectives 20*, 2, 105–111.

When did marital rape become a crime? (2018, 6 December) *The Week*. Accessed on 8/1/2020 at www.theweek.co.uk/98330/when-did-marital-rape-become-a-crime

CHAPTER 1

Restorative Hope

Keeping Families Together after Sibling Sexual Abuse

KATE BURN, ART THERAPIST

Introduction

What image comes to mind when thinking of a 'sex offender'?

When we hear this label in the news headlines, our minds can all too easily be drawn towards the stereotypical image of a cloaked stranger hiding in the bushes. Perhaps this feels easier? We don't have to accept that an 'offender' could be someone within our daily lives; or someone we love; or that sexual abuse is something which could affect us. We don't have to think about why this might happen, or see the vulnerability of the person who has offended. With rising media coverage, society is moving towards a more informed understanding of the reality of sexual abuse. However, there is still a long way to go before the feelings stirred up by this uncomfortable topic can be addressed widely, resulting in better outcomes for all involved.

I will explore the impact on families for whom this 'offender' has turned out to be their own child, forcing them to face the reality of sibling abuse. When this happens, all stereotypes are challenged. I will consider the complex work involved in processing sexual abuse when it has occurred between siblings. Sadly, the 'usual practice' in this situation is to separate the siblings, tearing families apart. Despite the intention of preventing future physical harm, this approach can cause psychological damage not only in the children involved but also in their wider family. The conflicting feelings held by these families in the aftermath of such abuse can be amplified through the physical separation imposed on their family unit. A new, more restorative, approach is needed to help families move forwards in a more integrated way.

In this chapter, I will introduce 'Restore', an innovative project in Bristol led by The Green House therapy service in collaboration with the North Bristol NHS Trust 'Be Safe' Service and the Bristol City Council Youth Offending Team (YOT). The aim of Restore is to change the outlook both for children who have been harmed as well as for those who have harmed. By recognizing the needs of the children and seeing both parties as vulnerable, Restore works therapeutically to hold a family together in cases of sibling sexual abuse. Professionals work holistically within a robust, communicative network, modelling the capacity to remain united in the face of division. I will draw on the comprehensive report by Streich and Spreadbury (2017) at the end of the Restore pilot to show the benefits of this initiative.

In parallel, I will explore how the art medium is able to contain the conflicting feelings in a way that enables them to be understood within the context of a therapeutic frame. I hope to draw comparisons between this process and the containing frame of Restore's holistic working. By way of illustration, I will present the work of a child in art therapy whose experience of sexual abuse from his brother left him fragmented in his feelings about their relationship.

For the purpose of this exploration, I will use a combination of direct clinical examples and composite situations from my own work, which I hope will enrich the discussion. Our clients are our greatest teachers, and I am indebted to their generosity in allowing me to use material from their journeys to illustrate a process that can be very difficult to articulate in words.

I will begin by exploring the unconscious dynamics rife in the aftermath of sibling sexual abuse.

Tension in the network

In cases of sexual abuse perpetrated by an adult, the unbearable feelings and thoughts associated with the abuse can be split off into this adult figure, and relief can be found through conviction or restriction orders; allowing the family some separation from the person who has harmed. Statistics from The Green House (Boulton 2018), however, suggest that only 46 percent of child sexual abuse cases investigated criminally proceed to a court case, with fewer still resulting in a conviction. With 92 percent of the referred cases of child sexual abuse involving a perpetrator known to the family (Boulton 2018), relief from the overwhelming feelings evoked by sexual abuse can be hard to come by.

Reporting of abuse between children is on the rise. A third of cases reported in the UK to the National Society for the Prevention of Cruelty to Children (NSPCC) in 2014 were in this category (Hackett 2014), whilst at The Green House in 2018 this had risen to over half the referrals. Yates (2017) cites a number of studies that suggest that between a third and half of these reported cases involve siblings (Allardyce and Yates 2009; Beckett 2006; Hackett, Print and Day 1998: Ryan 2010; Shaw *et al.* 2000).

When sibling sexual abuse is disclosed, parents are thrown into an impossible conflict of feelings. Both the 'victim' and the 'perpetrator' are under their care. Often in cases of non-sibling sexual abuse, the 'bad' feelings are attached to the 'perpetrator' and the 'good' feelings to the 'victim'. It can be hard to hold compassionate feelings within the 'bad' or difficult feelings within the 'good' (Klein 1946). However, when the two parties are separated, the need to contain these feelings together is reduced.

The harmful impact of these processes can be seen in the story of siblings, Jenny (aged 8) and David (aged 10). Jenny and David had been abused by their Uncle Peter, who had groomed them both and encouraged David to act out sexually with Jenny. Peter had since been convicted, and an injunction against him prevented any further contact with the children. Although the children's future safety from Peter was guaranteed, David's abuse of Jenny continued beyond the conviction. With support from therapeutic and social services, the abuse was stopped, and Jenny was referred by social services for art therapy sessions. David was referred to Be Safe for his own support.

In the art therapy assessment process, the mother of both children told me that Jenny was 'the good one' and that David was 'the difficult one'. She told me that Jenny always did everything she was asked and posed no problem in school, whereas David's behaviour was 'a nightmare'. She appeared to be struggling with the conflicting feelings she was left with around the abuse that had taken place. In order to manage this ambivalence, she seemed to have unconsciously assigned roles to the children, which they were acting out accordingly. The school reported that Jenny was almost impossibly 'good'; complying unfailingly and never seeming to challenge or question. David, meanwhile, was being held in isolation on a regular basis. David's role as a 'victim' of Peter's actions seemed to have been lost, both within the family and the wider network.

As Jenny's art therapy sessions progressed, her hurt and angry feelings began to emerge. She began to realize the role into which she had been trapped and to challenge this role with the uprising of previously suppressed thoughts and feelings. As a result, she began to assert herself and learn to say 'no'. After one particularly tearful session, her support worker commented to her, 'Oh no, Jenny, *this isn't you, what's the matter?*' I felt this comment further reflected the extent to which the projection had not only penetrated the family but also the network around it; everyone desperate for the feelings to remain contained where they had been projected.

At the 12-week art therapy review, my suspicions were confirmed as Mum reported back to me how Jenny had now become the 'nightmare'. She described defiant behaviour and a shift in presentation from the girl who always complied to a girl who had now begun to challenge. I noticed that, as she talked, her recognition of needs shifted, diminishing her concern around Jenny and beginning to ask when David might be offered a therapy space. 'I think he is depressed,' she offered, acknowledging David's vulnerability for the first time. The roles had been reversed. It seemed impossible for Mum to view both children in equal regard; both vulnerable and both with the capacity for 'positive' and 'negative' emotions.

When Jenny's agency began to return, and the original projections began to be challenged ('Why do I always have to be the good girl?' 'Is it okay for me to feel angry?'), the feelings needed to be rearranged within the family structure. With Jenny no longer offering a container for the vulnerability, this feeling was shifted on to David, and it seemed that Jenny was now seen as 'the bad one'. This reminded me of a paper by Gail Walker (2005), in which a group of primary-aged children were accessing a psychotherapy group. The roles assigned within the group helped to alleviate the anxiety and tension of ambivalence, to the point that, when the member of the group holding the rebellious, angry feelings was absent, another member asked, 'Who will be the naughty one now?'

Such is the power of childhood sexual abuse that the splitting can leak into the networks around the children. Often the helplessness felt by professionals leads them to locate difficult feelings in other parts of the network. Therapists can turn against social workers, referrers can turn against therapists, families can turn against professionals; each feeling the other is not doing enough to help the child. Feelings of powerlessness are rife within childhood sexual abuse and can be felt by the children, parents and professionals alike. It is painful to feel powerless, and nobody wants to be left with these feelings.

It can be tempting for a professional group planning the ongoing care of the family where sibling sexual abuse has happened, to deny that the children involved may share common needs. This often results in the neglect of the needs of one party or another. In cases of high and unbearable anxiety, overwhelming feelings can be flooded into individuals, providing absolute relief for some parts of the group, whilst sacrificing others into the scapegoat position. It takes the coming together of the network around the children to be able to consider a safety strategy whilst holding in mind the needs of both children simultaneously.

In order to tolerate the anxiety and risk where one sibling has sexually harmed another, the standard solution is often to remove the 'perpetrator' from the family home. This child, who will always have unconscious causes for their actions, can then feel the full force of the projection of 'badness' by being evicted. But does this solve the problem? It is imperative to face the reality and tackle the uncomfortable feelings if change is ever to come about. I will now present a vital new project in the UK which is working towards a different future for these families using a therapeutically based restorative approach.

The Restore Project

The Restore Project sees sibling abuse as a systemic issue. No one person holds all the responsibility for the harm that has been caused, and the motivating factors can be very complex. However, there is a recognition that, in order to foster successful and safe reunification of families in the aftermath of such abuse, identifiable change must first be demonstrated. Where the disparate parts of the family unit are being treated as separate, the whole system cannot be witnessed and untangled. In these cases, separation is the only way in which 'positive outcomes' can be realistically maintained. However, in the long term, the issue remains unresolved, widening potential for future repetition of harm. The family remains stuck.

In 2015, Stephen Barry, Service Manager and Lead Clinician at the NHS 'Be Safe' Service, approached Michelle Windle, Director of The Green House, about the possibility of working together to apply a multi-agency restorative justice approach to practice. He thought that a joined-up approach using a restorative justice model might contribute to more successful outcomes for the clients and families involved. The Green House, in collaboration with the Be Safe Service and the Bristol YOT was awarded a Community Safety Grant from Avon & Somerset Police & Crime Commissioner to run a pilot of The Restore Project for one year from April 2015 to April 2016.

Based on the practice of 'restorative justice', which often takes the form of 'a series of conversations leading to a meeting, and completion' (Streich and Spreadbury 2017), 'Restore' uses a *restorative approach* to work with families in which sibling abuse has occurred. This approach offers a more holistic form of care for these families, recognizing that 'each family is a system – a "traumatized system" so a restorative approach involves addressing the relational patterns within each traumatized system' (Streich and Spreadbury 2017). It recognizes the complexity of the family system and aims to work with this complexity, tailoring support that hears, values and responds to the needs of all the parties involved on a case-by-case basis. Although each case is individual, an established process contains the system within which flexibility can operate.

On receiving a referral for a family who might be considered within the Restore framework, the assigned therapist at The Green House offers the family information about the programme and gains consent for participation. Then links are immediately made between the organizations involved, and a network is established around the family. Communication continues throughout the course of the work, with joint review meetings every six to eight weeks, often involving the therapist and parents, as well as the social worker and sometimes a representative from Be Safe or the YOT. From the beginning of the work, the family is aware of this holistic approach, acting as a container for the often-fragmented parts of their experience. The Green House found that:

When family work is delivered holistically by both Restore partners, it can be particularly effective. In the partnership meetings held jointly with Be Safe, the voices of both the child who has harmed and the child who has been harmed are heard in an equal and supportive environment. Parents are also supported in an environment which hears and respects their conflicting and turbulent emotions. This is an unusual approach for agencies working with child sexual abuse, where agencies tend to work with one child or the other rather than address the feelings of both in the same room. Agencies working in isolation with the same family can contribute to the divisions within the family, mirroring the disconnection between supporting organizations. (Streich and Spreadbury 2017, p.20)

As a result of this shifted focus and the restorative approach, therapists at The Green House altered their assessment process to include talking with parents about their own difficulties. Bion (1962/1984) suggested that in order to have capacity to contain the distressing thoughts and feelings of their child, a caregiver must first feel a sense of being contained themselves. The Restore approach introduced a systemic aspect from the start; enabling the parent to have a role in the process and emphasizing the value of their own past and present experiences. Through the collaborative and systemic work that ensued, the organization saw a rise in the number of parents referring themselves for their own support with the adult therapy service. In several instances, this holistic approach prompted parents to disclose their own history of sexual abuse, providing hope that the cycle of harm across generations could be changed.

Regular network meetings meant that each member of the family could be heard and valued in the process. In being advocated for within these meetings, the harmed child could become empowered and feel heard, with decisions being made to benefit all parties concerned. Without the network of professionals collaborating robustly, it seemed that the powerful drive to split apart the conflicting feelings would eventually be inevitable. In two cases within the project, parents on the brink of separation 'reported that this collaborative approach prevented the breakdown of their relationships' (Streich and Spreadbury 2017).

With this approach embedded in the work around the whole family, difficult feelings can be safely faced and processed without needing to be acted out. Light is shone on the network, leaving no areas for shadows to go unnoticed. The conscious recognition of defensive mechanisms gives rise to the opportunity for reconciliation. Instead of setting the family up to repeat the same patterns of coping, fresh methods can be introduced. The Restore Project saw families reunified with the practical application of robust safety rules, and a psychological understanding of healthy communication within the system. It showed that the cycle of harm can be disrupted, offering hope for a more positive future.

The power of art

Through my work as an art therapist specializing in the field of childhood sexual abuse, I am often astounded by the power of art in its robust capacity to contain conflicting and muddled feelings on behalf of the child in a similar way to what is being pioneered in the Restore Project. Halton (1994) suggests that play can serve the same function for a child as projective processes, stating that 'relief from anxieties can arise from trying to contain conflicting needs and conflicting emotions' (p.14). This section illustrates how one child involved in the Restore Project was able to use this process in his exploration of the abuse he had experienced from his brother.

> When a child loves and hates the same person, wants to be with but is afraid of that person he ends up feeling chaotic. Because the child cannot trust his feelings, in that he experiences feelings that are exactly the opposite to what he thought he felt or thought he should feel, he is likely to cut off feelings. (Wieland 2006, p.41)

Art therapy is a powerful tool in enabling a child to contain and process the conflicting feelings evoked by the experience of sibling sexual abuse. Murphy (2001) comments that 'images could carry ambivalence and conflict which needed to find a means of expression when the perpetrator of the abuse was a person whom the child also loved and was sometimes the only person who had ever shown any affection to him or her' (p.7). The image within the containing therapeutic frame enables the capacity for holding mess and chaos safely outside the self, allowing the expression of feelings that may not yet have words, externally representing one's inner world to be explored at a safe distance. Boundaries that have been blurred in the course of sexual abuse can be expressed in mess-making, which challenges the conventional boundaries of art production. Art materials can be poured, spilled and mixed both within the frame of paper on a table, but also outside the paper, on the palette, the table or the floor (Aldridge 1998; Hanes 1997; Hastilow and Aldridge 2001; Murphy 2001).

In the work that follows, I hope to reflect on how the art making process helped Billy to express and contain some of his experiences. Billy was nine years old when he was referred for art therapy. He had been sexually abused by his elder brother. Both children were subject to a child protection order and Billy lived in a muddle of fear and sadness around his sibling relationship. He loved his brother dearly, and they clung to each other for comfort. However, he hated and feared the abuse he had suffered at his hand.

Billy and his brother were referred to the Restore Project. Alongside support for his brother from other services, Billy was offered 24 sessions of individual art therapy. These support services ran in parallel, with communication between the services and the parents facilitated through six-weekly review meetings, which also involved social services and the school.

Like many children who have experienced abuse in their young lives, Billy came into therapy fearful and mistrusting. The child of vulnerable parents who had experienced abuse and neglect in their own childhoods, he had low expectations of the world and its safety. He often appeared hyper-vigilant and used the creative process to show the utter terror he saw in everyday life. Amid the terror, he also expressed his feelings of sadness at missing his brother, who had been temporarily removed from the family home whilst a safety plan was established.

During his work with me, Billy created a powerful image of Pudsey Bear, the Children in Need mascot, on a busy and chaotic background. To one side of the main Pudsey, which claims the central position in the picture, he painted a smaller, fainter 'girl' Pudsey. He clearly defined the two Pudseys by gender as if suggesting a similarity as well as a difference. Could these bears, together amid this chaotic world, be siblings?

He was determined to create two parts of this second figure; the 'good' girl Pudsey, which is seen on the outside, and the 'evil' girl Pudsey, which lurks beneath. Billy told me that these were two parts of the same bear. He wanted to warn others not to open the flap that would reveal the 'evil girl Pudsey', by writing firmly in pencil 'Do Not Open'. In this gesture, he seemed to be demonstrating a desperate desire to know only one part, whilst also facing the reality of the other part hidden beneath. This double-part Pudsey led me to thinking about Billy's brother and the confusing experience of sibling sexual abuse. Billy's image holds both parts of this companion bear; not limiting the image to just one, definitive character.

Figure 1.1: Flap closed – 'Do Not Open' (see colour section)

Figure 1.2: Flap open – 'Evil Girl Pudsey' (see colour section)

Billy used large, coloured lettering to the right of the main Pudsey Bear figure to entitle the image 'Children in Need'. Although, of course, Pudsey is the face of the popular fundraising event, it seemed to me that Billy's message ran deeper into his personal experience. This powerfully poignant image illustrated what he needed me to know about his feelings.

In his image, Billy seems to have been able to capture the ambivalence faced by so many families in this position. The artwork shows a sophisticated expression of this intangible but very present feeling. If this second bear represented, as my interpretation leads me to believe, Billy's brother, Billy had been able to use the artwork to hold together the part of himself that felt comforted by his brother as well as the part that feared him, stating 'Do Not Open'. The capacity of art to hold the tension of this unthinkable situation enables a new level of understanding to emerge, acknowledging both the children indeed as 'children in need'.

Talking about this image and the confusion of understanding the bear's different 'parts' led Billy to a further exploration of what this could mean for him. He went on to create a 'scary mask', which he covered in glitter and feathers. It reminded me of a tribal costume. He gleefully wore the mask during the session, saying that nobody would be able to see the little boy hidden behind it, powerless to scare anyone. He told me that if people saw the mask, they would be frightened. When wearing the mask, he could take on a different character, which filled him with feelings of power and agency. We thought about the different positions he could adopt, whilst all the time being Billy. By embodying the different parts, Billy was able to make some sense of his experience and begin to explore the fear that can lie behind frightening behaviour. Using this understanding, and the imagery, I was able to translate Billy's experience in a more digestible way to the network and the family; helping his parents to see the feelings that were impossible to articulate.

I believe it is the inability to hold together the opposing feelings that can lead to both children 'in need' being lost. It is unbearable to think about both children as vulnerable, as this leaves the more aggressive and furious feelings with nowhere to go. Frequently, this tension results in one child being evicted so that the feelings can either remain with them as the 'bad one' or be located within the network that made this decision on behalf of the family. As organizations supporting families through the aftermath of sibling sexual abuse, we need to be more like the art medium, demonstrating the capacity to hold all the often conflicting and opposing parts of the experience of each individual family, so that nothing is left floundering or lost. As therapists, social workers and criminal justice workers around a family, we must unite to form a canvas on to which the difficulties can be painted and held within a robust and holding frame. It is this containing experience that offers hope for a future in which families can move forwards, together, after sibling sexual abuse.

Conclusion

In this chapter, I have tried to convey just some of the complexities of working with families where sibling sexual abuse has occurred. I hope these reflections can offer hope in the darkness of this field of work, for professionals and families alike.

The tension of feelings experienced in the aftermath of sexual abuse is amplified when the abuse has happened between siblings. This can leave families fragmented and despairing. As a professional group working amid this despair, capacity must be found for robust containment of the fragmented parts if progress is to be made. I hope that this discussion has highlighted possibilities for this capacity.

I have offered an example of how art therapy can form one element of the process, by facilitating a language to express and digest the complexities of intra-familial abuse. In addition to the alliance between the therapist and the child, the art medium allows space for tensions to be safely held within the boundaries of a trusting relationship. This can only operate effectively within a transparent and communicative system as described in the work of the Restore Project. It is the direct work in connection with multi-agency liaison in which real change can be seen.

The Restore Project continues to run beyond the pilot. As a result, the team has received enquiries from across the UK and Europe, wanting to know more about the approach. This is a project that, in isolation, risks maintaining the fragmentation already apparent in the work. It is vital to The Green House that as many organizations as possible hear about and disseminate the results of the project among their communities, with the aim that this approach becomes a standard through which all organizations can offer restorative hope.

References

Aldridge, F. (1998) 'Chocolate or shit: Aesthetics and cultural poverty in art therapy with children.' *Inscape 3*, 1, 2–9.

Allardyce, S. and Yates, P. (2009) *The Risks of Young People Abusing Sexually at Home, in the Community or Both: A Comparative Study of 34 Boys in Edinburgh with Harmful Sexual Behaviour.* Towards Effective Practice 8. Edinburgh: Criminal Justice Social Work Development Centre.

Beckett, R. (2006) 'Risk Prediction, Decision Making and Evaluation of Adolescent Sexual Abusers.' In M. Erooga and H. Masson (eds) *Children and Young People Who Sexually Abuse Others* (2nd edn). London: Routledge.

Bion, W. (1984) *Learning from Experience.* London: Karnac. (Original work published 1962)

Boulton, C. (2018) *Analysis of The Green House Children and Young People's Service April 2017– March 2018.* Bristol: The Green House.

Hackett, S. (2014) *Children and Young People with Harmful Sexual Behaviours.* London: Research in Practice.

Hackett, S., Print, B. and Day, C. (1998) 'Brother nature? Therapeutic Intervention with Young Men Who Sexually Abuse Their Siblings.' In A. Bannister (ed.) *From Hearing to Healing: Working with the Aftermath of Child Sexual Abuse.* (2nd edn). Chichester: Wiley.

Halton, W. (1994) 'Some Unconscious Aspects of Organizational Life: Contributions from Psychoanalysis.' In A. Obholzer and V. Zagier Roberts (eds) *The Unconscious at Work: Individual and Organizational Stress in the Human Services.* London: Routledge.

Hanes, M. (1997) 'Producing messy mixtures in art therapy.' *American Journal of Art Therapy 35,* 3, 70–73.

Hastilow, S. and Aldridge, F. (2001) 'Is It Safe to Keep a Secret? A Sibling Group in Art Therapy.' In J. Murphy (ed.) *Lost for Words: Art Therapy with Young Survivors of Sexual Abuse.* London: Brunner-Routledge.

Klein, M. (1946) 'Notes on some schizoid mechanisms' *International Journal of Psychoanalysis 27,* 99–110.

Murphy, J. (ed.) (2001) *Lost for Words: Art Therapy with Young Survivors of Sexual Abuse.* London: Brunner-Routledge.

Ryan, G. (2010) 'Incidence and Prevalence of Sexual Offences Committed by Juveniles.' In G. Ryan, T. Levers and S. Lane (eds) *Juvenile Sexual Offending: Causes, Consequences, and Correction* (3rd edn). Hoboken, NJ: John Wiley & Sons.

Shaw, J.A., Lewis, J.E., Loeb, A., Rosado, J. and Rodriguez, R.A. (2000) 'Child on child sexual abuse: Psychological perspectives.' *Child Abuse and Neglect 24,* 1591–1600.

Streich, L. and Spreadbury, K. (2017) *Disrupting the Cycle of Harm: Report on Developing a Restorative Justice Approach to Working with Children Who Have Been Sexually Abused, Those Who Have Harmed Them and Their Families: Early Findings from the Restore Project.* Accessed on 08/10/2019 at https://the-green-house.org.uk/wp/wp-content/uploads/2017/11/Disrupting-the-Cycle-of-Harm-Restore-Pilot-Evaluation-FINAL.pdf

Walker, G. (2005) 'Who will be the naughty one now?': Using observational skills in work with primary aged children in a small school-based group.' *International Journal of Infant Observation and Its Applications 8,* 1, 19–31.

Wieland, S. (2006) *Hearing the Internal Trauma: Working with Children and Adolescents Who Have Been Sexually Abused.* London: Sage.

Yates, P. (2017) 'Sibling sexual abuse: Why don't we talk about it?' *Journal of Clinical Nursing 26,* 15–16, 2482–2494.

CHAPTER 2

Story, Shadow, Shame and Risk

Dramatherapy with Male Personality-Disordered
Sexual Offenders in Medium-Secure Forensic Settings

KATE SMITH, DRAMATHERAPIST

Introduction

'How dangerous is it that this man go loose!' (Hamlet)

This chapter will look at the use of imagination and storytelling within long-term dramatherapy interventions with male personality-disordered sexual offenders in forensic settings. The chapter will start with a consideration of risk and why arts therapists must consider the reduction of risk in their interventions with offenders, how this is measured and the need for a patient-led approach to managing risk, briefly looking at the use of the Structured Assessment of Protective Factors for violence risk (SAPROF) assessment. I will look at the use of fairy tales and archetypal roles within dramatherapy, and the application of this with sexual offenders, looking at some of the unconscious processes behind this. Trust and the therapeutic relationship will be considered, and how this is built towards the emergence of drama and storytelling. Vulnerability is discussed in relation to the patient when in playful mode, and the risk of using play and accessing shame is discussed.

I will look at the therapeutic relationship after accessing play, and how this can lead to a greater understanding of the offender's life story (Adshead 2012). I will explore how accessing the life story of the offender can help the patient understand their own risk and the experience of their victims and how this could inform the management of their risk.

> Distinctive in the integrated theories and associated models of offending is the link between a sexual offender's own past and becoming a sexual offender...the experience of child sexual abuse could be expected to demonstrate disruption in the learning of social norms and the distorted thinking associated with becoming a perpetrator. (Winstone and Pakes 2007, p.87)

I have used a fictionalized case study throughout the chapter to give context to the theory. 'Dave' is a patient with mixed personality disorder who has been in secure services for 30 years, in a high-secure setting for 20 years and in a medium-secure setting for ten years. He is a paedophile with a number of convictions, including rape and indecent assault against children under ten. His childhood was disruptive and abusive; he was sexually abused by both his parents from one year old, and was removed and put into a care home aged eight, where he continued to be sexually abused until he was 15, when he ran away. His sexual offending against minors began when he was 14.

Risk

Within forensic settings, reducing risk is at the forefront of the work done by multi-disciplinary teams, and is the cornerstone of all psychological interventions. This is primarily to reduce recidivism to keep the public safe. In my experience of working in forensic mental health hospitals over the last decade, it has been interesting to note how thinking about risk has evolved in my clinical work, perhaps also paralleling the development of risk assessment in general during that time, and the move to evidence-based treatment in the arts therapies.

When I first started as a dramatherapist, I thought about risk in broad terms, thinking about it from a solely psychodynamic perspective, considering why high levels of risk had evolved, looking at relational dynamics, victim impact and patient trauma. I tried to introduce risk measures into my work, and found this a challenging new process, as my small arts therapies team had not previously assessed risk in a formal way. The measures I used were 'informal' – I adapted a self-reporting outcome measure created by Geese Theatre Company (Baim,

Brookes and Mountford 2002). Geese Theatre does theatre work with offenders, but it is clear that they are not dramatherapists.

What led to me using this model was a need to evidence the results of the therapy with patients and to evidence any change in risk. However, I had to accept the limitations of this outcome measure (it was not specific to sexual offending or dramatherapy or used within NICE guidelines), as it did not fit in with the formal measures used by the hospital at the time. Due to hospital culture at the time, I was not formally trained in risk assessment early in my career, but this changed as I moved into new services.

It was useful that, as arts therapists, we were working on the margins, because we could see patients from a different perspective; however, the outcome of years of dedicated work with patients must be formally measured. If the arts therapies are to be highly valued by the wider hospital teams, the impact of the interventions needs to be evidenced. The Geese Theatre outcome measure was based within a drama workshop model of working with offenders, so it fitted with dramatherapy more than a standardized risk assessment. Whilst perhaps lacking in the strong evidence base needed by tribunals, the evidence of change in risk allowed me to understand something fundamental about risk: by creating trust in a therapeutic relationship and process, risk of re-offending could be spoken about more openly. This meant that some risk indicators might seemingly increase due to the openness and insight in therapy.

For example, Dave initially self-reported at the start of therapy that he saw himself as at low risk of re-offending and was very keen to move to a low-secure ward. At the end of therapy, he was able to say that he was at high risk of re-offending and realized that being honest about his risk would potentially allow for more progression long-term. In a risk assessment such as the SAPROF, this actually indicates a reduction in risk as it begins to measure the insight of the patient and the protective factors that they identify, leading to a decrease in the likelihood of re-offending – that is, Dave was able to identify when risky thoughts arose, and the team could then arrange further treatment to help him manage these.

The SAPROF risk assessment (de Vogel et al. 2009) was developed for use with both violent and sexual offenders, but only in conjunction with a Structured Professional Judgement risk assessment such as the

Historical Clinical Risk Management-20 (HCR-20) and the Risk for Sexual Violence Protocol (RSVP). The risk assessment looks every six months at the protective factors surrounding the patient and how well they are or are not being met and whether any have developed. There is much more balance in this type of risk assessment than other types of violence risk assessment; it offers a holistic view of the offender, and there is a less punitive approach to the assessment, and this is more useful for both staff and offender. It takes a patient-led approach by recognizing that patients are individuals and that not all factors will be relevant or as developed as others. Strategies for improving risk management can be openly discussed and thought about together as a team, recognizing the protective factors that are already working. 'A protective factor is any characteristic of a person, his/her environment or situation, which reduces the risk of future (sexual) violence' (de Vogel *et al.* 2009, p.25).

In order to consider all protective factors, the SAPROF risk assessment looks at internal factors, motivational factors and external factors. Protective factors identified are valid for both violent and sexual offenders, since most risk factors for violence are also valid for sexual violence (Hanson and Morton-Bourgon 2009). However, Brown, Harkins and Beech (2012) argue that victim-specific empathy needs to be considered in relation to the treatment of sex offenders, including in risk assessment.

The protective factors that dramatherapists and other arts therapists may be able to identify and discuss in risk meetings, in relation to the patient's SAPROF risk assessment, are:

- victim empathy

- coping

- self-control

- motivation for treatment

- professional care.

These are qualities that would be evident and possibly enhanced by the therapy. Along with the discussion around protective factors, the clinical team develops a risk formulation, which includes a narrative that explains the underlying mechanism of violence and proposes possible actions to reduce the level of risk. Within the formulation, areas looked at are:

- the problem

- precipitating factors

- perpetuating factors

- protective factors

- predisposition factors.

The SAPROF is helpful in monitoring the stages of treatment and level of risk management and allows for treatment goals to be formulated and for recognition of which treatments are effective. In the first stages of admission and risk assessment it allows the clinical team to consider what to prioritize (de Vogel *et al.* 2009).

The effectiveness of the risk assessment depends on the quality of the assessor, and there is never a guarantee of prevention of future violence. In order for patients to be engaged in risk assessments, they must trust the team they are working with. Therapists and other clinicians can be healthy attachment figures who can open up a useful conversation about risk. Within forensic settings, attachment figures for some of the most challenging sexual offenders are arts therapists, as they can be the 'last hope', where traditional talking therapies have been tried with little success. Indeed, it has been put to me that we are the 'warm-up' act for hard-to-reach patients, in order to prepare them for other more evidence-based psychological treatments such as the Good Lives model. (This strengths-based model takes a holistic approach to sexual offending rehabilitation, helping offenders to make manageable realistic plans both to enhance their lives and lower their risk.) It is very important that these types of risk assessment are understood by a whole hospital team, where key professionals contribute to these valuable discussions.

Shadow and shame

In order to achieve an accurate, dynamic, effective risk assessment, transparency is needed from the patient in order to identify their own risk factors. Sexual offending is so often hidden in the shadows, in the sense that the offending often happens in secret and also because the patient retreats into their shadow self. 'The Shadow archetype is that hidden, repressed, for the most part inferior and guilt-laden personality whose ultimate ramifications reach back into the realm of our animal ancestors' (Jung 1991, p.285). This may lead to the patient hiding in the sessions, perhaps afraid and overwhelmed by the shadow and all that is unknown within it.

In the assessment sessions boundaries are often tested, grooming and seduction may be attempted, and the suggestion of play or creativity can be perverted into a form of sadistic expression. For example, when Dave came in for his assessment, he spoke about 'enjoying playing' and winked. He asked if I enjoyed playing and appeared to be sexualizing the idea of play within the therapy space. He seemed to want to take control, constantly moving about the space, looking at all the objects, fabrics and art materials, then picking things up and throwing them down. He talked about his offending behaviour with a smile on his face.

In her consideration of gender when working with perverse and violent patients, Yakeley (2014) suggests:

> Although perverse behaviors such as fetishism, exhibitionism, and sadomasochistic practices might appear to be sexually motivated, on closer examination they are revealed to be practices that are used, albeit unconsciously, by the perverse individual to aggressively control the other person and defend against anxieties of becoming too emotionally close and having his psychic existence obliterated. (p.86)

This may offer an explanation for Dave's boundary-testing and controlling behaviour within the dramatherapy. Time and trust allowed Dave to tell his story, something he had not been able to do before. The life story of the patient must be heard in order for them to stop hiding in the shadows and experience the possibility of new ways of connecting interpersonally with a healthy attachment figure. However, telling their story requires vulnerability, the very thing that may have led to their act of sexual violence.

The possible challenge in working therapeutically with antisocial or borderline patients is their experience of play in childhood and the inherent threat that may lie within this. Play may have been disrupted in childhood, not allowed, or distorted in some way for the pleasure of someone else. So, when asked to be creative in a session, the response from a patient may be resistance or withdrawal. For example, Dave had no memories of play, he was neglected throughout his childhood as he tried to survive. Normative relational socialization happens through play, so patients who never played may never have reached key neurological developmental stages, such as developing empathy (Jennings 2010). It is crucial that this is identified at the assessment stage, through the use of creative assessment tools.

For others, play may remind them of sexual and physical abuse, so the threat of repetition creates a palpable resistance in the therapy space. Life stories may have been manipulated by abusive adults, and lies created to distort the truth, as the patient's young mind formed. This can create confusion, distortion and a fragmented sense of self, or indeed no sense of self whatsoever. However, for some, there is a joy in play and a return to their inner child. They are able to experience wonder in accessing their imagination beyond the limitations of the shadow, and return to their playful self, and have this witnessed by a healthy attachment figure (the therapist).

For the hiding in the shadows to be named, trust must be built between the therapist and patient through containment and consistency. Sexual offenders with personality disorders can spend a lifetime relying on a strategy of 'smoke and mirrors' in order to remain unseen, alone and unchecked. This strategy can provide safety in childhood, but in adulthood it becomes a maladaptive coping strategy, leading to increased risk and impulsivity, and ultimately the potential for offending. Witnessing this process of hiding, and ultimately naming it in the therapy space, allows for an acknowledgement of the hidden part of the self.

The monstrous acts committed by sexual offenders often become entwined in their identity and define them, exacerbated by society and the law, and mirrored in the social microcosm of the hospital environment, and on a micro-level the treatment team. Often this 'monster' story is perpetuated by those around the patient and their life story is fixed within this. In therapy, it is important that the humanity of the patient is recognized and named, so that the patient has a space in which to tell their story and victim empathy can be fostered. Otherwise, the role of the monster keeps the patient separate, different, 'other' and lurking at the edges of humanity with the dark shadow of shame.

This recognition of their humanity can often be a painful process as it is a return to thinking and mentalizing (Fonagy and Bateman 2006), with the patient having to face themselves and their abusive violent acts. Landy (1993) talks about the role of the pariah as one inhabited by criminals and the mentally ill, occupying the underside of society and reminding the well and moral of the potential for this role to emerge in us all. The casting-off into the shadows of the pariah allows society to feel protected and in denial of their own shadow. Von Franz (1995) posits that if we lived alone away from others, it would be impossible to see our shadow; to be in therapy is to have an onlooker or witness to the story, where the patient makes use of the therapist's reactions and responses. For this to be useful, the therapist must be able to explore what is provoked in their own shadow within the countertransference, and to acknowledge their feelings of shame and revulsion (Geiser 1989).

Therapists therefore need rigorous supervision to work with this patient group. Assessment is the key, because it is a specific series of sessions designed to establish whether both parties can work together. It is important with such complex offending and trauma that both parties feel that trust can be possible and a therapeutic relationship established. There may be occasions when the countertransference is too overwhelming and the sadistic persona of the patient too unmanageable. This was the case for me during an assessment early in my career, when my own feelings of shame and sexualization of my body were too engulfing in the countertransference, so I could not work with that patient in a helpful way. Excellent supervision at the time reminded me that we cannot work with everyone. In such situations, the patient is referred to another therapist or put back on the waiting list.

Imagination and the importance of story

Slade (2009) suggests that narrative is the core of the recovery and change process in mental health. Narratives are the stories we tell of our choices and experiences that make up our identity and sense of self. Narratives are dynamic; over the course of a person's life span they change and shift. They are also formed by the systems around the patient, for example how often treating teams call the act of sexual violence an 'index offence'. Perhaps this is done to make the narrative more palatable for all involved and move away from the trauma of the event by not naming the sexual offence explicitly, such as 'rape, sexual abuse, etc.' But then the impact and meaning of the offence is dissipated within the narrative, so that the victim and the violence become distanced. In dramatherapy we are exploring the patient's narrative and attempting to make it coherent. 'Narratives are complex, layered, and integrate different perspectives of the self and social roles; they acknowledge that we may see things differently over time, and how we see ourselves may not be what others see' (Adshead 2012, p.1).

Dramatherapy is about exploring new narratives through distancing and metaphor. This possibility for a new way of thinking increases the capacity for patients to think about self and other. Often patients in therapy can be stuck in a narrative about themselves and the events of their offence, coming from a place of justification and externalization. There can also be inconsistencies in the storytelling and building trust in the first year or years of therapy; it is important to challenge these inconsistencies.

> Holding on to secrets cuts us off from the unconscious. Where there is a shaming secret, there is always a dead zone in the psyche, a place that does not feel or respond properly to the person's own continuing emotional life events or to the emotional life events of others. (Estes 1992, p.377)

The use of imagined stories through play helps access to the unconscious and holds the potential to move beyond defences and help the patient in accessing their vulnerability and their own life stories. Accessing vulnerability for traumatized patients must be done carefully, and the distance provided through story helps with this (Casson 2004). For men in secure settings, accessing vulnerability can also be challenging, as their need to survive the experience of a secure setting has meant that vulnerability equates to weakness, particularly for patients who will return to a prison environment post-treatment.

Fairy tales

Bettelheim (1991) explores the notion of the shadow within fairy tales and the inherent presence of this in cultural vernacular. He shows that through accessing story and archetypal fairy tales, shame and shadow can be spoken about in a distanced and curious way through using creativity and building imagined stories (Jones 2007). Fairy tales mirror collective unconscious material and yet hold within them morality tales and the polarizing opposites of good and evil (von Franz 1995). However, they also leave enough ambiguity for characters to be thought about in new and intriguing ways. The stories are rife with loss, violence, collusion and redemption. By using fairy tales in treatment, we access the stories that patients connected to at the earliest and often most traumatic parts of their lives, which allows them to reconnect to their own life stories. This process also gives the patient an opportunity to empathize whilst in role, something that is often too challenging for personality-disordered offenders to do in talking therapies.

The archetypal characters in fairy stories are developed and built on over a long period of time within the therapy and become safe, distanced touchstones in the treatment when the sessions become stuck or lose track. They also allow for the patient and therapist to be put into role, for the transferences to be heightened, projections to be identified and life stories to unfurl.

Through working with this patient group over a decade, I have noticed patients being drawn to similar archetypal characters in these stories, particularly the character of the witch. The witch role can be played by either patient or therapist at different times. The witch can lead to thinking about abusers, mothers, power, magical thinking, change, evil, relationships and childhood being threatened or destroyed. The witch stirs the cauldron of possibilities and challenges what is known and unknown; she embodies both innocence and sexual abandon (Martin 2010). Who could or would relate to a monster? Not a human, but perhaps a witch could? This role could also mirror the destructive ever-powerful internalized maternal fantasy, which is rooted in the patient's early relational experiences. The magical part of this character can speak to a need for change or an acknowledgement of difference, of being outside of the norm, something perhaps the patient has felt not only through their offending but also through their personality disorder. 'The witch is an archetypal aspect of the Great Mother. She is the neglected Mother Goddess, the Goddess of the earth in her destructive aspect' (von Franz 1995, p.121).

About a year into therapy, Dave wanted to move into some embodied work. He did not have a story structure as such but had created a 'troll' puppet over the previous three months. He asked me to play the character of the troll, whilst he took on the character of the witch. The setting was a wood, and the two characters walked into a clearing in the middle of which there was a deep clear pool. He wanted the character of the witch to end up falling into the water. As the story developed, he was lost in role, fully embodying the posture/voice and movement of the witch. When the witch arrived at the pool, she was thirsty and needed a drink; as the witch bent over the pool, she fell in. She yelled for the troll to help, but the troll could not reach her, and she disappeared into the blue fabric of the pool. This was a significant session, with Dave reflecting on the moment of being lost to the pool of water; he was quiet and subdued, thinking about the moment of needing help. The symbolic water (womb) could be seen as a return to the unconscious, in order to be cleansed, by considering the shadow aspects of self, which had been hidden for so long (von Franz 1980).

Risk also needs to be considered in relation to role and playing in the therapy sessions. There is an inherent risk for the therapist and the patient in the play dynamic, particularly with sexual offenders. There is potential for grooming fantasies to be enacted and control to be exerted. This can happen due to the fear of annihilation by the therapist (Glasser 1996), which may increase risk as there is a perceived threat from the therapist. The therapist needs to consider this in supervision and in session. To hold in mind risk, potentiality and change at the same time can be complex, indicating the level of experience needed by therapists to work with this patient group.

The need to see the humanity in sex offender patients is important. Whilst there is risk there is also opportunity. If a patient over-asserts control of the story or the character they have cast the therapist in, there is opportunity to think about this experience. We can consider what the need for control is about, discuss the challenging relational dynamic with the therapist, and think about whether these might mirror the distorted intimacy needs created in early childhood by the abusive (m)other. This can then be thought about in relation to the sexual offending. There needs to be a reflective space in the therapy room, away from the designated play space, where therapist or patient can go, to think and reflect on the ongoing dynamic in the play. It must also be a place of safety in which to return to self.

Life story

> Why are these feelings of shame and self-contempt so bottomless, chronic and almost ineradicable in the most violent men? It may be that the men I knew had been subjected to a degree of child abuse that was off the scale of anything I had previously thought of describing with that term. (Gilligan 2001, p.36)

The powerful themes that emerge in story and play often link unconsciously to the disturbed early experience of the patient. Empathy for the victim may never be possible for some pathologies, however, hearing the life story of the patient and their own experience of trauma can help the patient connect to their victim's experience. The story that is useful for the patient to tell is their full life story, not their life from the point they offended. Using play and returning to the fairy tale, building and unpacking the story allows for a connection to their early life and for a narrative to emerge. Patients who have not been able to speak about their early trauma are able to do this as they connect with the themes of the fairy tales. After his embodiment as the witch drowning in the pool, Dave was able to talk about his experience of being alone as a child, helpless to the abusers around him; he needed help but no one was there.

I have often heard expressions of surprise from patients that they are allowed to tell their story. So often, when the role of a man changes to that of an offender, the narrative of their life story starts from the point of their offending rather than what came before. In order to truly connect with the victim or victims of the offending, the full life story must be heard. For a patient to be able to think empathically about their victim's experience in any real way, their own experience of childhood abuse has to be acknowledged. For some patients in therapy, the realization that the abuse perpetrated *on* them is the equivalent to the abuse perpetrated *by* them is a deeply sorrowful moment. For those patients surviving in the shadows, this may never have come into true consciousness before.

Conclusion

The reduction of risk is only possible when there is an acknowledgement of the shadows, and the use of hiding in this space is thought of as a patient's coping strategy to tolerate their own disturbed mind and deep shame, and avoid their own and others' annihilation. If a patient can make these connections, then their ability to recognize their risk factors will be much more enhanced. Some sexual offenders have experienced such deep trauma that they may never move out of the shadows. But for others, an ability to acknowledge that the behaviours in the shadows – the avoidance, the hiding, the somatizing, the externalization and isolating themselves – are all warning signs that risk may be increasing, offers some hope. Hope that perhaps one day this insight can lead to their being psychologically safer and able to exist safely in society.

References

Adshead, G. (2012) 'Their Dark Materials: Narratives and Recovery in Forensic Practice.' Conference paper. Accessed on 1/12/2019 at www.semanticscholar.org/paper/Their-Dark-Materials-%3A-Narratives-and-Recovery-in-Adshead/1876a26f02dc54a694ce3f36bbc2b761329e207f

Baim, C., Brookes, S. and Mountford, A. (eds) (2002) *The Geese Theatre Handbook: Drama with Offenders and People at Risk.* Winchester: Waterside Press.

Bettleheim, B. (1991) *The Uses of Enchantment: The Meaning and Importance of Fairy Tales.* London: Penguin.

Brown, S., Harkins, L. and Beech, A. (2012) 'General and victim-specific empathy: Associations with actuarial risk, treatment outcome, and sexual recidivism.' *ATSA Journal of Sexual Abuse 24,* 12, 411–430.

Casson, J. (2004) *Drama, Psychotherapy and Psychosis: Dramatherapy and Psychodrama with People Who Hear Voices.* London: Routledge.

de Vogel, V., de Ruiter, C., Bouman, Y. H. A. and de Vries Robbé, M. (2009) *SAPROF: Guidelines for the Assessment of Protective Factors for Violence Risk.* Utrecht: Forum Educatief.

Estes, C. (1992) *Women Who Run with the Wolves.* London: Rider.

Fonagy, P. and Bateman, A. (eds) (2006) *Mentalization-Based Treatment for Borderline Personality Disorder.* Oxford: Oxford University Press.

Geiser, R. (1989) 'A therapist's exploration: Face to face with The Dark Side.' *The Arts in Psychotherapy 16,* 2, 133–136.

Gilligan, J. (2001) *Preventing Violence.* London: Thames & Hudson.

Glasser, M. (1996) 'Aggression and Sadism in the Perversions.' In I. Rosen (ed.) *Sexual Deviation.* Oxford: Oxford University Press.

Hanson, K. and Morton-Bourgon, K. (2009) 'The accuracy of recidivism risk assessments for sexual offenders: A meta-analysis of 118 prediction studies.' *Psychological Assessment 21,* 1, 1–21.

Jennings, S. (2010) *Healthy Attachments and Neuro-Dramatic Play.* London: Jessica Kingsley Publishers.

Jones, P. (2007) *Drama as Therapy: Volume 2.* London: Routledge.

Jung, C. (1991) *The Archetypes and the Collective Unconscious. Collected Writings: Volume 9.* London: Routledge.

Landy, R. (1993) *Persona and Performance: The Meaning of Role in Drama, Therapy and Everyday Life.* London: Jessica Kingsley Publishers.

Martin, K. (ed.) (2010) *The Book of Symbols: Reflections on Archetypal Images.* Cologne: Taschen.

Slade, M. (2009) *Personal Recovery and Mental Illness: A Guide for Mental Health Professionals.* Cambridge: Cambridge University Press.

von Franz, M-L. (1980) *The Psychological Meaning of Redemption Motifs in Fairytales*. Toronto: Inner City Books.

von Franz, M-L. (1995) *Shadow and Evil in Fairy Tales* (Revised edn). Boston, MA: Shambhala Publications.

Winstone, J. and Pakes, J. (2007) *Psychology and Crime: Understanding and Tackling Offending Behaviour*. Collumpton: Willan Publishing.

Yakeley, J. (2014) 'Therapist as "Perverse Female": The Implications of Therapist Gender for Working with Perverse and Violent Patients.' In J. Woods and A. Williams (eds) *Forensic Group Psychotherapy: The Portman Clinic Approach*. London: Karnac.

CHAPTER 3

Behind Closed Doors

Art Psychotherapy with Female Sexual Offenders

JESSICA COLLIER, ART PSYCHOTHERAPIST

Introduction: What it means to be female

'A storm of sorrow will break forth from this silence.' (Sophocles)

In England, prior to the Industrial Revolution, earning an income and the responsibility for childcare was a shared endeavour within the family. Particularly in rural areas, both women and men worked in the home and had an equal obligation to run the household and attend to the children. It was only in the 18th century that the division between the private and public domain, the separation of spheres at the heart of capitalism, became entrenched. The great myth of our times, that women are naturally predisposed to stay at home and care for the children while men must go out into the world and provide, is a relatively recent social phenomenon that benefits the wealthy and keeps both genders confined to damaging expectations (Friedan 1963). Even today, becoming a mother is the single objective women are expected to fulfil, female childlessness being regarded as inherently sad. For women, the act of mothering is seen as the natural expression of femininity. The signifiers 'woman' and 'mother' are often seen as synonymous.

Nowhere in the myriad of female experience do we find the possibility of the mother as both caregiver and sexual predator/manipulator. The taboo remains so entrenched that we cannot imagine a woman who might sexually abuse children as a means of exerting power or who may unconsciously enact her own early familial experience.

Such is the invisibility of these women in the discourse of our society, that when individuals are prosecuted, they are unable to recognize they have committed a crime. This apparent denial and blindness forms the theme of this chapter. Over many years, sexual abuse perpetrated by women has been ignored, disbelieved, minimized and even encouraged. Sanderson suggests that 'young boys being initiated into their first sexual experience is seen as innocuous and representative of all boy's fantasies' (Sanderson 2004, p.112). As a society, we must begin to understand and acknowledge that women are not domestic goddesses and recognize that an increasing number of women are being prosecuted for sexual abuse (Stemple, Flores Ilan and Mayer 2016). If we are to support these women in understanding the crimes they have committed, we must remove our own blindfolds and confront what can happen behind closed doors.

Women as victims and perpetrators of sexual abuse

Nearly all the British literature examining child sexual abuse focuses on male offenders as the perpetrators, notable exceptions being the seminal work of psychoanalyst Estela Welldon (1988) and forensic psychologists Saradjian (1996), Motz (2008) and Gannon and Cortoni (2010). In a search through the British art psychotherapy literature, there is not a single paper on women as the agents of these transgressions. Women and girls appear only as the time-worn stereotype: victims of male violence and coercion (Slater 2002). Welldon suggests that 'we have all become silent conspirators in a system which, from whatever angle we look at them, women are either dispossessed of all power or made into sexual objects and victims of their male counterparts' (Welldon 1988, p.86).

This observation does not contradict the evidence that men commit more violence; the Y chromosome is the single most compelling correlate of crime (Harris 2010). Rather, it is an argument to look more closely at what else is happening. To deny the possibility of female sexual perversity and violence is to deny the experience of the victims of these crimes, and the important reflection that offenders are often themselves both victim *and* perpetrator. Over half of incarcerated women report experiencing childhood abuse (Prison Reform Trust n.d.), and it is important to enquire as to where and how the anger they may feel is sublimated. As well as trusted male figures, the perpetrators of this abuse include mothers, sisters, aunts, babysitters, family friends and other responsible women in more cases than we might assume from the crime statistics, which show child sexual abuse as overwhelmingly committed by men. It is important to substantiate the fact that women, like men, are human beings, and consequently encompass the full human range of emotions and actions; some of which are troubling to accept.

There is still a view, reflected in part by notions of toxic masculinity, that young boys are lucky to be initiated into sex by older women. Neither the perpetrator nor the victim, nor even perhaps the victim's family, believes that this is a crime. Women equally report transgressive and sexually abusive relationships with female friends, carers or family members more often than might be expected. This would suggest that female sexual abuse is a seriously under-reported offence. 'The implicit denial of women's potential for sexual aggression…may ultimately contribute to the under-recognition of the problem in official sources' (Denov 2003, p.303). Our blindness to the possibility that women are perpetrators of child sexual abuse is then directly mirrored in the blindness of the female abusers themselves in failing to recognize what they have done as abuse.

Incest, rape and the law

Some sexual offences disclosed by female patients happen in incestuous relationships. Incest was defined, in part, by the late professor of criminology Herschel Prins as 'a man who has sexual intercourse with a woman he knows to be his granddaughter, daughter, sister' (Prins 1980, p.210). He goes on to explore incidences of father and sibling incest but does not discuss mothers committing incest. The mother is only acknowledged as sometimes 'prepared to collude in the practice' in 'cases where the wife is still physically present but where she has abrogated her sexual role' (p.211). The use of the verb abrogate implies a wife has a gendered duty to have sex with her husband, and that if she revokes this, the man may use his child to attain his gendered right to have sex.

This patriarchal outlook on sex within marriage was in line with judicial thinking up until the outlawing of marital rape, which only happened in Britain as recently as 1991. This reflected the long-held view that women were the property of men and therefore controlled in every sphere by men, a concept that continues to pervade marital rape ideology and laws around the world. This again suggests a blindness to the possibility that women can be aggressive perpetrators of sexual abuse as well as passive victims. Incest itself was not considered an offence until 1908, despite being one of the most widespread of all cultural taboos. Children continue to be reminded of 'stranger danger', while in reality, the overwhelming majority of child sexual abuse happens within the immediate or wider family context (Sanderson 2004).

The representation of incest in the arts

While there are examples throughout the history of art and literature of women who are violent and murderous towards children (Collier 2019a), the combined taboo of paedophilia and incest means that there are no depictions of child and adult female familial sex. Representations are found only when the perpetrators commit incest in acts of desperation or unknowingly, and never with infants or children.

Perhaps the most celebrated illustration of incest in the arts is to be found in Sophocles' play *Oedipus Rex* (2010), in which King Oedipus and his mother Jocasta unknowingly become lovers, only to discover that Oedipus has inadvertently murdered his father and taken both his crown and his queen. Oedipus' arrogant dismissal of the blind prophet Teiresias' warnings and his inability to see the truth because of his own excessive pride, culminate in his disgrace. At the end of the play, Jocasta kills herself and Oedipus gouges out his eyes in despair as his acts of patricide and incest finally become clear to him.

The literal and metaphorical references to blindness, seeing and truth that are fundamental to *Oedipus Rex* are deeply significant in thinking about female sex offenders. The myth of Oedipus is itself central to much psychoanalytic thinking. Freud's early formulation of the Oedipus complex suggested a continuity between maternal care and perverse sexual relations between mother and child. Indeed, Freud suggested that the mother 'herself regards [her child] with feelings that are derived from her own sexual life: she strokes him, kisses him, rocks him and quite clearly treats him as a substitute for a complete sexual object' (Appignanesi and Forrester 1992, p.404).

Female sexual offenders

The compulsion to deny that anything erroneous has happened is strong for perpetrator, victim and society when the abuser is female. This is elucidated further by Gilligan (2000), who suggests that violence sublimates feelings of shame into feelings of pride, thus transforming painful experiences into conquests or accomplishments. In art psychotherapy, this may be seen in images that contain elements of the sublimated feelings that result in violent and sexual offences (Collier 2019b).

While there is a paucity of literature and research on female sexual offenders, what research there is attempts to classify women who commit sex crimes into a number of categories. This may again reflect the resistance to recognizing sexual offending as part of a full human spectrum of behaviours; the inference being that women are not a heterogeneous population and individuals must be bad, sad or mad to abuse children. Nevertheless, these categories are relevant, as they include the possibility that women do not always perpetrate sexual offences in the context of a coercive relationship with a man, although this seems to be the most usual situation. As in the criminal justice system generally, the classification and treatment of women who commit sexual offences have been influenced by the research and management of men who have committed sexual offences, thus perpetuating the perception that these acts are uncharacteristic and anomalous. Harris (2010) suggests the following as useful typologies: women who abuse adolescent boys, women who abuse young children, women who have co-perpetrators and women who abuse adults.

Defining sexual offences

The Sexual Offences Act 2003 lists and defines 72 sexual offences, starting with rape and cataloguing transgressions such as causing a child to watch a sexual act and inciting a child family member to engage in sexual activity. The National Society for the Prevention of Cruelty to Children's website defines child sexual abuse as 'when a child…is forced or tricked into sexual activities', which may involve physical contact or non-contact activities and can happen online or offline. There is a comprehensive list of abusive behaviours, such as, in the contact section: 'making a child undress or touch someone else'; and in the non-contact section: 'exposing a child to sexual acts'.[1]

The vulnerability of female paedophiles in prison: A case study

The case study below concerns a woman who was found guilty of sexual offences, and who undertook art psychotherapy sessions for a year during her 18-year prison sentence. This was at times an exceptionally challenging piece of work, made more complex by the cultural taboos mentioned above. There were also potential consequences of the woman's charge being exposed to her peers and staff, making her vulnerable to violence and mistreatment (Collier 2019a; Higgins and Ireland 2009). Her difficulty in accepting responsibility for the offences required finding a way to work together that encompassed the disparity between her ongoing avowal of innocence and the court finding her guilty. I will consider the aetiology of the patient's sexual offending through a psychoanalytic lens as well as continuing my critique of society's idealization and denigration of women and the damage caused to victims of female sexual abuse due to the influence that 'societal perceptions of females as sexually passive and innocent appear to have…on the criminal law, on victim reporting practices, and on professional attitudes, reflecting an implicit negation of women as potential sexual aggressors' (Denov 2003, p.313). I will call this woman Linda, and I thank her for allowing me to use examples of our work together in this chapter.

'It was a normal boring childhood'

Linda was a robust, healthy-looking woman in her mid-fifties from the North West of England, who had been in prison for five years when we met. Due to her offence she had experienced bullying, and there was concern for her safety during the early part of her sentence. However, having moved prison, she was now doing well within the strict regime. When I asked Linda what she thought she might get from engaging in art psychotherapy, she said she did not know, but had been told she must do therapy to be eligible for parole. This is an interesting and

---

1   www.nspcc.org.uk/what-is-child-abuse/types-of-abuse/child-sexual-abuse/#what-is

common dynamic in prison psychological therapy provision, requiring more discussion than can be had here. Nevertheless, given the chaotic and often dangerous lives female prisoners lead when living in the community, working with them while they are 'safely' incarcerated is important and necessary (Collier 2015).

In our first meeting I asked Linda what her childhood had been like. 'It was a normal boring childhood,' she replied. Following this unconvincing assertion, she soon disclosed the reality of her experience growing up. She explained that her father and elder sister had been in an incestuous relationship that bore two children, one of whom survived. Thus, in the family home, Linda's father and sister shared a bedroom with their child, while Linda shared a bedroom with her mother. According to Linda, her father had been imprisoned twice for incest, but had returned home after his sentence and continued the incestuous arrangement, using extreme violence to maintain the family's acquiescence. Despite the obvious power imbalance in this dynamic, Linda blamed her sister for the relationship and insisted her mother was powerless to do anything.

Linda idealized her mother despite her apparent inaction and tolerance of the incest and was unable to move away from this position. She characterized her mother as a kindly woman who wasn't able to protect Linda because she herself was terrified. Saradjian found that women who abuse their children frequently idealized their own neglectful or abusive mothers and 'found reasons to excuse their mother…essentially blaming themselves… the women had to negate themselves and… received virtually no care, support or affection in return' (Saradjian 1996, pp.41–42). Linda looked after her mother to the detriment of her friendships and education until her mother died prematurely in her early fifties. 'She brought me into the world,' Linda said, 'the least I could do is repay the compliment.'

'I've always felt I was carrying her shame; I've been punished for what they did'

In the early stages of our work together Linda made drawings of her family life, both as a child in her own family and as the mother to her biological children and stepchildren, some of whom were the victims of her and her co-defendant's offences. The drawings of her childhood showed a lonely existence, including her childhood self alone in the front garden while other children played together on the verge; the high fence suggesting isolation and exclusion, even imprisonment (see Figure 3.1).

Figure 3.1: Childhood

Linda said, 'I have always felt guilty. I've always felt I was carrying her shame. I've been punished for what they did.' She described staying away from people in case the incest was uncovered. Meanwhile, the pictures she made of her own early adult family life were idealized images depicting playing in the park, baking together, family meals and seaside trips. Linda described losing all her photographs when she came to prison, and these images struck me as fantasies, replacements for the lost memories, an attempt to rebuild the narrative of her life to survive the reality of her current situation (Adshead 2011; Collier 2019a). Griselda Pollock (2008) suggests this idea when she asks, 'What do images remember for us in this paradox of retaining and disguising?' (p.79). Speaking to these images, Linda talked lovingly about her two children, especially her son Nicky. I felt moved by her stories of caring for them, despite the neglect and lack of interest from their father, and his eventual abandonment of the family, leaving Linda to care for the children alone.

'If I'd known what he was doing, I'd have kicked him into touch'

Some years after her first husband left her, Linda met another man and they started a relationship. They merged their families, making a large household of seven children ranging in age from around two to 14 years. Linda filled our sessions with descriptions of the special meals she made for the children, listing their dietary preferences and detailing the chores she did through the day, epitomizing the stereotype of the perfect mother in the domestic sphere: laundry, cleaning, cooking, school runs, and so on. She remained adamant that she was innocent, and I found as I was listening that I too was beginning to doubt the validity of the guilty verdict; perhaps unconsciously drawn into the mythical archetype of the nurturing mother. I experienced a keen sense of sympathy for Linda. When I asked why she thought the children had accused her of abusing them, Linda seemed genuinely hurt that this had happened. She denied all knowledge of what had gone on, blaming her husband and saying, 'If I'd known what he was doing, I'd have kicked him into touch.'

The reality and pain of incest and sexual abuse

Early in the sessions, I asked Linda how she would feel if she ever recognized her guilt for the offences. 'I would kill myself', she said simply. Troubled by my countertransference feelings of rationalization and concerned that I might be colluding in a 'cover story' (Collier 2019a) – consciously or unconsciously woven by Linda to protect herself from the appalling reality of what had happened – I read Linda's pre-sentence report. This is an assessment written by probation services for consideration by the court in sentencing those found guilty. The summary included detailed testimonies of the abuse that had happened in the family home and repeatedly described the children going to Linda for help. According to the report, Linda categorically denied the children's experience of familial rape and assault, despite her witnessing or taking part in the abuse. The assessment was upsetting to read and seeing it had an immediate effect on how I felt in the sessions. I now experienced Linda's stories of summer picnics and family meals as perfidious. I felt tired and impassive, and struggled to stay awake, perhaps a countertransference response indicative of Linda's protective 'false self' enfolding the space (Winnicott 1960).

Coinciding with my own new perspective, Linda simultaneously began to speak differently about her family. Slowly, she began to disclose the truancy, alcohol and drug abuse that affected her children from a young age. The wider family emerged as suffering from chronic illnesses, addictions, mental health issues, suicide, violence and poverty. The stories of picnics shifted into stories of social services visits, children running away, failing at school and entering violent and near incestuous relationships of their own. One of Linda's stepdaughters gave birth, below the age of consent, to two children with fetal alcohol syndrome, the youngest of whom was placed in the care of Linda and her husband, and whose later allegations of sexual abuse perpetrated by Linda were included in the prosecution. Linda's long and close relationship with social services again suggests the blindness of the system to imagining females as potential perpetrators of sexual abuse.

Alongside these disclosures, Linda began drawing her dreams. In one, a dark cloud encompassing a glaring face hovers over her as she sleeps (see Figure 3.2).

Figure 3.2: Dream 1

Linda described it as terrifying and identified the face as that of her abusive husband. The cloud appears almost breast-like above the bed, the sleeping figure tiny and childlike. I thought about the bed Linda had shared as a child with her idealized mother, and the terror her own children might have felt while being abused by their caregiver. Another showed Linda in a coffin in the ground. She described her horror as the worms and insects made their way into the space, intrusive and penetrating, leaving Linda exposed; another unconscious acknowledgement perhaps, of her own and her children's experiences (see Figure 3.3).

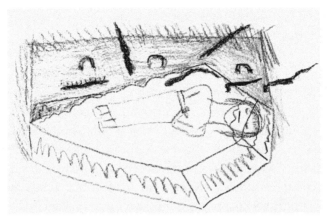

Figure 3.3: Dream 2

As her images became more revealing, Linda's continued attempts at re-imagining holidays with her children manifested on black paper, the darkness of the background making the pictures appear obscure and foreboding.

Linda said she was unable to think and drew an image of herself with cobwebs and spiders in her head. This, once again, brought to mind her mother's continued presence. I thought of the artist Louise Bourgeois' lifelong use of spiders as a motif symbolizing her own idealized 'Maman'. Bourgeois herself wrote: 'Aggression is used by guilt and turned against myself instead of being sublimated into useful channels' (Turner 2012). I considered Linda's aggression turned not towards herself, but towards her children. Estela Welldon's defining paradigm asserts that perverse mothers use their children as an extension of themselves in an attempt to master their own traumatic histories. She says: '...the opportunity that motherhood offers of being in complete control of a situation creates fertile ground for some women who have experienced injurious and traumatic events in their own lives to exploit and abuse their babies' (Welldon 1988, p.74). It seemed clear to me that Linda's attempt to simultaneously 'retain and disguise' her narrative was being enacted in her images and in my countertransference response, which moved from disbelieving to impassive, mirroring Linda's own response to her children's disclosures of abuse. Welldon further suggests that these enactments happen transgenerationally, echoing Freud's concept of the repetition compulsion in which unconsciously repressed incidents are enacted as contemporary experiences in an attempt to master them (S. Freud 1961).

Blindness as a means of survival

Despite the difficult sessions, Linda continued to attend and described stories of abuse and neglect without any emotion. I began to feel Linda's 'blindness' to the horror of what she was describing as an enactment of the abuse itself. My countertransference response to what I was hearing was to switch off and not say anything for fear that Linda might kill herself. I intuitively suppressed my own emotions and stayed quiet to prevent a potential act of violence. Linda gave several examples of hearing or being present during serious violence between adults in her extended family but refusing to help police inquiries 'because I didn't *see* it.' She refused, just as Oedipus refuses, to believe something she did not actually see, either literally or metaphorically, despite it being evident to others. We spoke at length about what she might have known or not known – seen or not seen – in her household, but Linda continued to avow her innocence. Linda told me she had Horner's syndrome, a rare condition caused by damage to the sympathetic nerves of the face, disrupting her peripheral vision. So innate was Linda's inability to see what was happening around her, so intrinsic was this 'blindness' to her psychological survival, it seemed to have been somatized in this unusual diagnosis.

Ending and loss

As we approached the year review session, Linda stopped making her own drawings and began to choose colouring sheets. She coloured a Geisha, heavily costumed, cutting into a small tree with scissors (see Figure 3.4). The Geisha, historically a performer who is submissive and respected for this false acquiescence, echoed the position Linda projected as woman and mother. However, the symbolism of the costume and the tree being cut, while in my mind elucidating the deceit, cover-up and violence of her painful familial experience, seemed absent in Linda's mind. This image took on further resonance as symbolic of cutting off any more potential growth when Linda decided to end our work together.

Figure 3.4: Geisha (see colour section)

In our penultimate meeting, Linda entered the room, sat down slowly and told me she had just heard that her beloved son Nicky had died of a drug overdose. She shared this news impassively, and I found myself equally unable to feel anything, unable to process this suffering. The tragedy of this young man's life and death seemed overshadowed by Linda's literally inexpressible pain. As she finished her final drawing, a prison-like building with a seemingly dormant volcano in the background, Linda vigorously covered over the entire image with a white pencil. I asked Linda what she was doing, and she told me, 'It's the fallout.'

Conclusion

To me it seemed that Linda's final action and comment was an unconscious attempt to simultaneously acknowledge and conceal that the abuse she and her husband had meted out to their children had led, eventually, to the death of her son. There had been a tangible consequence to the pattern of trauma: 'the fallout'. It seemed that, alongside most of society, Linda was incapable of seeing herself as both a loving mother and a perpetrator of sexual violence against her children. Anna Motz writes:

> Understanding the female sexual offender requires the capacity to suspend stereotypes about 'maternal instincts'... They are acting out, through their children's bodies, experiences that are too difficult to think about. What cannot be borne mentally becomes enacted through this sexualised violence. (Motz 2008, p.69)

It is important to reiterate that Linda maintained her innocence throughout our work together, and to note that denial does not necessarily increase an individual's risk of recidivism, but can be seen as a cognitive distortion, perhaps a means of psychological survival (Yates 2009). Linda grew up in an incestuous family. This parental failure meant boundaries between generations were blurred and fragmented. The normal generational differentiation of roles was absent. For Linda, the unconscious defences of projective identification and denial made her own role as parent possible. She may have promised herself that she would never allow her children to suffer what she had been through, that she would never be 'blind' to the abuse as her mother had been. Nevertheless, Anna Freud suggests that, without the experience of maturational insight, parents treat their children exactly as they themselves were treated (A. Freud 1939). In an unconscious attempt to master the original overwhelming trauma, Linda unconsciously transformed her previously passive role into that of the violent aggressor. Linda repeated her original trauma, whilst denying its existence and her involvement. Unconsciously, by making her own children vulnerable and helpless victims, Linda perhaps temporarily rid herself of her own vulnerability and helplessness and so found a way to survive. The sudden and unexpected death of her son might have brought Linda too close to 'seeing' what she had done, and in an attempt to stay alive, she drew our sessions to a close, at least for the time being.

When we finished, Linda acknowledged the transgenerational pattern of abuse in her family and said the sessions had made her think differently about her life. She asked for the possibility to continue therapy at a later date to be kept open. Linda left her images with me, and perhaps in time she will be ready to return to therapy and think more about her innate shame and how this has blinded her to the trauma she experienced and inflicted on the people she loved most. In Sophocles' play, Teiresias attempts to speak the truth to Oedipus when he tells him, 'I say with those you love best you live in foulest shame unconsciously, and do not see where you are in calamity' (Sophocles 2010, ll.422–424).

References

Adshead, G. (2011) 'The life sentence: Using a narrative approach in group psychotherapy with offenders.' *Group Analysis 44*, 2, 175–195.

Appignanesi, L. and Forrester, J. (1992) *Freud's Women*. London: Weidenfeld & Nicolson.

Collier, J. (2015) '3 man unlock: Art psychotherapy with a woman with severe and dangerous personality disorder.' *Psychoanalytic Psychotherapy; Applications, Theory and Research 29*, 3 243–259.

Collier, J. (2019a) 'Cover Stories: Art Psychotherapy with Mothers in Prison Who Have Killed or Harmed Their Children.' In A. Foster (ed.) *Mothers Accused and Abused: Addressing Complex Psychological Need.* London: Routledge.

Collier, J. (2019b) 'Trauma, Art and the "Borderspace": Working with Unconscious Re-enactments.' In P. Windham Stewart and J. Collier (eds) *The End of the Sentence: Psychotherapy with Female Offenders.* London: Routledge.

Denov, M. (2003) 'The myth of innocence: Sexual scripts and the recognition of child sexual abuse by female perpetrators.' *Journal of Sex Research 40*, 3, 303–314.

Freud, A. (1939) *The Ego and the Mechanism of Defence*. London: Hogarth Press.

Freud, S. (1961) *Beyond the Pleasure Principle*. New York, NY: W.W. Norton.

Friedan, B. (1963) *The Feminine Mystique*. New York, NY: W.W. Norton.

Gannon, T. and Cortoni, F. (eds) (2010) *Female Sexual Offenders: Theory, Assessment and Treatment.* Chichester: Wiley-Blackwell.

Gilligan, J. (2000) *Violence: Reflections on Our Deadliest Epidemic.* London: Jessica Kingsley Publishers.

Harris, D. (2010) 'Theories of Female Sexual Offending.' In T. Gannon and F. Cortoni (eds) *Female Sexual Offenders: Theory, Assessment and Treatment.* Chichester: Wiley-Blackwell.

Higgins, C. and Ireland, C. (2009) 'Attitudes towards male and female sex offenders: A comparison of forensic staff, prison officers and the general public in Northern Ireland.' *British Journal of Forensic Practice 11*, 1, 14–19.

Motz, A. (2008) *The Psychology of Female Violence: Crimes Against the Body.* London: Routledge.

Pollock, G. (2008) 'Beyond Oedipus: Feminist Thought, Psychoanalysis, and Mythical Figurations of the Feminine.' In V. Zajko and M. Leonard (eds) *Laughing with Medusa: Classical Myth and Feminist Thought.* Oxford: Oxford University Press.

Prins, H. (1980) *Offenders, Deviants or Patients.* London: Brunner-Routledge.

Prison Reform Trust (n.d.) Welcome to the Women's Programme. Accessed on 29/6/2019 at www.prisonreformtrust.org.uk/WhatWeDo/Projectsresearch/Women

Sanderson, C. (2004) *The Seduction of Children: Empowering Parents and Teachers to Protect Children from Child Sexual Abuse.* London: Jessica Kingsley Publishers.

Saradjian, J. (1996) *Women Who Sexually Abuse Children: From Research to Clinical Practice.* Chichester: Wiley.

Slater, N. (2002) 'Re-visions on Group Art Therapy with Women Who Have Experienced Domestic Violence and Sexual Violence.' In S. Hogan (ed.) *Gender Issues in Art Therapy.* London: Routledge.

Sophocles (2010) *Oedipus the King* (trans. David Grene). Chicago and London: University of Chicago Press. Accessed 29/6/2019 at https://studylib.net/doc/8130696/oedipus-the-king-pdf

Stemple, L., Flores Ilan, A. and Mayer, H. (2016) 'Sexual victimization perpetrated by women: Federal data reveal surprising prevalence.' *Aggression and Violent Behavior 34*, 302–311.

Turner, C. (2012, 6 April) 'Analysing Louise Bourgeois: Art, therapy and Freud.' *The Guardian. Accessed* 29/6/2019 at www.theguardian.com/artanddesign/2012/apr/06/louise-bourgeois-freud

Welldon, E. (1988) *Mother, Madonna, Whore: The Idealization and Denigration of Motherhood.* London: Karnac.

Winnicott, D.W. (1960) 'Ego Distortion in Terms of True and False Self.' In D.W. Winnicott (ed.) *The Maturational Processes and the Facilitating Environment: Studies in the Theory of Emotional Development*. London: Karnac.

Yates, P.M. (2009) 'Is sexual offender denial related to sex offence risk and recidivism? A review and treatment implications.' *Psychology, Crime & Law 15*, 2–3, 183–199.

CHAPTER 4

Exploring Maternal and Erotic Transference in Dance Movement Psychotherapy with a Sex Offender

PREETHA RAMASUBRAMANIAN AND DAWN BATCUP,
DANCE MOVEMENT PSYCHOTHERAPISTS

Introduction

This chapter focuses on learning experiences during an internship as a trainee Dance Movement Psychotherapist under supervision as a part of the MA programme in the UK. It is based on work in a medium-secure forensic psychiatric hospital setting in London. In presenting this case study that focuses on the therapeutic relationship with a sex offender, we have attempted to understand the multiple levels of relationship that emerged as erotic, maternal and analytical, which were the main flavours of the narrative during therapy and supervision.

Preetha, first author, refers to herself as 'I' when she is in the clinical sessions with the client and with the supervisor in supervision. Dawn, second author, is the supervisor.

According to the Association for Dance Movement Psychotherapy (2012):

Dance Movement Psychotherapy is a relational process in which clients and therapist engage in an empathic creative process using body movement and dance to assist the integration of emotional, cognitive, physical, social and spiritual aspects of self. It is founded on the principle that movement reflects an individual's pattern of thinking and feeling. Through acknowledging and supporting clients' movements, the therapist encourages development and integration of new adaptive movement patterns, together with the emotional experiences that accompany such changes. DMP is seen to be beneficial for a wide range of individuals, for those who are considered healthy as well as those who are emotionally distressed and physically or intellectually disabled.

Dance movement psychotherapy sessions with the client of this chapter evoked maternal and erotic feelings in the trainee. This transference became interwoven in each step of the therapy process. The complex task of understanding client material that surfaced as movement, play, metaphors, words, imagination, self-reflection and links made, contributed to the interplay between the client, the trainee therapist and the supervisor. Racker (1968) writes that the psychoanalytic therapy relationship is complex and the interaction between two people occurs at multiple levels. Considering this, we portray how the maternal and erotic transference was supported by the psychotherapeutic relationship and formed reciprocal, parallel and constant themes in the relationship.

This chapter focuses only on a set of pivotal DMP sessions, which include the beginning of therapy up to a point at which an important transition was made. These sessions are described in detail, and also the supervision sessions reviewing the therapy sessions.

Tom – the client

Tom, a pseudonym, was in his thirties and diagnosed with schizophrenia. He broke into his former girlfriend's residence to sexually assault her. His belief that she had had sex with his father triggered the assault, compounded by his tremendous fear of castration by his father. Tom was admitted to the medium-secure forensic unit of a psychiatric hospital, where the trainee worked with him using dance movement psychotherapy (DMP). Tom's referral to DMP was prompted by female psychologists and nurses who remained intimidated and uncomfortable in his presence, even though he had completed psychological work focusing on sexual offending. The team wondered if using the body in a more process-oriented way could help Tom gain insights that provided him with the resources to communicate non-verbally in less intimidating ways.

Considering the nature of Tom's offence, the team suggested that sessions should be conducted in the activity room in his ward, as it was considered safer to be closer to the team, as compared to the DMP room in an outpatient setting further from a response team. Tom was offered 20 weekly individual hour-long sessions over five months. The sessions were structured as is usual (Sandel 1993), with an initial verbal check-in followed by a body warm-up and movement encouraging creativity and rhythmic activity. This then leads to internal and perhaps less conscious material emerging, following which the client is encouraged to reflect on the process verbally.

DMP assessment

Tom came into the room looking relaxed and sociable. I was anxious and recalled the previous conversations with the psychologist who had worked with Tom, but slowly felt my anxiety fade. His free and light body movements suggested a 'dream state', which in Laban Movement Analysis (LMA) is a particular combination of weight and flow effort qualities suggestive of the Jungian archetype of sensing and feeling (Bloom 2006). Tom sat with folded arms and spoke in a quiet voice, alluding to his offence without sharing details. Tom blamed the offence on illicit drugs and mental illness and said he was happy about DMP treatment on an individual basis, which led me to think about his possible need to be the centre of attention. Tom mentioned his future discharge, accompanied by 'shadow movements' (North 1972) of fast rhythmic tapping of his thighs, while the rest of his body was static. I thought these might indicate a strong desire to be released from the closeness of the current therapeutic interaction as well from the confinement of the unit.

In discussing our working alliance and Tom's expectations of therapy, he asked my opinion of his appearance, followed by several personal questions. My anxiety increased and I wondered if the intimacy of the therapeutic relationship was too intense for him. I struggled to reflect and find the most helpful way to use his intense curiosity about me. Focusing on changes in his body attitude helped me to think, and I noticed he had shifted to 'vision drive', which has direct, bound and sudden LMA effort qualities (Bloom 2006). I experienced Tom's non-verbal behaviour and communication becoming too close, and felt bodily and psychologically invaded and afraid. This led me to end the session sooner than intended.

I discussed this in supervision and how I found it difficult to be alone with Tom. We explored ways to build the therapeutic alliance and maintain boundaries. I believed that his desire for therapy was probably led by self-centredness and he eroticized the therapeutic relationship by flirting. This made it hard for me to empathize. Solomon (1969, cited in Koo 2001) points out that a preoccupation with sexual matters, in fantasy or in acting-out behaviour, may be entirely separate from meaningful human relationships, and suggests that the eroticized transference may defend against a true object relationship. This seemed reinforced by Tom's movement responses. I wondered if Tom found it easier to deflect focus away from his crime by focusing on me instead. I also discussed with my supervisor my inability to think in Tom's presence. She quoted Bion (1967) on how attacks on thinking become attacks on possible links by fragmenting and numbing of thinking. This leads to incoherence of thoughts communicated by the patient to the therapist.

Intrusion

Tom wanted to cancel the next session, saying he felt vulnerable after an attack by another patient and was frightened to leave his bedroom. I invited Tom into the session room, and he sat down but kept dozing off to sleep. I suggested movements to keep him awake. He started to mirror me, which was intense. To reduce this intensity, I introduced movement props (fabrics, balls, bean bags, foam yoga blocks, etc.) into the space between us, as had been discussed in supervision. Tom chose a ball and threw it at me fiercely while maintaining an intense gaze. I acknowledged the force he used and gently bounced the ball back, modelling how strong force could be safely redirected to the floor through the bounce. But Tom repeated his fierce throw, which felt like an invasion of my personal space, so I held the ball and made a verbal intervention, requesting him to reconsider the forcefulness of the throw. I suggested that there might be a link between force and anger, which Tom said he would think about.

Cordess and Williams (1996) write that the criminal act is experienced jointly by both client and therapist during therapy. To ensure my psychological survival through what had felt like projected destructiveness, I demonstrated how anger might be safely communicated through cathartically throwing the ball to the floor, thus ensuring others' safety. In response, Tom said I was like his girlfriend. This was the person he had sexually assaulted. He probed me with personal questions while looking directly at me. Given the continued intensity, I wondered if he had drawn a parallel between me, the index offence and the fierce ball throwing. Tom closed his eyes, smiled and whispered my name under his breath, which symbolically invaded my personal space further and angered me. This anger resulted in my ending the session early again, as my capacity to think and feel safe in the room with Tom was impaired (Ogden 1993). With the session ending, Tom noticed my frown; this surprised me as I was not aware of the continued closeness of his scrutiny – this may have also been a countertransference response (Alexandris and Vaslamatzis 1993; Meekums 2007).

During supervision, we considered my feelings and reflected upon Winnicott's (1971) writing about how infants watch their mother's face closely, so even the smallest facial twitch can induce an uneasy response in the infant as '*what* she looks like is related to what she sees there' (p.131). We explored movements that might help Tom understand us as separate people collaborating in therapy. For example, instead of sharing movement props, we considered exploring different props simultaneously, as this might help to lessen the sense of intrusion. It was important to consider Ruszczynski's point (2010), where parental figures are threatening for the forensic patient because they invite closeness and intimacy, but only in order to inevitably betray them.

During reflection, it seemed that the dissociated part of Tom's psyche became more evident as he re-enacted anger in movement, projecting it while not fully relating to the feeling. I associated my early session termination with Tom's transference of primitive and eroticized emotions. I felt guilty, de-skilled and inadequate as a trainee therapist, and wondered whether this was also countertransference, reflecting Tom's experience of relationships. The creative process may have helped Tom link his inner and outer worlds, and perhaps led him to experiences that he was unprepared for (Meekums 1999). Tom may have also explored less conscious motivation and partially acknowledged that suppressed feelings could lead to uncontrolled outbursts (Smeijsters and Cleven 2006). It already seemed apparent that the use of metaphors could be important for Tom to reconnect with his previously overwhelming and difficult-to-address emotions (Cox and Theilgaard 1987; Govoni and Weatherhogg 2007; Shuttleworth 1985).

The containment in supervision helped me feel safe enough to connect with my feelings, versus acting out during the session. This seemed similar to the pre-verbal communication between mother and child through projective identification, whereby the baby projects intolerable feelings on to the mother, who then contains and detoxifies them, and feeds them back to the child in a more tolerable form. This enables the child to manage experiences and develop the capacity to think and communicate. I realized that retaining my capacity to think in the therapeutic space was important for Tom too, as this could enable the exploration of his feelings in a safe and contained way (Bion 1967). I then had to cancel the next session due to heavy snow.

Merging and connecting

Tom began the next session with renewed curiosity about me. I supported his curiosity and reflected on the impact of the unplanned break and our developing professional relationship. In response, Tom stared at me and I felt uncomfortable. To break the silence and the stare, I suggested using movement. To redirect his attention and gaze, I asked Tom to explore his personal space in movement. Being mindful of proximity, I suggested that we each use our own movement prop and find different ways of exploring them.

Tom bounced a ball off the wall, calling it his 'world of natural disasters'. I mentioned that his world sounded unsafe, to which he agreed and repeated bouncing the ball. I wondered if the cancelled session amplified the 'disaster' as it represented his commitment to therapy.

He then offered me one end of a large blue cloth and although I did not want to share props, I accepted his initiation as I imagined he would have felt rejected had I not. Holding the cloth together gave us a connection on to which Tom placed the ball, and we started to sway it. He said that the movements were soothing, but for me it invoked a strong sense of holding him, which raised my discomfort with the closeness and intimacy of the act.

Tom moved the cloth quickly, causing the ball to bounce and said the ball 'felt chaotic'. I responded that although the ball felt chaotic, it might feel safer held in the cloth, to which he agreed. He used the ball to explore a range of thoughts, from chaos to calm. I felt calmed by the indirect use of touch through the movement prop (Meekums 2002), and this contributed to a more thoughtful connection with Tom. Reflecting verbally on the movement, Tom said it helped him relax, which suggested that my direct instructions may have helped him with grounding and embodying his feelings. He commented that rocking the ball soothed him and the bouncing was chaotic for him. I wondered if I was being a safe enough container to help Tom explore his feelings.

Tom wanted to set a therapy goal, which we defined as 'to explore and find out what comes up during movement'. He said he would now know what to say when asked about DMP sessions. I responded by saying that the therapeutic relationship could be confusing, as it deals with intimate feelings, so a goal could be containing.

I noticed that when Tom left the room after this session, I felt abandoned. I wondered about the complex nature of this as a potential countertransference. I walked back from the therapy smiling and then realized that I had overrun by five minutes. I recognized that the feelings of wanting to be close during swaying could be linked to maternal erotic transference, which made it difficult to end the movement.

In supervision, I admitted my internal conflict about enjoying the connection with Tom while sharing the blue cloth during movement. We discussed closeness in therapy versus the state of symbiosis, where the couple blurs boundaries and creates the illusion of oneness. Mann (1997) writes that some patients only form relationships using erotic transference because they don't know any other way. This made me think further about becoming overly close and enmeshed in physical and psychological proximity, during movement.

Orbach (1999) writes that the therapist can become less afraid of her responses if she keeps herself consciously aware of them long enough to ponder, rather than banish them, which reminded me of my fear in sharing the blue cloth. Kumin (1985) talks about erotic horror during therapy and describes how the situation excites both the therapist and the client, requiring a rule of abstinence to prepare both for the predictable frustration from the lack of achieving their desires. Tom's frustration about the session cancellation may have been a representation of this commitment and relationship, hence referred to as a 'natural disaster'.

The phallus

The session started with discussing the broken CD player (in the activity room where we had sessions), which Tom said he had accidentally jammed earlier. He talked about writing music and discussed the prevalence of violence, drugs and sex in rap music. Tom said that his rap music was different and called it 'rap poetry'. In response, I caught myself giggling flirtatiously, which I guessed was my flattered reaction to him wanting to impress me with his 'rap poetry'.

I reached for a big scarf to use to amplify the space between us, which provided me with time to regain my professional stance. The scarf promoted whole-body interactive movements, flexibility in response and movement interactions with a shared focus, cooperation and creativity (Stanton-Jones 1992). This took me out of the previous pattern of a potentially flirtatious interaction.

I watched as Tom then built a three-foot-tall vertical tower using foam yoga blocks and then balanced a ball at the top. He called it the 'Tower to Heaven'. The phallic shape of the tower made me wonder about Tom's confined state and struggle to make meaningful sexual relationships with others. He talked about how people could not reach heaven through the tower and as he talked, he changed the yoga block formation into a man. Suddenly, he became silent and had a horrified look on his face while staring at the man he had made. Tom's body became tense and bound (Bloom 2006) and he curled up into a seated fetal position. I sensed a deep connection Tom had made, perhaps to masculinity, and potentially to his offence, through the phallic object he had created. Tom and I sat in silence together for the last few minutes of the session.

Chace's approach to DMP (cited in Sandel 1993) included image-making; as the image shifted, the clients' movement shifted from being a simple action to a symbolic act. This stimulated the connection between a feelings state and symbolic representation, which in turn transformed into symbolic communication. Tom's curiosity seemed to be evolving as his focus gently moved away from me to his own reflective process, which may have given him more insight through starting to use creative externalization (Blatt 1996; Sutherland cited in Lewis 1987).

Supervision was also helping me externalize through talking honestly about my feelings, which developed my understanding that Tom's curiosity about me need not be destructive to the therapeutic relationship. In the session, it had seemed important to sit with him in the silence, being emotionally present to my own sadness, as the use of words at this point might have minimized his experience and understanding of the tower's symbolism and potential to transform (Lewis 1987). The session may also have touched upon learning about 'self' and reduction of denial (Lewis and Perkins 1996) and was perhaps more consciously experienced when Tom made a non-verbal link to the figure. I thought that it was difficult to express in words what the tower may have represented, and apparently, so did Tom. I noticed that I did not want to end the session and took this to supervision.

I discussed the session with my supervisor and was honest about giggling flirtatiously; we noted together how this connection may have been a response to Tom wanting to impress me. I also wondered if my response was tantalizing. Orbach (1999) explains that, until recently, therapists believed it was best to deny their patients' arousal in order to protect themselves. It was often only addressed in supervision if they perceived it becoming unprofessional rather than being instrumental in communication and part of the psychotherapeutic work as a whole.

The phallic tower that Tom created made me wonder if it also linked to sadistic fantasies of wanting to gain power and control. Nneke (2003) says that in transference, the therapist becomes the object of the feelings repressed by the patient. These feelings return and are expressed in therapy, where the patient exhibits aggressive tendencies, sexuality or near-senile compliance toward the therapist, accompanied by an arsenal of other defensive measures. Coen (2007) states:

> …narcissistic patients seek to draw the analyst into a shared narcissistic splendour, as they once experienced with a parent, seductively trying to pull the analyst into their world. … If this is performed subtly and skilfully, a sufficiently needy and vulnerable analyst may not grasp what is being repeated. (pp.1179–1180)

I recalled not wanting to end the session. My supervisor suggested that the tower may have also represented Tom's isolation and loneliness.

Love, lust and passion

Tom came in looking excited and wondered aloud about how it would be to meet me socially and wanted to know more about me. I said that it must be frustrating for him to make sense of the boundaries of the caring, professional relationship. Searles (1959) said that during the Oedipal phase, it was beneficial for his patients when he allowed them to see candidly that they moved him deeply, helping them recognize the therapeutic relationship.

In using movement, Tom kicked and punched the air. I attuned to the fighting qualities of his movements without mirroring and mentioned that perhaps built-up frustration was emerging. He picked up a cloth and gave me one end to hold and folded it until it became very small. I released the cloth, creating more distance between us and wondered if the physical proximity was tantalizing. Searles (1959) writes that the patient's romantic and erotic demands astonished the therapist because of the incest taboo. Tom found it difficult to understand the therapeutic relationship partly due to his struggles with attachment, care and intimacy, and wanted to minimize the space between us.

Tom then handed me a stretch-cloth and whilst holding on to the other end, he leaned away, trusting me to hold his weight. I held it tightly, not wanting him to fall. I had an image of the cloth being an umbilical cord, supporting Tom while he trusted me to hold him securely. This also made me wonder if Tom wanted to see how much I could hold him on an emotional level. He said, 'You are a strong woman, Preetha.' I replied, 'It looks like this support is important to hold you securely.' This was followed by silence, and Tom stood again fully on his own two feet, looking upset.

Tom folded the stretch-cloth, and I sensed my desire to be physically close to him but reminded myself to ponder this thought, potentially maternal, rather than act on my desire. I imagined Tom as a rejected child who was trying to figure out how he could be close to his maternal figure without upsetting her. This made me feel guilty for letting go of the cloth earlier.

Tom then wrapped a ball in scarves and threw it to me, calling it the 'ball of fire'. He said that it symbolized his love, lust and passion for me. Tom said he was struggling with the idea of not being able to hold it for long, as he might get burnt. He also mentioned how hard and frustrating it was for him to understand the therapeutic relationship. I wondered how I could be 'good enough' (Winnicott 1971). Koo (2001) suggests that eroticization permitted her male client to express his need in a way that was more socially acceptable; that is, gender norms where a man's sexual passion for a woman is deemed more acceptable than dependency, which could imply being weak and needy.

I felt guilty when I left the ward and worried that I was tantalizing Tom. I questioned whether I was working with Tom to satisfy my own narcissistic need and to avoid feeling inadequate, needy and dependent. After discussing this with my supervisor, I could think about this more as a potential countertransference and a way into understanding Tom's confusion about closeness and intimacy. I also sensed Tom's perception of me as a purely eroticized object slowly diluting over time, as he trusted me to literally hold his weight when he leaned away using the stretch-cloth, signifying his perception of me as someone who holds.

When I was holding Tom with the stretch-cloth, the verbal intervention I made provided Tom with an insight into his being held in therapy. Dosamantes (1992) stated: 'To interrupt the symbiotic merger, therapists must create the distance required so that what has been enacted by the patient and themselves unconsciously may be consciously understood.' By attaching meaning to the patient's experience, a shift may have occurred in the type of relationship that existed between us. I was also aware of Tom needing and enjoying physical proximity (Koo 2001) as he initiated sharing movement props with me and never missed a session. I started to believe that DMP was helping Tom decrease his sexualized behaviour (Stanton-Jones 1992), as he did seem to use the movement props and the relationship to explore his intense feelings in a more appropriate manner.

Erotic maternal countertransference/breastfeeding

Tom walked into the room with questions that felt like piercing arrows. He then said we were all made 'wonderfully fearful'. While I was trying to understand this, he leaned forward and said, 'Do you know it's been so long since I did it?' His proximity made it difficult for me to think and I moved away. I tried to make a transition into using movement, moving the right arm and leg simultaneously, and Tom followed, and then suddenly jumped towards me. I was startled by his unexpected movement, maybe as he had been by mine.

Tom wrapped a large cloth around himself and said it was for protection, then he folded it and put it aside. I was no longer afraid but was struggling to understand – possibly like Tom. I commented that perhaps he needed to make his 'wonderfully fearful' feelings less intense so that he could put those aside too, like the cloth. Milliken (2002) writes how DMP helps forensic clients to explore coping with intolerable feelings.

Tom recalled an earlier DMP session and mentioned how this had inspired his folding and putting aside of the cloth. I commented on how likewise his earlier life had impacted his present life and how his present would affect his future. Tom nodded in agreement. Winnicott (1958) discusses how the mother enables the infant's ability to use illusion to help him contact the psyche and the environment. Tom may have begun to feel secure in therapy, as he did seem able to think about what I was saying.

I talked with my supervisor about Tom's sudden jump and my fear. She helped me understand how the movement I had attempted to introduce may have taken him by surprise. We also looked at how using the same arm and leg activated one half of the body, which may have linked to early child development movements. For instance, body-half movements happen within the initial months of infancy and are typically seen when babies are contentedly being breastfed. Early traumas and rejections may be remembered bodily and then accessed during the DMP sessions. This could have been partly why Tom jumped. Hartley (2004) wrote regarding somatic resonance:

> …the therapist feels something of the client's somatic experience within her own body. Sensations within her body are evoked by, or resonate with, the client's psychic and somatic experience in the moment; recognition by the therapist of her own somatic experience, evoked by the client's process, facilitates the awakening of awareness in the client, and the release or transformation of energy. (p.23)

Rescue team

Tom came in saying that I was part of the staff team and wondered aloud how our sessions contributed towards his progress. He also commented on the ambiguity of facing what might come up. Tom looked at the props bag and asked, 'What *is* in that bag?' I responded by attuning to his curiosity and repeating the tone of his voice but changed the words to reflect a question concerning what was in the therapeutic relationship whilst bringing the bag to the centre of the room.

Tom pulled out the movement props and then abruptly stopped, saying it was messy. I suggested we take out one prop at a time. Tom chose large foam blocks, laid them on the floor and initiated a game where we took turns walking on them. He said that they were wooden pieces floating on water. Tom handed me one end of a cloth, calling it 'the rescue line' and we used it for support to stay on the blocks. Tom lost his balance, let go of the rescue line and fell into the water. I threw the rescue line to him and he climbed back to safety. The theme of rescue started to build. In DMP sessions, participants explore play as it emerges in the session. Meekums (2002) writes that during this process, the unconscious and conscious aspects of both client and therapist can coexist.

Tom again lost his balance and was about to fall into the water, he said that he might drown. As he was in close proximity, I grabbed his wrist and helped him to stay afloat. This touch evoked strong and powerful feelings as both of us looked at each other and then moved away in an awkward silence.

While reflecting on the session with Tom, he spoke about the theme of rescue and how I was a part of the professional team trying to help him recover, but neither of us acknowledged the use of touch. Towards the end of the session, when I reminded Tom about my planned break, he spoke about his fears of his violent father. As it was important to keep to the strict time boundary, there was no time to discuss this further with him.

After the session, I thought that Tom was beginning to trust me since he mentioned his father. In supervision, we discussed the psychodynamic significance of the violent father being discussed before the therapy break, leaving no time to explore it, and how the break may have felt 'violent'. I also talked to my supervisor about touching Tom and my horrified feelings. I was aware that while body boundaries could be better understood through the use of touch, it could also evoke erotic and sexualized feelings (Freud 1973). I think it was my maternal instincts that took over to help Tom survive the calamities of the emerging narrative.

When focusing on touch, Ramsden et al. (2006) state that to touch one's own skin is to touch one's own source of memories. Therefore, to use touch with the forensic patient who is scared of his/her own hurtful memories can be frightening and re-traumatizing because of complicated early childhood experiences, where touch is often associated with cruelty, corruption and fear.

We wondered how the use of touch was perceived by Tom. My grabbing him and initiating the use of direct touch in the session seemed to be linked to his thoughts about me as part of the recovery team, and not primarily as an erotic attachment. Avstreih (1981) points out that when a child in distress experiences a dissolution of ego, the mother's touch, her secure holding, can restore a sense of intactness for the child. Therefore, when touch was used, Tom perhaps perceived it as a secure holding that restored a sense of intactness for him.

I wondered about Tom's relationship with his father, whom he described as a strict disciplinarian. As it was the first time that Tom had spoken about his childhood, I pondered the timing of this information surfacing. Due to the upcoming break, I felt extremely guilty and wondered if this was my maternal or paternal countertransference reaction. In rescuing Tom from falling into the water, I thought about the creative process of bringing inner reality to bear on outer reality (Winnicott 1971). I also considered the importance of the therapeutic process as co-creational and how I might have added to the event, which Meekums (1999) described as a projection of the client, to help shape the emerging self.

Supervision – the dyad becomes a triad

The most important aspect of this work was the triadic relationship involving the client, myself and my supervisor. As a trainee supervisee, it was important for me to have a sense of being held in supervision and have a third perspective from my supervisor (Cavell 1998). This need was amplified further as working with a sex offender through erotic transference was challenging enough, but I also experienced constant self-doubt, anxiety, fear of failure, ethical dilemmas and other conflicts. Through the course of this work, supervision, theoretical frameworks and personal therapy were the main elements that kept me and the client safe and enabled a coherent story about the work we were doing. In supervision, we looked keenly at ethical and physical boundaries, safety, shame, containment and other less conscious narratives that emerged in and around the therapy. The supervisory sessions facilitated and supported a strong learning alliance (Govoni and Pallaro 2008).

The psychodynamic theoretical framework was also brought to the supervision. This helped to understand transference, countertransference, theory and the client. It was also helpful in understanding and noticing the multi-layered relationships arising during sessions. I felt held and contained during supervision and the non-judgemental atmosphere enabled useful disclosures, which we also used to generate information about the client. Personal therapy was also crucial in helping me make sense of myself in the sessions (Penfield 2008).

Conclusion

This chapter has focused only on the pivotal DMP sessions, which include the beginning of therapy and those at the transition that Tom made from sensing me as an eroticized object to a nurturing object. This transition was particularly important to highlight. Because the erotic transference could be fully explored in the security of supervision, this served as a bridge that enabled Tom to use me and the therapy as a secure base where he could explore and collaborate in creating a coherent narrative about current and past relationships more safely.

When Tom made romantic and erotic demands in therapy, it shocked me, possibly due to the incest taboo (Searles 1959). But instead of denying those feelings, it was important to acknowledge and work with them (Mann 1997; Orbach 1999). I also think that the romantic and erotic feelings were made more available by the use of the body as the therapeutic medium. Lewis and Perkins (1996) state that the main aim of using psychotherapy with sex offenders is to reduce the dangerousness and/or frequency of re-offending. They also state that object-relationships and negotiating new relationships play important roles during psychotherapy. As Tom and I negotiated our way through the erotic and maternal transferences, the supervisory relationship helped in understanding and analysing the therapy sessions better. I sensed significant changes in Tom's attitude towards women and therapy.

DMP also led to being able to contemplate less conscious motivation and acknowledge that suppressed feelings could lead to hurtful outbursts (Smeijsters and Cleven 2006). Significant issues can be difficult to identify, hence structuring the sessions, body action, time and relationship boundaries may be important in establishing what 'the problem' is (Lewis and Perkins 1996; Meekums 2002). Learning about myself, being honest and reducing denial, projection and blame (Lewis and Perkins 1996) was also an important parallel process in building meaningful therapeutic and supervisory relationships.

References

Alexandris, A. and Vaslamatzis, G. (1993) 'Countertransferential Bodily Feelings and the Containing Function of the Analyst.' In A. Alexandris and G. Vaslamatzis (eds) *Countertransference: Theory, Technique and Teaching.* London: Karnac.

Association for Dance Movement Psychotherapy (2012) 'What is Dance Movement Psychotherapy?' Accessed on 7/12/19 at https://admp.org.uk/dance-movement-psychotherapy/what-is-dance-movement-psychotherapy

Avstreih, A. (1981) 'The emerging self: Psychoanalytic concepts of self development and their implications for dance therapy.' *American Journal of Dance Therapy 4,* 2, 21–32.

Bion, W.R. (1967) *Second Thoughts.* London: Heinemann Medical.

Blatt, J. (1996) 'Dance Movement Therapy.' In C. Cordess and M. Cox (eds) *Forensic Psychotherapy: Crime, Psychodynamics and the Offender Patient.* London: Jessica Kingsley Publishers.

Bloom, K. (2006) *The Embodied Self: Movement and Psychoanalysis.* London: Karnac.

Cavell, M. (1998) 'Triangulation, one's own mind and objectivity.' *International Journal of Psychoanalysis 79,* 3, 449–467.

Coen, S.J. (2007) 'Narcissistic temptations to cross boundaries and how to manage them.' *Journal of the American Psychoanalytic Association 55,* 4, 1169–1190.

Cordess, C. and Williams, A.H. (1996) 'The Criminal Act and Acting Out.' In C. Cordess and M. Cox (eds) *Forensic Psychotherapy: Crime, Psychodynamics and the Offender Patient.* London: Jessica Kingsley Publishers.

Cox, M. and Theilgaard, A. (1987) *Mutative Metaphors in Psychotherapy: The Aeolian Mode.* London: Tavistock Publications.

Dosamantes, I. (1992) 'The intersubjective relationship between therapist and patient: A key to understand denied and denigrated aspects of the patient's self.' *The Arts in Psychotherapy 19,* 359–365.

Freud, S. (1973) *Introductory Lectures on Psychoanalysis.* London: Pelican Books.

Govoni, R.M. and Weatherhogg, A.P. (2007) 'The body as theatre of passions and conflicts: Affects, emotions, and defences.' *Body, Movement and Dance in Psychotherapy 2,* 109–121.

Govoni, R.M. and Pallaro, P. (2008) 'The Supervision Process in Training.' In H. Payne (ed.) *Supervision of Dance Movement Psychotherapy.* London: Routledge.

Hartley, L. (2004) *Somatic Psychology: Body, Mind and Meaning.* London: Whurr.

Koo, M.B. (2001) 'Erotized transference in the male patient–female therapist dyad.' *Journal of Psychotherapy Practice and Research 10,* 28–36.

Kumin, I. (1985) 'Erotic horror: Desire and resistance in the psychoanalytic situation.' *International Journal of Psychoanalytic Psychotherapy 11,* 3–20.

Lewis, P. (1987) 'The expressive arts therapies in the choreography of object relations.' *The Arts in Psychotherapy 14,* 321–331.

Lewis, P. and Perkins, D. (1996) 'Collaborative Strategies for Sex Offenders in Secure Settings.' In C. Cordess and M. Cox (eds) *Forensic Psychotherapy: Crime, Psychodynamics and the Offender Patient.* London: Jessica Kingsley Publishers.

Mann, D. (1997) *Psychotherapy: An Erotic Relationship, Transference and Countertransference Passions.* London: Routledge.

Meekums, B. (1999) 'A creative model for recovery from child sexual abuse trauma.' *The Arts in Psychotherapy 26,* 247–259.

Meekums, B. (2002) *Dance Movement Therapy: A Creative Psychotherapeutic Approach*. London: Sage.

Meekums, B. (2007) 'Spontaneous symbolism in clinical supervision: Moving beyond logic.' *Body, Movement and Dance in Psychotherapy 2*, 2, 95–107.

Milliken, R. (2002) 'Dance/movement therapy as a creative arts therapy approach in prison to the treatment of violence.' *The Arts in Psychotherapy 29*, 203–206.

Nneke, A.M. (2003) *The Psychodynamics of the Unconscious: The Origins, Controversies, Disputes, Principles and Practice of Psychodynamic Psychotherapy*. London: Intapsy Publications.

North, M. (1972) *Personality Assessment Through Movement*. Trenton, NJ: Princeton Book Company.

Ogden, T.H. (1993) 'The Analytic Management and Interpretation of Projective Identification.' In A. Alexandris and G. Vaslamatzis (eds) *Countertransference: Theory, Technique and Teaching*. London: Karnac.

Orbach, S. (1999) *The Impossibility of Sex: Stories of the Intimate Relationship Between Therapist and Client*. London: Karnac.

Penfield, K. (2008) 'Three Makes One.' In H. Payne (ed.) *Supervision of Dance Movement Psychotherapy*. London: Routledge.

Racker, H. (1968) *Transference and Countertransference*. New York, NY: International Universities Press.

Ramsden, E., Pryor, A., Bose, S., Charles, S. and Adshead, G. (2006) 'Something Dangerous: Touch in Forensic Practice.' In G. Galton (eds) *Touch Papers: Dialogues of Touch in Psychoanalytical Space*. London: Karnac.

Ruszczynski, S. (2010) 'Becoming neglected: A perverse relationship to care.' *British Journal of Psychotherapy 26*, 1, 22–32.

Sandel, S.L. (1993) 'Imagery in Dance Movement Therapy Groups: A Developmental Approach.' In S.L. Sandel, S. Chaiklin and A. Lohn (eds) *Foundations of Dance/Movement Therapy: The Life and Work of Marian Chace*. Columbia, MD: The Marian Chace Memorial Fund.

Searles, H.F. (1959) 'Oedipal Love in the Countertransference.' In H.F. Searles (ed.) *Collected Papers on Schizophrenia and Related Subjects*. London: Hogarth Press.

Shuttleworth, R. (1985) 'Metaphor in Therapy.' *Journal of Dramatherapy 8*, 2, 8–18.

Smeijsters, H. and Cleven, G. (2006) 'The treatment of aggression using arts therapies in forensic psychiatry: Results of a qualitative inquiry.' *The Arts in Psychotherapy 33*, 37–58.

Stanton-Jones, K. (1992) *An Introduction to Dance Movement Therapy in Psychiatry*. London: Routledge.

Winnicott, D.W. (1958) 'Transitional Objects and Transitional Phenomena.' In D.W. Winnicott (ed.) *Collected Papers: Through Paediatrics to Psychoanalysis*. London: Tavistock Publications.

Winnicott, D.W. (1971) *Playing and Reality*. London: Routledge.

CHAPTER 5

The Use of Art Therapy to Address Dynamic Risk Factors in Sex Offender Treatment

AMY PFENNING AND MARIAN HUSTED, ART THERAPISTS

Introduction

This chapter describes the variety of art therapy work with sex offenders in a hospital in California. This work includes art therapy groups, art groups, open studio groups and ceramic groups. We show how all of these can contribute to sex offenders' learning about different aspects of relationships, and how this can lead to patients enrolling voluntarily in a Sex Offenders Treatment Program (SOTP). The case studies show how sex offenders with different problems and difficulties can learn enough to make themselves safe enough to be released into the community.

Currently there are approximately 114,000 registered sex offenders in the state of California. The facility where the two of us work houses approximately 1200 sex offenders, or 'sexually violent predators' as they are called under the civil commitment law. In addition, mentally disordered offenders and mentally ill inmates from the Department of Corrections are also treated at the facility. The population is male with a small percentage who have gender dysphoria.

The patients in the hospital have completed their prison sentences and have met criteria to be civilly committed, meaning they are being detained involuntarily because they are still considered to be a risk to society. Sex offender treatment is not mandatory; however, many patients choose to participate in the SOTP offered.

Sex Offender Treatment Program
Risk-need-responsivity model

The program uses a risk-need-responsivity model (RNR) and incorporates other modalities in its treatment. The *risk principle* involves matching the intensity of treatment to the individual's risk level of reoffending, with high-risk offenders receiving more intensive and extensive treatment than low-risk offenders. Offense risk is determined by the combination of static and dynamic risk factors. Static risk factors, such as past offenses, cannot be changed, whereas dynamic risk factors can change, such as substance abuse and self-regulation. Some of the dynamic risk factors that we address through art therapy include lack of concern for others, lack of intimate relationships with adults and poor problem-solving.

The *need principle* focuses on assessing dynamic risk factors and targeting them in treatment. Dynamic risk factors are defined as enduring but changeable features of an offender. They are amenable to interventions, and when successfully addressed result in a decrease in risk of recidivism.

The *responsivity principle* states that services should be delivered in a manner that is engaging and consistent with the learning style of the individual. Examples include: fostering strengths; establishing meaningful relationships; and attending to relevant characteristics such as age, cognitive skills, cultural factors and emotional regulation issues. It also states that the primary treatment components should use social learning and cognitive-behavioral approaches. Empirical studies indicate that adhering to RNR principles can maximize treatment effects and reduce recidivism (Bonta and Andrews 2007).

The SOTP at the hospital is for the patient to acquire prosocial skills and to prevent recurrence of sexual offending. Some of these skills include relationship skills, empathy, anger management and coping skills. The program combines components of a self-regulation model and a strength-based model that helps offenders adhere to a meaningful and well-rounded lifestyle. These models operate in conjunction with the principles of risk-need-responsivity. This combined approach strengthens the individual's self-regulation skills to prepare him for a life free of sexual offending. Patients in SOTP address their behavioral patterns that led to their offending, learn avoidance strategies, cognitive strategies, and emotional and behavioral strategies. In addition, there is a community preparation and integration component.

There are several dynamic risk factors included in the Sex Offender Need Assessment Rating (SONAR). Some of the risk factors considered important treatment targets for this population include intimacy deficits related to lovers and intimate partners, general social rejection, loneliness and lack of concern for others. Also important is general self-regulation, indicated by poor cognitive problem-solving skills and negative emotionality/hostility (Witt and Schneider 2005).

Ward and Beech (2016) discuss a multi-factorial explanation for sexual abuse, including genetic predisposition, adverse developmental experiences, psychological dispositions, empathy deficits, emotional skill deficits and interpersonal problems, among others.

Insecure attachment and poor early learning experiences can result in a lack of interpersonal skills in relationships, leading to further social deficits, such as intimacy problems, that can then lead to sexual offending (Ward and Beech 2016). Many of our patients have difficulty forming emotional intimacy with other adults, and this has led some of them to offend against children, whom they felt they could relate to better than adults. Or they may have been sexually abused as children and repeat this behavior as adults. Developmental problems can lead to low self-esteem, poor school performance, isolation, anger and addiction issues, and these may be precursors of offending. Many sex offenders feel socially rejected and lonely, another risk factor for sexual offending (Ward and Beech 2016).

SOTP – not for everyone

Recent statistics show that the SOTP's 'one-size-fits-all' approach to treatment is not effective; it is sometimes described as hierarchical in that it makes the assumption that everyone has the same cognitive abilities. It is a classroom model with workbooks, handouts, homework, paper and pencil. The SOTP curriculum presupposes that everyone is literate, that they don't have compounding issues such as a history of trauma, an Axis I mental illness, a personality disorder, low IQ, illiteracy issues, and so on. No one person has exactly the same problems as the person sitting next to him. A variety of treatment options might better serve the diverse population that we treat.

Some patients would arrive at the hospital thinking that if they 'pass' the recommended groups, they would then be discharged within a short time. Seldom does it work that way, especially if the patient is not willing to really examine himself. Some initially refused to participate in SOTP. They reported that their attorneys said that participation in SOTP would be an admission of guilt. Some felt they could not trust other patients in the SOTP groups as they were hypocritical and said 'just what the facilitator wanted to hear', then immediately demonstrated through their behavior that they did not mean what they said in the group. Another common refrain is 'We don't want other patients spreading our business around.' The sex offenders we work with are known for being highly manipulative, so there is no real proof that the patient has learned anything. Some illiterate patients have confessed that they had a 'friend' to help them fill out their workbooks. The only real way of knowing if the treatment has worked is through the review of recidivism statistics.

Art therapy treatment

The art therapy program is designed to help our patients address the risk factors described above, as our case examples will show. Art therapy can help the therapist meet the patient where he is at and enable him to look at himself more carefully and gain more meaningful insight. Art therapy may be a superior delivery modality for addressing the dynamic risk factors of sex offenders, as the creative process addresses multiple social psychological and physiological facets of wellbeing. It is also an effective way to begin work with patients who resist treatment, through activities such as painting, clay work, crochet and leatherwork, to name just a few. In the non-threatening environment of a leisure group setting, patients develop relationships with the therapist and are assisted in learning through subconscious material or any physical struggle revealed through the creative process. One patient was asked to throw clay against the wall and say one thing he was angry about when he did it. Afterwards, he said that he was surprised that he had that much anger inside him. While some patients have been released by the courts due to the insight and interpersonal skills gained through SOTP, in some cases, patients have been discharged based on their progress made through alternative therapies such as art therapy as a stand-alone therapeutic modality.

After over 12 years working with this group of sex offenders in a maximum-security facility, we have been able to witness the successes and failures of SOTP. In addition, we have also experienced rejection by some in the 'scientific community' as they minimize, deride or dismiss art therapy for its qualitative nature. This is despite the fact that we have used standardized testing combined with art therapy to address all facets of offending, and have helped patients address their dynamic risk factors, and ultimately, be released back into the community. We have helped patients organize informal creative events, in addition to our clinical work and documentation responsibility that is shared with the social work and psychology departments. We are held to the same standards as other clinicians. We are encouraging other staff to view art therapy with the same high regard that we have for it.

There is a need for more empirical studies to demonstrate that art therapy is an effective way of enlightening patients and helping them to develop empathy or relationship skills. Empathy is an important component of social wellbeing and developing healthy relationships. The other need is to address learning barriers, 'those factors which inhibit or block learners' preparedness for the experience, their active engagement in it, and their ability to reflect rationally on it with a view to learning from it' (Boud, Cohen and Walker 1993, p.80).

Art therapy may be an effective delivery modality for addressing the static and dynamic risk factors of sex offenders. Art therapy can lead to greater personal insight by addressing subconscious material revealed through the creative process.

> Art is life itself. If we can sustain our arts in a diversity as rich as our social and political and religious diversity, then our artists can indeed play a most valuable role. They can sustain and inspire us, but they can also lead us – directly or, more likely, indirectly – from darkness to light. (Rockwell 2001, p.3)

Art therapy with civilly committed sex offenders

Several of the patients included in this chapter have participated in many art therapy groups over the 14-year span that the hospital has been operating. The art therapy process is much more revealing than cognitive therapy alone. The creative process is ripe with metaphor. The therapist makes observations during the patient's process to help assess and evaluate the patient's abilities. Are the patients able to follow instruction, complete a task, are they able to be socially appropriate, can they problem-solve? Are they able to seek assistance, do they share, are they timely, are they easily frustrated or patient? Can they accept defeat, can they demonstrate learning through the process, can they demonstrate kindness and support their peers? Art therapy can also build self-esteem in the patient through learning and mastering a new skill or being recognized for doing something positive. An art therapist will also address a patient's need for an adaptive approach for successful learning. Anywhere in the creative process where the patient is struggling, an art therapist will find a metaphor and an opportunity to provide insight through open-ended questions about how this process relates to his social or offending behaviors.

In a group setting each patient will produce a completely unique visual representation of the directive given to share with the group. Often patients will identify with the images of others, and patients say the visual aspect helps them talk about issues that are too complex to put into words.

> The images of the unconscious place a great responsibility upon a man. Failure to understand them, or a shirking of ethical responsibility, deprives him of his wholeness and imposes a painful fragmentariness on his life. (Hocoy 2007, p.23)

Through art therapy, patients can address their dynamic risk factors. In one juvenile sex offender case, art therapy helped the offender to take responsibility for his actions and identify feeling states. In addition, he learned how certain feelings created a sense of powerlessness, which triggered a reaction in order to regain a feeling of power (Wadeson 2000).

The facility hires clinical rehabilitation therapists, including art, music and recreation therapists, in part to address 'quality of life' issues. With approximately 20 art therapists working at the facility, many different kinds of art therapy group have been offered to address dynamic risk factors for sex offenders.

Art therapy groups are offered in 12-week quarter-year blocks. The group meets once a week for a 100-minute session. An art therapy directive is given, and after the art making is complete, patients are invited to talk about their artwork and offer feedback to peers.

One of the first art therapy groups offered at the facility addressed lack of concern for others, due to poor empathy for others. Offenders with this risk factor are selfish and indifferent to others' welfare, and can be cruel in order to meet their own needs (Mann, Hanson and Thornton 2010). A lesson plan on empathy was developed, using the Interpersonal Reactivity Index (IRI) to capture changes in the patient's empathy from the beginning of the quarter to the end of the quarter. The IRI looks at four components of empathy, including empathic concern, perspective taking, fantasy and personal distress.

Empirically, addressing general empathy, versus victim empathy, has been shown to be more helpful for offenders. Art therapy groups are used to help patients understand and practice feeling empathy for others. Some basic directives include: 'What is empathy?'; 'A time you felt empathy for someone'; and 'A time you lacked empathy'. Other directives are used to demonstrate that empathy can include positive feelings as well as negative ones or focus on helping the patient be more in touch with his feelings generally. More advanced directives encourage patients not only to feel empathy, but to show it through comforting or compassionate actions.

Case examples
Mr. B
Mr. B is a Caucasian man in his thirties. His crimes included molesting children and distributing child pornography. In the 'Empathy through Art Therapy' group, one of the directives was 'Create an image about a time you hurt someone'. Mr. B chose to draw about one of his victims. He drew a powerful image of a girl being torn in half by the experience of being molested. In one hand she holds an angel to represent her innocence. In her other hand is a devil to represent the abuse she suffered. There is a shadow looming over her to represent the sexual abuse perpetrated by Mr. B. She is standing in water that represents the feeling of drowning (Figure 5.1).

In response to another directive, 'Represent a time that you felt empathy and it prevented a negative behavior or action', Mr. B drew about a time that he had an opportunity to molest a child, and he did not. He was a teenager at the time and was attending a barbecue where children were present. He saw a young girl enter a tool shed, and he followed her there. When he saw her, she was crying, and she told him that she was sad because she didn't have a father. He saw that she was hurting and did not want to hurt her any more by molesting her, so he left the tool shed.

Figure 5.1: A time you hurt someone

His image depicted the girl in the tool shed. He is the figure holding a red stop sign up to his demons to prevent them from hurting the girl (Figure 5.2). In the group, Mr. B reported that he had never talked about this incident before, but the directive triggered this memory. This is a good example of how art therapy can help clients process past events as well as material that has been repressed or is subconscious.

Figure 5.2: A time empathy prevented a negative action

Mr. D

Mr. D is a Caucasian man who was admitted to the hospital when he was in his mid-twenties. Some of his crimes included attempted lewd and lascivious acts upon a child and indecent exposure. Upon admission he was sullen and angry but enrolled in therapy groups on the advice of his treatment team. He enrolled in the 'Empathy through Art Therapy' group, and participated in the first art therapy directive, 'What is empathy?' He drew a path using a drawing pencil, and above the path he drew a question mark (Figure 5.3). He also completed the IRI (Table 5.1). He subsequently dropped out of the group.

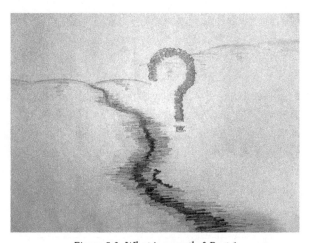

Figure 5.3: What is empathy? Part 1

Mr. D went on to participate in some studio art groups, art therapy groups, and the SOTP offered at the hospital. Five years later, I asked Mr. D to do another drawing about what empathy meant to him. This drawing was done with chalk pastel. It depicted him observing a person yelling at another person. In the picture he is imagining a time when someone yelled at him, relating to that feeling, and then feeling empathy for the person being yelled at (Figure 5.4).

Figure 5.4: What is empathy? Part 2 (see colour section)

At this time, I also asked Mr. D to complete the Interpersonal Reactivity Index again (Table 5.1). His scores showed improvement in all four areas of empathy. His scores went up in the fantasy, empathic concern, and perspective taking categories, all falling in the average range. His score went down in the area of personal distress which showed improvement as the more personal distress a person has, the harder it is for that person to feel empathy for others.

Table 5.1: Interpersonal Reactivity Index, pre- and post-treatment

	Fantasy	Empathic Concern	Perspective Taking	Personal Distress
2009	9	13	16	8
	Low	Very Low	Average	Average
2015	15	18	20	2
	Average	Average	Average	Low

The art created in groups is a powerful look into the subconscious and it can bring awareness to aspects of the self that may elude the patient. When Mr. D first arrived at the hospital, he was very angry, storming up and down the halls of his unit, saying he would kill someone if he was not moved to another unit. He refused SOTP or any treatment. On leaving work one day he was discovered by one of us hiding behind the unit door crying. He was young, big, tall and full of rage. We asked him if he had any coping mechanisms that worked for him at times like this. He said that when he was in prison he would draw. The therapist encouraged him to share his work. He yelled, 'But you are going home!' A half-hour delay to review his artwork revealed an angry young man's creative talent. Mr. D was encouraged to start coming to the Art Center to attend an open clay studio offered as a leisure group, as he was averse to treatment.

Not only did he show up, but his work was ambitious, and he demonstrated a sharp intellect. The ability to follow instructions was hampered initially by his ego and anger; however, over time he was able to learn new skills, such as mold-making and creating his own chess set. Mold-making was an excellent skill to teach him because he had the creative capacity to visualize the finished project before it began. This activity requires the student to think about each step of his process and his end goal and requires a good deal of thought before beginning. The metaphor was not lost on him and a new level of self-esteem began to emerge. He learnt to run a kiln and was able to teach others. He was able to learn to work through situations that left him feeling frustrated and angry, and he started to show a sense of humor.

Mr. D wanted to make a detailed replica of a lighthouse that his family lived near. He was assisted in learning simple clay techniques and how to use the slab roller and extruder. He was successful in building his lighthouse and demonstrated all the new techniques he had learnt. He was informed of the fact that, as clay items are processed, a certain degree of shrinkage occurs. If a project has two pieces that are to fit together upon completion, they need to be made together, so that any shrinkage problems can be addressed before firing.

Mr. D wanted his lighthouse to be a lamp, sitting on a small island of rocks. He ignored the shrinkage issue and made the base after the lighthouse was totally complete. One day upon entering the Art Center, I found Mr. D already attempting to create his rocky base. He yelled, 'I am going to smash this thing into a million pieces.' When I asked what was angering him, he said that every time he tried to fit the completed lighthouse into the green ware base it broke. I picked up one of the rocks, dipped it in slip and stuck it back on, and asked why he was angry at the clay. We were able to have a five-minute conversation to look at what it feels like when consequences arise as a result of avoiding the proper protocols, and how that translated to his being locked up in a maximum-security facility.

> Our own personal awareness, our instinctive feelings, can also alert us to barriers. Heeding our own comfort level within a given situation can bring us to an awareness of our abilities, or lack of them, to work with experience as a source of learning. Being in touch with oneself within the experience is an important way to appreciate one's potential, or lack of it, to learn from the experience. (Boud *et al.* 1993, p.82)

Shortly after that event, Mr. D had to see a doctor in the community. He had been very frustrated with the doctor, because on a prior appointment he felt dismissed and that his serious medical issue had been minimized. After the appointment, he was excited and proud to share that he had been able to hold his anger in check when the doctor again seemed dismissive, by thinking about the rock that fell off the base of the lighthouse, and how one action or person's opinion did not remove his responsibility to control himself.

Mr. D was not only able to improve his problem-solving skills through ceramics, but through other art projects as well. He also enrolled in a Box Making group where he decided to construct his dream house. He completed his measurements to scale and carefully cut strips of chipboard to build a solid infrastructure for his house. He was organized and methodical in his work (Figure 5.5).

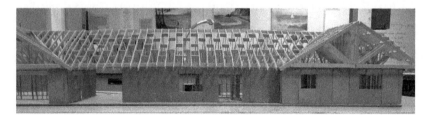

Figure 5.5: House

Mr. D was discharged from the hospital after spending eight years here. His social skills and anger management skills had vastly improved. He was discharged through the hospital's conditional release program, in which he receives supervised housing, therapy and activities. He is currently taking college classes, including ceramics and drawing, which he says he enjoys. He has the support of his family and has been able to make friends out in the community. He has had no violations and hopes to be unconditionally released from supervision in the next few years.

Mr. M

Mr. M is an example of a patient with self-esteem and intimacy issues, described above. Art therapy is especially useful in addressing intimacy difficulties. In an art therapy group designed to address this, patients may be asked to draw what they think intimacy is, or a time they were intimate with another adult.

Mr. M is an African American man in his sixties. He is a serious person with a tendency towards perfectionism in his artwork. He served time for rape and attempted rape. When he first arrived at the hospital, he did not participate in sex offender treatment. Art therapists encouraged him to enroll in art groups, which he did. Through these groups he learnt new skills, such as ceramics, which increased his sense of mastery and accomplishment. He also practiced and improved his social skills through his interactions with peers and staff. He later enrolled in several art therapy groups. He recently decided to enroll in sex offender treatment.

Mr. M was shamed by his mother when he was young. He was hidden away because she was embarrassed that he was an illegitimate son. In a 'Self-Esteem through Art Therapy' group, Mr. M drew an image of low self-esteem as himself huddled in a box. He depicted himself alone with walls rising up around him.

Mr. M was asked to draw an image about intimacy. He drew a picture of intimacy as a dance where the woman was showcased and the man was hidden (Figure 5.6). This showed that his feelings of rejection and not being recognized, internalized from interactions with his mother, continued to be an issue for him as an adult.

After Mr. M talked about his drawing and received feedback from therapists making this connection, we asked him to create another drawing about intimacy that might portray a more equal partnership. His second drawing was much more detailed, and depicted the man participating in the relationship more fully (Figure 5.7).

Mr. M also participated in a 'Grief, Hope and Loss' group for years. Mr. M denied that he was angry about anything. He persistently stated that he was innocent and was just a 'convenient person for the police to use to clean up unsolved rapes in the area', but said he was not angry about that. For two years he maintained his innocence to the point where the facilitators looked into his arrest files and found descriptions of a man that could be no other.

Figure 5.6: What is intimacy? Part 1

Figure 5.7: What is intimacy? Part 2

One day the directive was for the patients to create a target on a 6' x 4' sheet of paper, and then stand across the room from the target and throw balls of clay at it, while yelling out something that they were angry about. Mr. M passed the ball of clay back and forth in his hands for several seconds. After some deliberation he leaned in towards the therapists and said that he was 'scared of his anger'. This was a breakthrough for him. Truth and empathy began to develop, and he was able to receive more information with regard to his impact on the community. Ultimately, after several years of different therapies and his growing ability to trust the facilitators, his participation in art therapy led to enrolment in SOTP. He improved his social skills and emotional regulation, and even became a peer mentor in the Art Center, helping other patients learn skills and undertake ceramics projects.

Mr. R

Mr. R is another example of a patient with a deficit in emotional intimacy skills. He is a Latino male in his thirties. He served time in prison for child molestation and distribution of child pornography. He presents as an outgoing and talkative man with a sense of humor. After being admitted to the hospital, Mr. R participated in various groups and activities where he was able to develop rapport and trust with staff and was able to talk about his past experiences and share his feelings with others. He reported having a dysfunctional family dynamic. He wrote: 'As a child, my family used everything to hurt me. My innocence and being carefree was used against me. I stopped being those things. I shut everyone out. Trust has never come easily.' His image to represent the directive of 'A time you trusted a woman' was a hand shattering glass, the shards of the glass jagged and sharp; hence, dangerous.

Mr. R never married or had a serious romantic relationship as an adult. For a directive about emotional intimacy, he drew a picture about a relationship with a woman he met in college. The drawing depicted a woman trying to stab him with a knife. In another part of the paper, he drew a metaphor of himself playing basketball with the woman, describing himself as playing defense.

Mr. R never engaged in sex offender treatment, but he participated in art therapy groups that addressed how his past impacted his life.

He also engaged in art therapy groups on self-esteem and empathy, as well as studio art groups where he could practice his social skills and problem-solving abilities. He was recently unconditionally discharged from the hospital after eight years of treatment.

Further examples

In the group that addresses hostility toward women, patients may be asked to draw a mother figure or a time that they felt deceived by a woman. Through exploration of these risk factors, the patients can learn to challenge their cognitive distortions and long-held beliefs, so that they can begin to learn the skills needed to form a healthy intimate relationship, both emotional and physical.

In an Open Art Studio group where no directives are given, patients are often able to address their dynamic risk factors and other concerns. One patient may reveal his inability to follow directions even after he has sought out assistance; therapists can address the risk factor of lack of cooperation through supervision with him. Another patient may be able to work on his interpersonal skills through working on a group painting in the Mural group. Patients who have difficulty asking for help demonstrate a basic inability to solve problems. For the patient who is unable to stay with his frustration and wants to destroy his artwork for the smallest mistake, maintaining a helpful attitude and looking to problem-solve can be very helpful. The therapist can use the art process as a metaphor for how the patient coped with past issues, and how he deals with current difficulties.

One challenge with trying to foster skills in this population that strengthen relationships is the concern that the offender will use these skills to groom or manipulate potential victims. Sex offenders can be angry and aggressive, but they can also be very charming and manipulative, with a high incidence of psychopathy. Through the art therapy work, the therapist may be able to see when a patient is more genuine or more defended.

Many patients who resist treatment will start their journey towards treatment through leisure art groups such as Painting, Leatherworking or Ceramics. These groups can seem less threatening to a patient new to treatment. After rapport and trust are developed with the therapist, patients feel more comfortable opening up and sharing their stories.

The Art Center where these leisure groups take place becomes a safe and enjoyable environment which is conducive to therapy.

Conclusion

At this facility, the art therapist is able to observe a patient's creative process and assist with problem-solving in a way that is less threatening than through talking therapy alone. Often parallels between the creative process can be drawn by the therapist that will assist the patient in becoming more self-aware, eventually leading many patients to continue seeking enlightenment through art therapy or the SOTP. Sometimes, the patient may be released based on the insight they have gained using alternative treatments to the SOTP, such as substance abuse treatment, dialectical behavior therapy and/or expressive therapies, to develop more self-understanding as well as the skills needed to succeed in the community at large.

Therapy with repeat sex offenders is a long-term endeavor, sometimes with little progress or even a sense of worsening behavior at times. The patient needs to be sincerely motivated to change his behavior, and have the perseverance to overcome legal and psychological setbacks in his treatment. One patient recently told me that his biggest obstacle is himself. The therapist requires strong boundaries as well as the ability to maintain hope in herself and her patient. The ability to develop rapport and hold the space for these damaged individuals, to trust the process and remain patient in the face of long-term treatment all contribute to the capability of the patient to succeed in therapy and in preventing himself from re-offending.

References

Bonta, J. and Andrews, D. (2007) *Risk-Need-Responsivity Model for Offender Assessment and Rehabilitation.* (Cat. No. PS3-1/200706). Public Safety Canada. Accessed on 13/4/2020 at www.publicsafety.gc.ca/cnt/rsrcs/pblctns/rsk-nd-rspnsvty/rsk-nd-rspnsvty-eng.pdf

Boud, D., Cohen, R. and Walker, D. (eds) (1993) *Using Experience for Learning.* Philadelphia, PA: Open University Press.

Hocoy, D. (2007) 'Art Therapy as a Tool for Social Change: A Conceptual Model.' In F.F. Kaplan (ed.) *Art Therapy and Social Action.* London: Jessica Kingsley Publishers.

Mann, R., Hanson, R. and Thornton, D. (2010) 'Assessing risk for sexual recidivism: Some proposals on the nature of psychologically meaningful risk factors.' *Sexual Abuse: A Journal of Research and Treatment.* Accessed on 21/5/19 at http://responsesystemspanel.whs.mil/Public/docs/meetings/Sub_Committee/20140225_CSS/Materials_Presenters/07_RiskFactors_Mann_Hanson_Thornton_2010.pdf

Rockwell, J. (2001, 23 September) 'The aftermath: Peering into the abyss of the future.' *New York Times*. Section 2, p.1.

Wadeson, H. (2000) *Art Therapy Practice: Innovative Approaches with Diverse Populations*. New York, NY: John Wiley & Sons.

Ward, T. and Beech, A.R. (2016) 'The Integrated Theory of Sexual Offending – Revised.' In *The Wiley Handbook on the Assessment, Treatment, and Theories of Sexual Offending*. Palo Alto, CA: John Wiley & Sons. Accessed on 21/5/2019 at https://onlinelibrary.wiley.com/doi/full/10.1002/9781118574003.wattso006

Witt, P. and Schneider, J. (2005) 'Managing sex offenders by assessing dynamic risk factors.' *Sex Offender Law Report* 6, pp.49, 54–57.

CHAPTER 6

Beauty and the Beast

Trauma-Informed Dramatherapy with a
Male Patient in a Forensic Setting

EVA MARIE CHADWICK, DRAMATHERAPIST

Introduction

This chapter introduces and describes a trauma-informed dramatherapy framework, which is explored through the case study of a male patient with self-reported gender dysphoria and a history of sexual offending who engaged in individual dramatherapy for 16 months in a private forensic hospital in the UK. To date, this is the first documentation of trauma-informed dramatherapy in a forensic setting – a practice that is now ongoing within the forensic unit I work in, with men who have committed sexual offences and who endure complex trauma and pathological issues.

The dramatherapy referral was for offence-related work, a premise that suggests the patient needs to gain insight and awareness into their behaviour and reduce their risk of re-offending. Because of the links that his cross-dressing had with his offences, the hospital supported his initial aim for therapy, which was to feel 'comfortable as a man'. For the purpose of this publication, the patient chose Christina as a pseudonym whilst no preference was indicated regarding pronoun. Christina presented both male and female aspects of self, as documented in this chapter, whilst feelings of gender dysphoria that were explored suggested gender non-conforming, where a person identifies with both sexes.[1] During the

---

1   See www.genderedintelligence.co.uk; www.gic.nhs.uk

length of the intervention the patient referred to themselves with their male name and pronoun. It therefore seemed appropriate to use *he* as a pronoun – to authenticate the work, hold both male and female aspects in mind, and highlight, for the reader, the ongoing conflict this provided while working with Christina and the ambivalence he experienced.

Details of the case study, whilst they shed light on the complexities of unprocessed trauma – the symptoms and behaviours that developed as a way of coping – are presented as a way of demonstrating the principles of a trauma-informed dramatherapy approach. They are not limited to this case, but are flexible enough to be used with a variety of cases, in which the clinical perspective shifts from 'what's wrong with you?' to 'what happened to you?'[2] This chapter will not claim to provide a solution to the aetiology of gender dysphoria, and respects that there are many people with this distressing condition that do not have a background of trauma.

During the intervention it became apparent that female clothing provided a number of functions for Christina: a coping mechanism that enabled him to re-invent himself and escape the sexual abuse he experienced as a child; a mastering of his early experiences where female clothing featured in his own experience of abuse (Herman 1992; Perry 2008); and a source of intense desire and aggressions in his offending behaviour. In the context of Christina's life therefore, his wanting to be female ceased to be a stand-alone issue. What became important was understanding the variety of symptoms and behaviours that stemmed from cumulative unexpressed traumatic events, which took place outside of his control (Herman 1992). Through the complexity of these presenting issues (above), as well as my own somatic responses while working with him (Greenberg 2016; Rutstein n.d.), I began to develop a trauma-informed dramatherapy approach that focused on Christina's early life narrative and 'complex trauma'.

My dramatherapy practice aims to provide patients with the ability to access and explore their emotions, provide opportunity to work through unconscious material associated with their pathological difficulties, life narrative and offending behaviour. The hospital has both medium- and low-secure wards and provides long-term care for an all-male patient population on multiple pathways. This includes

---

2 See www.samhsa.gov

those that come from one of the four high-secure settings in the UK, or transfer from medium-secure and/or prison.

Christina was on a low-secure ward and had a great desire for his story to be told. He advocated for a creative approach himself, citing: 'I don't need medication, I need dramatherapy!' The dramatherapy methods and techniques drawn on in the therapy included art making, small object work, writing and role-play. In addition, a combination of specialist trauma-informed methods and approaches were employed from fields outside of dramatherapy to address the various issues as they arose. These included Peggy Pace's Lifespan Integration method (2015); Pat Ogden's defensive gestures (Ogden, Minton and Pain 2006); and exercises from Eye Movement Desensitization and Reprocessing (EMDR) (Shapiro 2012). These methods, along with a working understanding of the psychological and physical processes of trauma, as advocated by Pat Ogden (Ogden, Minton and Pain 2006), Peter Levine (1997), Janina Fisher (1999, 2017), Bessel van der Kolk (2014) and Stephen Porges (2011), complemented the physical nature of the dramatherapy intervention. In practice, this resulted in a trauma-informed approach with a particular focus on the body.

Part 1 of the case study below describes Christina's background history, highlighting complex issues which led to my research into theories and methods on trauma treatment. Part 2 highlights areas within the clinical work that were a part of Christina's therapeutic journey, using a trauma-informed dramatherapy approach, which enabled him to process trauma and reduce the anxiety and conflict that led to the complex coping mechanisms he developed.

The index offence will not be focused on as the details of the offence do not represent the level of risk he posed, and there is also a risk of anonymity being compromised for the people involved. The chapter will not try to find a solution for Christina's gender dysphoria, but will represent issues contributing to his distress, trauma and risk to self and others, focusing on the methods that were integrated.

My reflections on process will be demonstrated by art images drawn directly after the sessions, that enabled me to process and illuminate unconscious communications present in the work. Reflecting in this way has become a customary practice within my work, providing a means of exploring the dynamics as well as illustrating the felt responses, projections, transferences and countertransference.

PART 1
Christina's background history

Christina is a bisexual man in his mid-sixties who has identified with himself as being 80 percent a woman since adolescence, cross-dressing in secret and developing an array of female personas. At the time of the intervention he was detained under the Mental Health Act and had spent 45 years inside secure psychiatric and prison settings, following a sexual offence. Christina suffered extensive physical and sexual abuse perpetrated by his father, which began when he was aged three. He was kept in a state of constant fear, by means of threats of violence. His mother was reportedly unaware of the abuse and described by Christina as emotionally distant and removed.

Christina's adolescence was characterized by intense feelings of gender dysphoria (DSM-5; previously called 'gender identity disorder'). He began living a double life and related having an obsession with the need for altering his gender and wearing women's clothing. Many of the female personas he developed were constructed around sexual play/role-play, though others seemed to offer him the feeling of being blissfully safe.

There seemed to be no healthy sexual boundaries within Christina's family life. He became preoccupied with sexual feelings towards his mother in his adolescence; sexually abused his younger brother while a minor himself; and engaged in many one-off situations with female members of his family. All of these situations involved him wearing female or baby clothing, whilst there were times when these role-plays would not result in sex.

Cross-dressing and role-play were also a part of his father's sexual perversion, where he made his son wear female outfits before sexually abusing him. The aetiology of Christina's gender dysphoria and cross-dressing became a part of the therapeutic process and was linked to his offending. He remains of the belief that he would not have been abused himself if he had been female (see Figure 6.1).

As a young person, Christina ran away, prostituted himself and tried to take his life on many occasions. As an adult, he was diagnosed with emotionally unstable and dissocial personality disorder (DSM-5), while during the course of the dramatherapy intervention it emerged he had begun to hear voices.

Issues brought to therapy are summarized as complex, whilst the therapeutic inquiry involved a process that would both respect his need to protect and/or cope in the world, relieve the burden of trauma he carried, and lessen his anxiety and conflict, in view of his offending and risk.

Figure 6.1: Storyboard Theatre scene – 'You can't touch me, I'm a woman!'

Development of a trauma-informed dramatherapy approach

There is a rich history of dramatherapy practised in forensic settings across the UK and abroad (Jones and Dokter 2008; McAllister 2002; Ramsden and Guarnieri 2010; Rothwell 2016; Seebohm 2011; Stamp 2008; Thorn 2011). I will briefly summarize the psychological theories, methods and practices influencing my development of a trauma-informed dramatherapy approach, including an understanding of the physical and psychological effects of trauma, and the three stages of trauma treatment suggested by Judith Herman (1992): stabilization, processing and integration.

I worked with the understanding that trauma is held in the physical body (Fisher 1999; Levine 1997; Ogden *et al.* 2006; Rothchild 2000; van der Kolk 2014). In accessing unprocessed trauma, I was mindful of the potential for flooding or dissociation, resulting in the risk of re-traumatizing in the process. Stephen Porges' Polyvagal Theory (2011) provides an understanding of the physical processes a person undergoes during trauma, from the inability to move/freeze during the incident, to the ability to unlock and process these in therapy (Dana 2018).

I developed methods and techniques that are informed by his theory, involving physical techniques and step-by-step processes. These included Lifespan Integration (LI) (Pace 2015), involving working at speed with the trauma story or life narrative, in order to stay within a person's 'window of tolerance'. Adult and child ego states are coached by the therapist to inform the self-system that the trauma is in the past. EMDR (Shapiro 2012), likewise, is a method that provides a patient with comprehensive physical exercises, to enable them to reduce and/ or be released from the activating triggers that suggest the trauma is in the present. While, in addition, Pat Ogden's sensorimotor approach maintains the importance of working with the body to effect lasting change, described as a somatically driven approach to trauma treatment (Ogden *et al.* 2006).

Enabling the body to be released from past trauma is one aspect of 'bottom-up' trauma treatment (Ogden *et al.* 2006), while the psychological aspect of becoming stuck in the past is another. Fragmentation and arrested development or sense of being stuck at developmental phases is well documented, whilst Fisher (2017), Pace (2015) and Schwartz's work in particular influenced the intervention (Anderson, Sweezy and Schwartz 2017). Pace suggests that split-off aspects of self develop their own neural pathways, lives and narratives, while we require a supportive adult to co-construct our life narrative and a sense of ourselves as a whole. Schwartz's Internal Family Systems approach explores the constructs we have created, the protective factors of the personality that develop to keep the exiled and wounded parts safe. These constructs and internal family systems illuminate our shared and individual coping styles in a normal and healthy environment, while magnified and extreme for a person with a history of complex trauma.

These theories and methods influenced the development of a trauma-informed dramatherapy practice, while factors as regards sexual offending and cross-dressing were influenced by Glasser's core complex (Glasser 1979), a psychological framework for understanding sexual violence and the need to be in control and master the intensity of inner conflict. In summary, his theory suggests that there is a vicious circle embedded within the conflict of the sexual desire to merge and fear of annihilation by the other. This merging includes the desire to wear female clothing as a pseudo-experience of being within the feminine body and/or the womb and he suggests there is both 'excitement...and peace', and 'intense destructiveness securely contained' in this process (Glasser 1979, p.303). Glasser also illuminates the link between anxiety and aggression as a disturbance of 'psychic homeostasis' (Glasser 1979, p.282) and the conflict of wanting to 'maintain the relationship, and... break it' (Glasser 1979, p.303).

Glasser's psychology of sexual offending, and the theories and methods used in trauma treatment, broadened my understanding of the physical and psychological effects of complex trauma. It provided me with conceptual frameworks, and techniques to draw on, enabling me to develop a trauma-informed approach emphasizing the use of body-based techniques, creativity and safety.

PART 2

The trauma-informed dramatherapy intervention will demonstrate:

- the importance of a step-by-step approach
- how creative work provided a reflective function for both therapist and patient
- means of coping with projections
- processing trauma without re-traumatizing.

Benefits of this integrative approach will highlight how Christina was able to access and reflect on unconscious material associated with the complexities of his psychopathology and offending behaviour; gain insight via a range of creative methods; and experience a more integrated sense of self. The development of a therapeutic alliance, described below, demonstrates the importance of collaborative relationship for people with complex trauma (Fisher 1999; Herman 1992; Terre 1994).

Developing a therapeutic alliance

Christina presented as a quietly spoken and predominantly cheerful happy-go-lucky person, with a childlike sense of vulnerability. He was eager to come to dramatherapy having waited many months to start. Therefore, there was a feeling of urgency during the early sessions, noted by the speed of his delivery and the sense of spilling and flooding of explicit information, as if he could barely contain himself. I felt the prevalence of his sexual preoccupation as an overwhelming force, causing feelings of dizziness, blurry vision, physical arousal, and sense of claustrophobia. These feelings were so overwhelming that I felt almost unable to stay in the space and wondered if I could continue with the intervention. Developing my understanding of these somatic responses as well as strategies to work with them became a focus in peer and clinical supervision. These included offering creative work – in effect redirecting the focus/projections onto small objects, drawing and spectrograms. This enabled me to have space to think without feeling overwhelmed, while the creative medium effectively expressed Christina's unconscious material. I was able to identify my experience as projective identification – the split-off intolerable feelings/projections – Christina being unable to acknowledge, hold or own them himself (Bion 1967).

I also began drawing images directly after sessions as a way of processing feelings that I felt unable to verbalize immediately. Figure 6.2 illustrates the sense of chaos in the unconscious communication, noting that the figure in the background was representative of how Christina presented. This drawing was also extremely useful in illuminating Christina's splitting and rawness of feeling. Both my somatic experiences and the images suggested there was a large amount of unprocessed trauma within Christina (Herman 1992), and I felt the need to protect myself, wearing tight inner clothing around my solar plexus during the sessions.

During this initial phase, Christina tried to kill himself while on leave in the community. It transpired that Christina had begun to hear 'command hallucinations' – a voice telling him to harm himself. There had been no evidence to suggest he was suicidal or experiencing hearing voices at this time. However, my process image (Figure 6.2) and experiences within the unconscious communication in these sessions revealed feelings of immense chaos, disturbance and trauma still present within him. It became evident that my use of self and faculty for attunement was invaluable in alerting me to Christina's mental and emotional state (Greenberg 2016; Schur 1994).

Re-contracting with Christina, I invited him to work with a new level of honesty, that would keep us all safe in the process. This also entailed becoming more directive in my approach as a therapist, recommended for stabilization in trauma treatment. As if adopting a tough-love style of mothering, the role of the therapist becomes that of teacher and/or guide (Fisher 1999). In summary, using myself as a guide in gauging the unconscious dynamics within the alliance; responding with creative methods to direct the focus of the work; and empowering Christina with becoming more transparent in his communication enabled us a way forward.

Figure 6.2: Process image – Unprocessed

The six sections below demonstrate the integration of trauma-treatment methods and the phases of stabilization, processing and integration. The integration of these techniques and methods are presented as examples of practice, providing evidence of how these may be transferable in developing a trauma-informed dramatherapy practice.

1. Voice-hearing

Christina said his voice-hearing never occurred whilst staff were present, relating 'it wouldn't dare' – suggesting that whilst figures of authority were around, Christina would be safe. It seemed Christina continued to experience himself as a child and victim of abuse and could not tell past from present (van der Kolk 2014), while the extent to which Christina's father terrorized him seemed to have morphed into the voice he was hearing, either belittling or commanding him to harm himself. Christina related feeling utterly helpless, terrified, and unable to defend himself.

VIGNETTE

In order to help him cope with this experience, I began to explore strategies and techniques, influenced by Shapiro's EMDR work, encouraging Christina to imagine this voice as a humorous and/or cartoon-like image, as a way of distancing himself from the experience (Shapiro 2012). This was integrated into drawing pictures representing situations in which he experienced hearing the voice, resulting in a series of storyboards (see Figure 6.3).

Figure 6.3: Storyboard street scene

Adapting dramatherapeutic methods with Ogden's defensive gestures, the dialogue in the storyboards was explored between both himself and the character, before the practice of acting it out was developed. This involved writing a series of verbal responses while devising a gesture with each one, such as 'Stop', 'You can't hurt me now', 'Go away', and so on. This became an ongoing practice for Christina, who employed a word and gesture whenever the tormenting voice emerged, and in whatever situation he was in, relating 'I don't care what others think', because the technique works, the voice disappears.

REFLECTIONS
This practice helped towards stabilizing Christina and empowered him with techniques which he used outside of the therapy space. He became less fearful and related feeling 'stronger' in himself. It would seem this physical approach enabled him to re-pattern his emotional responses, reduced his anxiety and experience of voice hearing, whilst positively affected his psychological health.

2. Processing trauma
At Christina's request, sessions were planned and put aside to process a number of violent sexual attacks he'd experienced by his father, and in which he was made to wear female clothing. Mindful of Christina's tendency to flood and, therefore, the potential for him to become hyper-aroused (Pace 2015) I used the lifespan integration method to keep him within his window of tolerance.

VIGNETTE
The process entailed talking through the narrative whilst holding a cushion as if it were his child self. Christina worked through each story in separate sessions, pausing to breathe and to flex arms and limbs so as to remain alert and present after each repetition. I coached his adult self at various junctures to help him affirm the child self, with words such as 'I'm here now, and holding you; it happened a long time ago; and you're safe now'.

REFLECTIONS
Christina related experiencing that a 'weight had been lifted off', whilst there were no signs of re-traumatization in the process. These were distressing stories to hear as a therapist, however, and my way of avoiding vicarious trauma was to draw the narratives, the child's unspoken words, and the adult's affirmations. The creative process enabled me to get it out as opposed to retain it within my own body. Reflecting on these images illuminated the continued processing work required to enable Christina to experience the trauma as past and to support him in the fact that he survived it.

3. Beauty

Christina was not physically well enough to have a sex-change operation, and he had not been allowed to wear female clothing in this hospital, due to the associations this had with his offence. However, it was evident that he continued to have an overwhelming desire to merge with/or into a female.

VIGNETTE

I encouraged Christina to use creative mediums with which to describe the narrative of his cross-dressing experiences, while it emerged that he had created many personas. They had different functions and roles and included: a housewife, prostitute, office girl, princess/bride, schoolgirl and baby. Christina drew each one, their thoughts and feelings, roles and/or motivations, as if creating a catalogue, noting that the style of clothing, materials/fabrics were important factors.

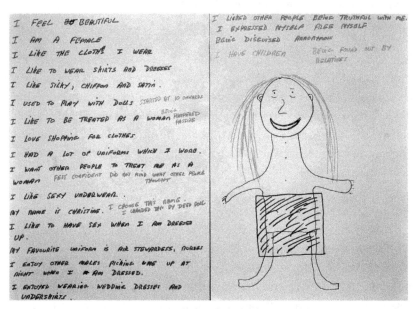

Figure 6.4: Being a female (see colour section)

This piece of work continued for a number of weeks, whilst Christina described having felt 'beautiful' as a woman, and a sense of freedom in becoming anonymous (see Figure 6.4). He suggested feeling both relief and pleasure in the moments he'd see his masculine-self disappear when he looked in the mirror, and a sense of blissful peace.

REFLECTIONS

Christina identified that cross-dressing had provided him with a sense of autonomy, a way of coping with the overwhelming nature of the sexual abuse he was experiencing at home. Relieving anxiety was concurrent with Christina's self-reporting (Glasser 1979; Holmes and Holmes 2009), while issues regarding 'gender dysphoria' seemed enmeshed with Christina's complex trauma, as further exploration will demonstrate below (see Figure 6.5).

Figure 6.5: Process image – Disappearing

4. Mastery

Finding ways to cope with the extensive abuse he experienced was further reflected upon within the next phase of the work: What did he do with his experience? How did he cope with it? How did this go undetected by others? Where did he put his pain, his anger, and so on? The vignette below demonstrates how the act of cross-dressing crossed over into sexual role-play scenarios.

VIGNETTE

Christina drew an image that demonstrates the extensiveness of the life he'd developed during his adolescence, involving sexual encounters he initiated, cross-dressing and role-play (see Figure 6.6). He reflected upon this as becoming an addiction that was getting steadily out of control, whilst relating that the 'angry monster' had begun to creep in and was threatening to take over. In this respect, he related being glad that he'd been caught when he was, unsure of what he might have done if not.

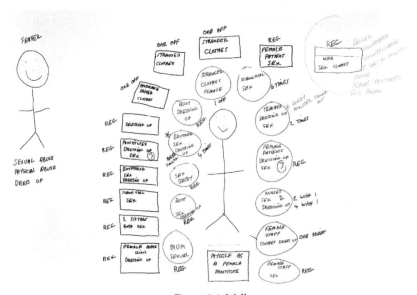

Figure 6.6: Wall

Christina could step back and view the shape of the image itself, reflecting alongside myself at the layers built up around him, as if he'd cocooned himself. He also noted with amazement the amount of people that played a part, in contrast to the feelings of isolation and abandonment he'd experienced as a young boy. This was a profound realization, affecting his relationships with hospital staff, whom, it seemed, he was subsequently better able to view as supportive and caring.

REFLECTIONS

Whilst Christina came to view his cross-dressing as a defence mechanism, he also related experiencing immense pleasure in the process: he could disappear, re-invent himself, be free of an unwanted aspect of himself as a boy, be treated well by others, and have sexual interactions that he could both instigate and be in control of.

Christina's self-reported preoccupation with situations in which he wore female clothing for sex (such as he wore for his father) suggested he was re-enacting his own trauma and the masochistic pleasure he gained was his overwhelming urge to master the pain of abuse (Shaughnessy, cited in Jones 2016).

5. Beast

As therapists working with offenders will know, the victim-perpetrator has enormous fear and anger, associated with their offences and/or self-destructive behaviours (Liebmann 2008), which may include a fear of their own anger too, and the challenge of being able to express this (Glasser, Kenefick and O'Leary 1966). By the time Christina was able to access this anger, he had a range of techniques to work with that enabled him to explore this self-named Angry Monster within him.

VIGNETTE
Using the creative mediums, he identified the angry monster through choosing an object representing himself as male. Further explored through image-making, we then cross-referenced him with an image from the catalogue (Figure 6.7), a female character with clothing that incited the angry monster in him. Christina was able to articulate that it was the fabric/material that a woman wore that incited his sexual desire, which was so strongly enmeshed with anger that he'd do 'whatever it takes' to have it.

The anger and desire for revenge were encapsulated safely in these images and objects. However, a few weeks later, confronting and owning his unwanted feelings seemed to depress him, and he experienced feelings of hopelessness and a difficulty in being able to reflect or move, as if stuck in an emotional freeze. I invited him to engage with his body, to use his weight to push against the stuckness, combining an understanding of the body's capacity to hold trauma and, likewise, the ability to move through it (Levine 1997; Ogden *et al.* 2006; van der Kolk 2014).

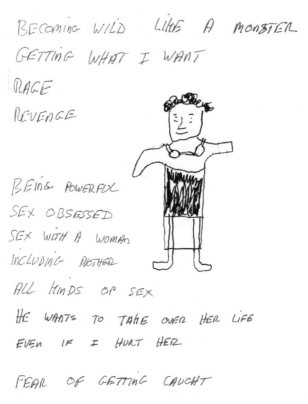

BECOMING WILD LIKE A MONSTER

GETTING WHAT I WANT

RAGE

REVENGE

BEING POWERFUL

SEX OBSESSED

SEX WITH A WOMAN

INCLUDING MOTHER

ALL KINDS OF SEX

HE WANTS TO TAKE OVER HER LIFE

EVEN IF I HURT HER

FEAR OF GETTING CAUGHT

Figure 6.7: Angry Monster

REFLECTIONS

Using the body to make contact with emotions, while, at the same time, grounding himself in the present, enabled Christina to work in the here and now and experience himself as safe, enabling him to reflect on his life with a sense of distance.

I was mindful of Christina's assertion he was 80 percent female, suggesting 20 percent male and, as such, conforming to both genders, albeit unevenly. The function of cross-dressing, enmeshed as it seemed with Christina's complex trauma, provided evidence he had strong needs for safety, comfort and contact. Processing his trauma, the anger and pain, was imperative in reducing risk – his need for revenge, and harm to self or others.

6. Hatred

Christina identified negative thoughts within his internal dialoguing through drawing an image he entitled 'Hatred'. It seemed both burdensome and painful for him to share the fact he had these thoughts, whilst it was also evident that Christina was developing autonomy within his therapeutic process, and the ability to take ownership of his material.

VIGNETTE

The process of naming the hateful things that happened to him, alongside the hatred that he felt in response, was extremely painful, achieved through image-making and physical release exercises (Levine 1997; Ogden *et al.* 2006). Christina reflected that these negative thoughts seemed to emulate the voice he heard – stemming from the deep hatred he felt towards his father, which had fuelled his own violence, sexual aggression and drive for revenge.

REFLECTIONS

A process image of mine conveyed the overbearing feeling of weight Christina relayed through the experience of his complex trauma, the crushing feelings that were being released gradually and the deep pain of hating someone he had wanted to love, namely his father.

Discussion and conclusion

This chapter describes the development of a trauma-informed dramatherapy framework using body-based/bottom-up approaches to trauma treatment. These approaches were integrated into a 16-month dramatherapy intervention in a forensic setting.

Conceptual frameworks regarding the presentation of a complex sexuality and sex-offending history were held in mind. This helped to formulate the intervention, providing an understanding of the psychopathology of sexual aggression, within the context of Christina's deep disturbance and/or disrupted childhood development.

The integration of trauma-treatment methods and techniques helped to provide:

- a more directive approach within the therapeutic alliance

- a step-by-step approach and the provision of techniques

- the ability to cope with projections from the patient as they arose

- processing of trauma without re-traumatizing the patient, through the understanding of both the physical and psychological effects of trauma.

The creative work also provided a reflective function for both therapist and patient alike, whilst deepening the level of engagement with the unconscious processes, provided insight and understanding of his psychopathology and offending behaviour.

The therapeutic journey summarily focused on Christina's early life narrative and complex trauma, coping mechanisms, and sexual offending. No attempt was made to dismantle Christina's gender confusion, nonetheless the distress/dysphoria within his desire to cross-dress seemed to ease as he experienced a newfound strength of character, along with a sense of being more comfortable as a man. Through the co-construction of his life narrative, split-off and/or unacceptable aspects of self were acknowledged, and Christina began to experience a more integrated sense of self.

My use of self in the process of working with Christina was imperative in identifying his unprocessed trauma, and assessing the risk to self and others, whilst the development of the trauma-informed dramatherapy approach kept us both grounded and safe from overwhelm in the process.

Figure 6.8: Process image – 'I can do what I want'

Reflecting on my process image at the end of the intervention (Figure 6.8), there is a sense of celebration in the narrative: Beauty and the Beast are safely integrated, and Christina's autonomy and choice are being exercised. This celebration also includes the fact that my unconscious bias about a gender binary system has been irrevocably challenged, for which I am immeasurably grateful.

The intervention closed when Christina transferred to another hospital, whilst he asserted there was 'a lot more to do'. In this regard, he demonstrated having become more aware of himself and his recovery needs. He was also heartened and empowered by his ability to process trauma, and had developed the necessary tools to function day to day, suggesting he had largely stabilized.

References

Anderson, F.G., Sweezy, M. and Schwartz, R.C. (2017) *Internal Family Systems Skills Training Manual: Trauma-informed Treatment for Anxiety, Depression, PTSD & Substance Abuse.* East Claire, WI: PESI Publishing & Media.

Bion, W.R. (1967) *Second Thoughts.* London: Heinemann Medical.

Dana, D. (2018) *The Polyvagal Theory in Therapy: Engaging the Rhythm of the Regulation.* New York, NY: W.W. Norton.

Fisher, J. (1999) 'The Work of Stabilisation in Trauma Treatment.' Paper presented at The Trauma Centre Lecture Series.

Fisher, J. (2017) *Healing the Fragmented Selves of Trauma Survivors: Overcoming Internal Self-Alienation.* London: Routledge.

Glasser, D., Kenefick, D. and O'Leary, V. (1966) *The Violent Offender.* Washington, DC: US Department of Health, Education, and Welfare.

Glasser, M. (1979) 'Some Aspects of the Role of Aggression in the Perversions.' In I. Rosen (ed.) *Sexual Deviation* (2nd edn). Oxford: Oxford University Press.

Greenberg, E. (2016) *Borderline, Narcissistic, and Schizoid Adaptations: The Pursuit of Love, Admiration, and Safety.* Scotts Valley, CA: CreateSpace Independent Publishing Platform.

Herman, J. (1992) *Trauma and Recovery: The Aftermath of Violence – From Domestic Abuse to Political Terror.* New York, NY: Basic Books

Holmes, S.T. and Holmes, R.M. (2009) *Sex Crimes: Patterns and Behaviour* (3rd edn). New York, NY: Sage.

Jones, L. (2016) 'Conceptualising Trauma and Trauma Informed Care in Forensic Settings.' Paper presented at the DFP and Forensic Faculty Conference, Winchester.

Jones, P. and Doktor, D. (eds) (2008) *Supervision of Dramatherapy.* London: Routledge.

Levine, P. (1997) *Waking the Tiger: Healing Trauma.* Berkeley, CA: North Atlantic Books.

Liebmann, M. (2008) *Art Therapy and Anger.* London: Jessica Kingsley Publishers.

McAllister, M. (2002) 'Dramatherapy and psychosis: Symbol formation and dramatic distance.' *Free Associations 9,* 3, 353–370.

Ogden, P., Minton, K. and Pain, C. (2006) *Trauma and the Body: A Sensorimotor Approach to Psychotherapy.* New York, NY: W.W. Norton.

Pace, P. (2015) *Lifespan Integration: Connecting Ego States through Time.* Eirene Imprint.

Perry, B. (2008) *The Boy Who Was Raised as a Dog.* New York, NY: Basic Books.

Porges, S. (2011) *The Polyvagal Theory: Neurophysiological Foundations of Emotions, Attachments, Communication, and Self-Regulation.* New York, NY: W.W. Norton.

Ramsden, E. and Guarnieri M. (2010) *Dramatherapy and Victim Empathy: A Workshop Approach in a Forensic Setting.* London: Routledge.

Rothchild, B. (2000) *The Body Remembers: The Psychophysiology of Trauma and Trauma Treatment.* New York, NY: W.W. Norton.

Rothwell, K. (ed.) (2016) *Forensic Arts Therapies: Anthology of Practice and Research.* London: Free Association Books.

Rutstein, J.S. (n.d.) *Self-Care for Those Who Work with Trauma.* Accessed on 13/4/20 at https://soundstrue-ha.s3.amazonaws.com/mandala/microsites/healing-trauma-summit/bonus/Self-Care-for-Those-Who-Work-with-Trauma.pdf

Schur, R. (1994) *Countertransference Enactment: How Institutions and Therapists Actualize Primitive Internal Worlds.* Lanham, MD: Jason Aronson.

Seebohm, H. (2011) 'On Bondage and Liberty: The Art of the Possible in Medium Secure Settings.' In D. Doktor, P. Holloway and H. Seebohm (eds) *Dramatherapy and Destructiveness.* London: Routledge.

Shapiro, F. (2012) *Getting Past Your Past: Take Control of Your Life with Self-Help Techniques from EMDR Therapy.* Emmaus, PA: Rodale.

Stamp, S. (2008) 'A Place of Containment: Supervising Dramatherapists in a Secure Setting.' In P. Jones and D. Doktor (eds) *Supervision of Dramatherapy.* London: Routledge.

Terre, L. (1994) *Unchained Memories: True Stories of Traumatic Memories, Lost and Found.* New York, NY: Basic Books.

Thorn, R. (2011) 'Sugar and Spice and All Things Nice: A Black Woman's Anger in a Forensic Setting.' In D. Doktor, P. Holloway and H. Seebohm (eds) *Dramatherapy and Destructiveness.* London: Routledge.

van der Kolk, B. (2014) *The Body Keeps the Score: Mind, Brain and Body in the Transformation of Trauma.* London: Penguin.

CHAPTER 7

Development of Self-Perception

*Art Therapy with Sex Offenders in a
Therapeutic Community Prison*

SIMON HASTILOW, ART THERAPIST

Introduction

This chapter outlines my thinking around my work on a prison wing
run as a therapeutic community. Throughout this chapter I will refer
to this simply as the Wing. I will explore the development of self-
representational images made in art therapy. I draw upon literature
pertaining to distorted cognitions and the significance of self-esteem
in sexual offending. I make links to the men's thinking about how
their understanding of themselves evolves during therapy. Not all
group members make images of themselves, and there are many other
images and themes that are not included here. I am not claiming that a
development of self-depiction is the only sign of progress, or that
people therefore need to make images of themselves to progress. It is
possible for someone to make well-rounded pictures of themselves and
still have low self-esteem and distorted cognitions. People might also
make images of themselves that do not change, but the way they think
about themselves does. My aim here is to present my understanding of
a phenomenon I observe in my group within the context of sex offender
literature.

The Wing model and where art psychotherapy sits within it

The Wing houses up to 40 men, all of whom have committed sexual offences. For those who are unfamiliar with the term, a therapeutic community is a group of people living together to undertake therapy in which everyone acts as everyone else's therapist (Rapoport 1960). The men attend talking therapy groups, known as small groups, large wing meetings and engage in jobs on and off the Wing. The aim is to create an environment in which both the effect of group therapy and the generative power of everyday life can be used for everyone's therapeutic benefit.

The Wing is communal in terms of the emphasis on shared amenities, encouraging closer relationships and informality between staff and residents alike. The Wing runs along these lines, but as a part of the prison establishment there are some rules that are non-negotiable, applicable to all prisoners throughout the prison establishment. A majority of staff are uniformed prison officers who have a dual role; they facilitate therapy groups, but they also enforce the security on the Wing.

The aim is to address offence-specific needs; making people aware of the impact of their actions, enhancing victim empathy and developing an understanding of aspects leading to re-offending. There is work done on offence-related factors, such as beliefs of sexual entitlement or having particular sexual interests.

Art therapy is offered to all men who have been in verbal therapy for at least 12 months. The art therapy group has a membership of six men and meets for two hours every week. There is often space at the beginning of sessions for group members to check in an issue that has been on their minds or from their small group. The group then works in silence for 30–45 minutes before coming back to the circle of chairs. The men are encouraged to be curious about their own and others' artmaking, often asking thoughtful questions or offering insightful observations.

The significance of implicit theories and schemas

Although I had worked with offenders for 18 years when I started on the Wing, I soon felt a need to acquaint myself with approaches to sexual offending via the vast body of literature pertaining to this client group.

I was looking for theories linked to the way in which men perceive themselves. The core themes resonating with my understanding relate to implicit theories and schemas. Implicit theories are a means by which people understand relationships, interpret other people's behaviour and generally make sense of the social world (Ward 2000). Schemas are internalized structures containing beliefs and attitudes, usually evolving along a particular theme. They are formed during our earliest interactions as we develop our sense of self (Mann and Beech 2003).

Implicit theories can play a significant role in sexual offending. It is suggested that the person's perception of their victim leads them to misattribute the significance of what they say and how they behave (Ward 2000). For men who have committed rape, it was found they identified with beliefs that women are unknowable, that women are sex objects, that male sex drive is uncontrollable, that men are entitled to sex and that the world is a dangerous place (Polaschek and Gannon 2004). Another study identified a 'suspiciousness schema', outlining how sexually aggressive men held beliefs that women are deceptive and play games with men's affections (Mann and Shingler 2006). Whilst implicit theories and schemas might identify some beliefs held in common by men convicted of sexual offences, they don't necessarily identify how those men feel about themselves. Schemas are generally considered as affecting the mind's information-processing at an unconscious level (Mann and Hollin 2010).

What seems useful is the idea that schemas have their roots in childhood. For a child growing up in a dysfunctional family, developing schemas may have been a means of making sense of experiences. Coming to believe a parent behaves the way they do because they are inherently deceitful might have given a child a means to understand and predict that behaviour. When the child becomes an adult, however, attributing deceitfulness to someone's ambiguous behaviour is likely to lead to difficulty in building trusting relationships. Social interactions are further disadvantaged when the belief system, employed at an unconscious level, is hyper-sensitive to factors confirming the belief. The person will screen out information contradicting their belief but be completely unaware they are doing so (Mann and Beech 2003). Not only are beliefs activated and functioning at an unconscious level, they can also evoke intensely uncomfortable feelings (Brazão *et al.* 2015). Having an emotional blueprint, that unconsciously triggers feelings and behaviour in the present, that have their roots in the past, seems a lot like Freud's original concept of transference (Freud 1964).

Self-esteem and sexual offending

Self-esteem and implicit theories are closely linked. Self-esteem relates to one's own estimation or evaluation of oneself. The idea that the way in which someone sees themselves links to their propensity for committing sexual offences is not new. Low self-esteem is linked to people having difficulties forming meaningful relationships, being rejected by peers, and experiencing anxiety and depression (Dubois and Tevendale 1999). If someone sees themselves as unattractive and unworthy of romantic relationships, they are more likely to find other ways to meet their sexual needs. They might turn to the internet and pornography, or they might decide to take what they want by force or coercion. However they saw themselves prior to offending, for men who are convicted of a sexual offence, the situation can only get worse.

Within the prison system there is an inmate hierarchy where people bolster their self-esteem in relation to the nature of offences. People who commit sexual offences are at the bottom of this hierarchy. In order to survive prison, men have to hide what they have done and generally avoid showing aspects of themselves that will be perceived as vulnerable. This denial of one's true self is detrimental to self-esteem (Dubois and Tevendale 1999). Furthermore, when someone's perception of their offence evokes shame, they see themselves as being a bad person to the extent that they can only see themselves as an irredeemable offender (Marshall *et al.* 2009).

But there is more to it. Having high self-esteem has been found to make people more prone to aggression and defensive behaviour and thinking (Baumeister, Smart and Boden 1996). When someone feels good about themselves in a way that depends on making themselves look better than others, any threat to this is perceived as a threat to their ego (Waschull and Kernis 1996). Therefore, simply thinking of high or low self-esteem is unhelpful. What seems more useful to think about is how stable someone's level of self-esteem is. When someone has stable self-esteem their overall view of themselves is less likely to fluctuate. When self-esteem is less stable, that person's view of themselves is less clear and more vulnerable to being swayed by life's events (Kernis 2005).

Self-esteem can also be thought about as being explicit or implicit. Explicit self-esteem links to conscious thoughts someone has about their self-worth, self-liking and acceptance. Implicit self-esteem links more to less conscious perceptions, those that are automatic and learned from an early age, akin to schemas (Zeigler-Hill 2006). This goes a step further when you consider it is possible for our explicit self-esteem to be at odds with our implicit self-esteem. We might think highly of ourselves at a conscious level, but under the surface we feel insecure and unworthy.

Other perspectives on human figure drawing

It is worth noting that art therapy is not the only profession to consider the importance of how people draw human figures. In 1948, John Buck, a psychologist, developed the House-Tree-Person technique as a means of gaining insight into an individual's personality and cognitive functioning (Buck 1948). Amongst other things, this was seen as having relevance to assessing someone's attitude towards sex. An overemphasized neck could indicate conflict between sexual drives and intellectual control. Similarly, an overemphasized waistline could be taken as a sign of difficulty expressing and controlling sexual urges (Hammer 1954). Over the years various studies have questioned the validity of using drawing a person as an accurate assessment tool, citing a lack of corroborative evidence (Allen and Tussey 2012).

Case material

The following case material uses a pseudonym and some of the details have been changed to ensure anonymity. Stuart is a white British male in his early forties. He has been in the art therapy group for just over two and a half years. Stuart grew up with his mother, father and a younger brother, seven years his junior. He described his family life as good but stated there was no communication about feelings or emotions, and although there were never any arguments, he felt his parents were just ignoring problems. Further, Stuart felt unable to express his emotions to his parents. Stuart always saw them as knowing what was best and described them as very strict; in order to avoid conflict, he did not argue or disagree with them.

Stuart stated that, looking back, there were a couple of things he found difficult: first, his younger brother being diagnosed with cancer; and second, his parents' divorce. When his brother was diagnosed Stuart accepted it as 'something that happened'. However, his parents' divorce had a more personal impact on him. Stuart was embarrassed by his mother having an affair and was extremely angry with her and did not speak to her for over two years after that. Stuart described feelings of rejection throughout his life, saying his parents focused on his brother when he was ill, and left Stuart with neighbours, feeling confused. He also described feeling rejected by girls at school, when he tried to initiate relationships with them, and developed the view that he was 'ugly'. Stuart struggled to cope with these feelings of rejection and jealousy.

He started using pornography at the age of 13, usually on a daily basis. From this he reported developing a distorted view of sex and relationships. He described developing a habit of masturbating as a way of coping with these uncomfortable feelings.

Stuart had a previous conviction for sexual offences committed against female strangers. Whilst in prison Stuart actively engaged in the treatment available. He completed the Core Sex Offender Treatment Programme (SOTP) in 2007 and Extended SOTP in 2010. The index offence occurred when Stuart was released on licence, having been identified as posing a reduced risk of re-offending. He had been in the community for just six days. Stuart reported he felt lonely on release from prison and described being sexually preoccupied. He was using extreme pornography as a coping strategy. On the day of the offence, he saw families and couples out Christmas shopping, which triggered grievance thinking related to being owed something. He reported seeing a woman alone in a car park and thinking he would 'take what he never had'. He asked her to have sex with him and when she refused, he told her he had a knife. He knocked her to the floor, was disturbed by passers-by and fled the scene. Stuart admitted the offence when questioned by police officers. Stuart was convicted of attempted rape for which he received a sentence of Imprisonment for Public Protection.

When Stuart was assessed for the Wing, his feelings of inadequacy were a central risk factor. Stuart held a very negative view of himself, and this prevented him from attempting to initiate relationships, fearing being hurt. So, his sexual fantasies were about contacting strangers in order to experience sexual gratification, without the need to experience emotional intimacy. Stuart acknowledged he felt sexually entitled within his offending, believing he was owed sex. He did not identify a schema directly related to entitlement thinking during the Extended SOTP, however he did identify a belief 'I can't be loved' that contributed to his offending, which he believed was the only way to achieve sexual intimacy.

His fear of being rejected by women seemed to be related to his own self-esteem. On the Wing he was initially quiet and withdrawn. He struggled to challenge people and was almost incapable of speaking directly to some of the female staff. Part of the therapeutic culture on the Wing is for men to challenge people who they perceive as displaying antisocial or offence-paralleling behaviour or language. It wasn't long before Stuart found his voice and was able to speak out. He was also able to build relationships with female staff. Stuart seemed to find solace in the logic of therapy, recognizing it was possible to make sense of past events by thinking about how they resonated in the present.

Figure 7.1: Assessment piece

The image represented in Figure 7.1 was made in Stuart's individual assessment prior to starting in the group. I asked him to make an image to introduce himself to me, which could include anything he felt significant. Stuart made an image of a tiny stick figure, surrounded by green, with six small black shapes that seemed to be guarding the figure. The rest was a sea of red with a thin black border.

Stuart talked about the red as anger, which surrounded him. The border was about how he had contained the anger all his life and only recently started letting it out. He said green was the jealousy that surrounded him. He felt jealous whenever he saw other people whom he perceived to have a good relationship, something he had never had. He hadn't realized until he made the image quite how close the jealousy was to him. The black shapes were skulls, representing the darkness/ evil he felt he had become. He explained the small size of the figure represented how insignificant he felt.

I commented on the confidence of his brush strokes, and how he placed himself in the centre of things. I contrasted this to his perception that it made him look insignificant. I said the green and the black seemed to protect him, but also kept him in the same place. I noted he had given himself a lot of space to grow into, once he released himself from his jealousy. We talked about the nature of jealousy, how it is based on fantasy and obliterates any sense of self-value. Initially, I didn't think much about the figure being a stick man, assuming it could be an expedient way to draw a small figure.

Another thought about stick men is they could be an attempt at protecting unstable self-esteem. By working on an easy task, someone can protect themselves from discouraging feedback (Waschull and Kernis 1996). When men first join the art therapy group, they may anticipate some level of criticism or ridicule of their artwork. If they have implicit theories that lead them to feel that whatever they do won't be good enough, they will be particularly sensitive to nuances in the way their artwork is received. When the evidence is consistently different from their expectations, they may find they can question the evidence for their perception of their unworthiness. The size of the figure is worth further consideration. The size in which someone represents the human figure has been explored in relation to self-concept; image size was found as not significant, but the amount of detail was; and participants in high and moderate self-concept groups were seen to produce a more complete image of better quality (Prytula et al. 1978).

After being in the group for eight months, Stuart made an image that showed a face, a pair of legs and penis and the word 'Scarred'. These were surrounded by a brown border, outside of which were the words 'stay away'. Unfortunately, the pencil drawing was so faint it was not possible to photograph it in a way that would enable it to be reproduced for this chapter. I was immediately struck by the increased level of detail in the way Stuart depicted himself. He explained the image related to an issue he had raised in his small group. He talked about having a problem with his penis when he was growing up. It was painful and uncomfortable, but he didn't tell his parents because they were not very approachable, and he felt too awkward to talk about this with them.

When he was first in prison it got diagnosed as a problem that could be fixed with surgery. He described being in hospital after surgery and the horrified response of the escorting prison officer, when he caught a glimpse of Stuart's penis while the dressing was being changed. Stuart felt his penis was disgusting and didn't feel a woman could ever find it attractive. The image of his face related to teenage acne, which had been bad, but reasonably bearable in comparison to the penis issue. The making of this image enabled other group members to talk openly about their perceptions of their own genitalia and the impact this had on their self-esteem.

It is tempting to see a parallel between the brown border in this image and the border in the image in Figure 7.1. The border functions to keep people out and to keep Stuart's anger in, but there is more space surrounding it. Even though the border is reinforced with the repetition of 'stay away', the surrounding space feels like room for people to approach, whereas in Figure 7.1 there is no room for anything or anyone else. The shift to a more detailed image felt significant.

In a formal programme of art therapy designed to promote self-esteem in sex offenders, Joy Ackerman (1992) found that after ten sessions her clients paid more attention to detail in their drawings of human figures. Other studies have noted a correlation between a lift in emotional mood and increased realism in artwork (Gussak 2009), as well as the creative process facilitating the integration of uncomfortable feelings (Gerber 1994). In Stuart's case it might not have been a lift in mood, but there was certainly an increased level of self-worth, enabling him to talk openly about uncomfortable personal issues.

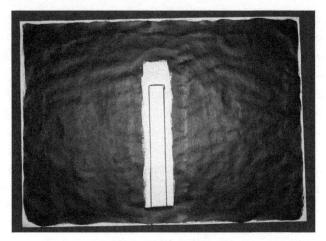

Figure 7.2: The column

Two months later Stuart produced the image depicted in Figure 7.2. It shows a tiny light-blue figure standing on a tall column surrounded by black. Stuart linked the image to where he felt he was now, having dealt with feelings evoked by an interaction on the Wing where another community member challenged Stuart over the way he had presented his opinion on a situation on the Wing. We thought about this in terms of his feeling uncomfortable after being challenged and disliking the feelings. I commented this was actually an ordinary aspect of getting on with people, how people who have grown up with friendships are used to falling out with people and then making up again. Stuart understood this and accepted he might have to get his head around it.

What seems striking is the way Stuart had reduced himself to being small and insignificant again, as in Figure 7.1, swamped by the surrounding feelings. There's something paradoxical about his size in the figure and the giant pedestal he'd put himself on, possibly signifying the extent to which he felt exposed by being criticized. The other parallel with Figure 7.1 is the use of paint to depict an emotion. I wondered whether the fluidity of the medium was significant. Whilst the black is much thicker than the red, the emotion itself was undefined by Stuart, a more general sense of discomfort compared to the more specific nature of the anger.

The image depicted in Figure 7.3 was made when Stuart had been in the group for just over two years. The page is divided diagonally with blue zig-zag arrows, with two red hearts in one half and a black skull and crossed bones in the other. In the middle of the arrows is a tiny blue figure. Stuart explained that the hearts represented the loving aspects of a relationship, whilst the skull represented anger and mistrust. The mistrust was in relation to thoughts about how open he felt he could be with a potential partner about his offence history; if he's completely open, he risks losing a relationship, if he's not open then he's being deceitful. This linked to Stuart's growing realization that he might actually be capable of forming a genuine romantic relationship at some point, something he'd previously believed would be impossible.

Figure 7.3: Choices

Stuart described himself as oscillating between the two different positions, hence the arrows. I commented that the arrows seemed like stitches, bringing the two aspects together, as a real relationship would not be one or the other but a combination of both. He reflected on the role model of his parents' relationship, where uncomfortable feelings bubbled away under the surface but were not talked about. He linked this to the skull not having a mouth. At the time I didn't make the connection, but the skull is reminiscent of the skulls in Figure 7.1 which represented the darkness/evil he felt he had become. Where he previously saw himself as being defined by these qualities, the image in Figure 7.3 seems to indicate these had become qualities he could reflect on and understand. Another group member wondered whether the skull represented poison, indicating toxic relationships. Stuart felt anger and mistrust were toxic to relationships if they were not acknowledged and spoken about. In my mind this indicated a sense of agency in dealing with uncomfortable feelings and situations. His parents couldn't deal with their interpersonal difficulties, but Stuart could recognize where he might end up if he didn't voice things.

As with Figure 7.1, I was struck by the small size of the figure. I was sad, but not entirely surprised, that three days after making this image, Stuart started having suicidal thoughts. In this instance, he was not overwhelmed by one particular emotion, but by finding himself caught between conflicting positions, similar to the depressive position (Klein 1946).

Figure 7.4: 'I fucking matter' (see colour section)

Seven weeks later Stuart made the image depicted in Figure 7.4. At the start of the session, Stuart said he was feeling angry. He described a recent encounter with another community member who asked Stuart about the procedure for getting a job. Because they didn't like the answer, they became snippy with Stuart. Stuart got angry, pointing out how hurtful their comments were, that he had tried to help them, and their response was unacceptable. The other person then apologized. Stuart was pleased with the outcome but still felt uncomfortable. He made an image of him standing on a hill with his face red and his arms trembling. He was saying the thoughts that had gone through his head at the time of the encounter. On the hill were the words 'I fucking matter'.

We explored the image and how valuable it was that he could stand up for himself and feel he was significant. I commented on how he'd pictured himself as full-bodied and solid compared to the previous stick man images. The red background echoes the red in the assessment image, but this time Stuart drew himself as big and solid, with a voice. The boundary from Figure 7.1 no longer contained the anger but had become the place from which Stuart could give voice to his feelings.

Conclusion

It seems useful to think about how someone sees themselves and others, and to consider the experiences that have shaped these beliefs. Art therapy provides a good opportunity for men who have committed sexual offences to think about who they are, what they have done and why. Stuart's early life left him with a confused and critical sense of who he was. His self-worth was low, and his sense of himself as someone who could love and be lovable became distorted. During his time in art therapy, Stuart grappled with his identity, and this is reflected in his images. As his sense of self grew clearer, his ability to use the group as a space to explore uncomfortable issues also evolved.

Other art therapists have found their clients reported improvements in their level of self-esteem and their capacity for self-disclosure (Green, Wehling and Talsky 1987; Hartz and Thick 2005; Heenan 2006). In a study involving emotionally disturbed adolescents, Terry Tibbetts and Beth Stone (1990) found that engaging in art therapy led to participants forming a more realistic view of themselves and their environment.

This has not been a linear process. Working on deeply personal material is, I believe, inherently unsettling. This has been reflected in Stuart's images, with him oscillating between stick men and more rounded forms. What stands out for me is not just the way he'd depicted himself, but also his relationship to his feelings. What started out as something that isolated Stuart from others – his anger – became something he could own and express, not as a destructive force, but as a force for change. The change in the images may link to the increase in stability and level of self-esteem. Stuart's father was often critical and withheld approval, so he may have expected a similar response from me or from other group members. By being met with empathy, acceptance and emotional support, Stuart was able to increase his overall evaluation of himself and perceive himself as capable and able to change.

References

Ackerman, J. (1992) 'Art-therapy intervention designed to increase self-esteem of an incarcerated pedophile.' *American Journal of Art Therapy 30*, 4, 143–149.

Allen, B. and Tussey, C. (2012) 'Can projective drawings detect if a child experienced sexual or physical abuse? A systematic review of the controlled research.' *Trauma, Violence, & Abuse, 13*, 2, 97–111.

Baumeister, R.F., Smart, L. and Boden, J.M. (1996) 'Relation of threatened egotism to violence and aggression: The dark side of high self-esteem.' *Psychological Review 103*,1,5.

Brazão, N., Da Motta, C., Rijo, D., do Céu Salvador, M. *et al.* (2015) 'Clinical change in cognitive distortions and core schemas after a cognitive–behavioural group intervention: Preliminary findings from a randomized trial with male prison inmates.' *Cognitive Therapy and Research 39*, 5, 578–589.

Buck, J.N. (1948) 'The H-T-P technique: A qualitative and quantitative scoring manual.' *Journal of Clinical Psychology 4*, 4, 317–396.

Dubois, D.L. and Tevendale, H.D. (1999) 'Self-esteem in childhood and adolescence: Vaccine or epiphenomenon?' *Applied and Preventive Psychology 8*, 2, 103–117.

Freud, S. (1964) 'The Dynamics of Transference.' In J.E. Strachey (ed.) *The Standard Edition of the Complete Psychological Works of Sigmund Freud: Volume 12*. London: Hogarth Press.

Gerber, J. (1994) 'The use of art therapy in juvenile sex offender specific treatment.' *The Arts in Psychotherapy 21*, 367–374.

Green, B.L., Wehling, C. and Talsky, G.J. (1987) 'Group art therapy as an adjunct to treatment for chronic outpatients.' *Psychiatric Services 38*, 9, 988–991.

Gussak, D. (2009) 'The effects of art therapy on male and female inmates: Advancing the research base.' *The Arts in Psychotherapy 36*, 5–12.

Hammer, E.F. (1954) 'Guide for qualitative research with the HTP.' *Journal of General Psychology 51*, 1, 41–60.

Hartz, L. and Thick, L. (2005) 'Art therapy strategies to raise self-esteem in female juvenile offenders: A comparison of art psychotherapy and art as therapy approaches.' *Art Therapy 22*, 2, 70–80.

Heenan, D. (2006) 'Art as therapy: An effective way of promoting positive mental health?' *Disability & Society 21*, 2, 179–191.

Kernis, M.H. (2005) 'Measuring self-esteem in context: The importance of stability of self-esteem in psychological functioning.' *Journal of Personality 73*, 6, 1569–1605.

Klein, M. (1946) 'Notes on some schizoid mechanisms.' *International Journal of Psycho-analysis 27*, 99.

Mann, R.E. and Beech, A.R. (2003) 'Cognitive Distortions, Schemas, and Implicit Theories.' In T. Ward, D.R. Laws and S.M. Hudson (eds) *Sexual Deviance: Issues and Controversies*. Thousand Oaks, CA: Sage.

Mann, R. and Hollin, C. (2010) 'Self-reported schemas in sexual offenders.' *Journal of Forensic Psychiatry & Psychology 21*, 6, 834–851.

Mann, R.E. and Shingler, J. (2006) 'Schema-driven Cognition in Sexual Offenders: Theory, Assessment and Treatment.' In W.L. Marshall (ed.) *Sexual Offender Treatment: Controversial Issues*. New York, NY: John Wiley & Sons.

Marshall, W.L., Marshall, L.E., Serran, G.A. and O'Brien, M.D. (2009) 'Self-esteem, shame, cognitive distortions and empathy in sexual offenders: Their integration and treatment implications.' *Psychology, Crime & Law 15*, 2–3, 217–234.

Polaschek, D.L. and Gannon, T.A. (2004) 'The implicit theories of rapists: What convicted offenders tell us.' *Sexual Abuse: A Journal of Research and Treatment 16*, 4, 299–314.

Prytula, R.E., Phelps, M.R., Morrissey, E.F. and Davis, S.F. (1978) 'Figure drawing size as a reflection of self-concept or self-esteem.' *Journal of Clinical Psychology 34*, 1, 207–214.

Rapoport, R. (1960) *Community as Doctor*. London: Tavistock Publications.

Tibbetts, T.J. and Stone, B. (1990) 'Short-term art therapy with seriously emotionally disturbed adolescents.' *The Arts in Psychotherapy 17*, 136–146.

Ward, T. (2000) 'Sexual offenders' cognitive distortions as implicit theories.' *Aggression and Violent Behavior 5*, 5, 491–507.

Waschull, S.B. and Kernis, M.H. (1996) 'Level and stability of self-esteem as predictors of children's intrinsic motivation and reasons for anger.' *Personality and Social Psychology Bulletin 22*, 1, 4–13.

Zeigler-Hill, V. (2006) 'Discrepancies between implicit and explicit self-esteem: Implications for narcissism and self-esteem instability.' *Journal of Personality 74*, 1, 119–144.

CHAPTER 8

Diagnosis, Ethics and the Sexual Offender Subject

A Lacanian Psychoanalytic Perspective

ALICE MYLES, ART PSYCHOTHERAPIST

Introduction

In this chapter I will discuss how ideas within Lacanian psychoanalytic theory can inform clinical practice with sexual offenders. Focusing on the modality of art psychotherapy, I will draw on the case material of a patient detained by forensic section under the Mental Health Act (1983, amended 2007) to secure hospital treatment for a mental health disorder associated with a sexual risk to children. There is a great deal to be found in the psychoanalytic teachings of Lacan that may be of interest to us in the fields of art psychotherapy and forensics, but I will limit my discussion to two themes I feel to be of salience: diagnosis and ethics.

Jacques-Marie Lacan taught a weekly public seminar in Paris from 1952 to 1980, focusing on the theory and ethics of clinical work in the psychoanalytic field. Why, though, should we be looking to import French 20th-century intellectual goods of this type to the specifics of working with sexual offending in a secure unit in the UK today? More broadly, how can psychoanalysis, which focuses on speech and language, be of use to us when the practice of art psychotherapy deals primarily with the image?

Diagnosis, symptom and signification

Lacan's interventions in psychoanalytic theory emerged from his working since the early 1930s as a consultant psychiatrist at the Sainte-Anne hospital in Paris. One effect of this background was undoubtedly his development of a new and clear distinction between diagnostic categories and the theorizing of an aetiology of, and direction of the treatment for, psychosis. Whereas Freud had shied away from the question of psychosis and had viewed it as a contra-indication for psychoanalysis, Lacan brought forth significant contributions that opened up psychoanalysis as a viable treatment for the psychotic subject.

By the early 1950s, Lacan had evolved a clinically oriented theory of signification influenced by the then-new sciences of social anthropology and structural linguistics. The essential idea that Lacan drew from, was that language and culture are structural equivalents, in that the symbols and artefacts of culture function like individual elements of language, meaningful only in their conjunction rather than in isolation. Language was seen as a social bond, a means to establish identity through difference, not merely as a way to communicate. Lacan argued that clinical work should privilege the differential elements within language: signifiers, as distinguished from signs. While signs might correspond to a commonsense understanding of language as having a fixed meaning, the signifier only 'represents a subject for another signifier' (Lacan 1981, p.207).

What does this mean? Simply that what someone says may not be what they mean, and in clinical work the former is to be privileged ahead of the latter. The person in analysis or therapy is a 'speaking subject', and their communications are unable to be fully apprehended outside the closed circuit of their own subjective significations. The work of analysis, Lacan argued, is to bring these significations to the fore in order to free the subject from their symptomatic effects. This is done through free association, critical self-reflection and interpretation within the dynamics of transference. The goal is not merely to uncover the full import of the subject's thoughts and ideas but to help them, through the analytic relationship, to forge new meanings free of the toxic effects of their erstwhile significations.

On a first approach, we may understand these seemingly obscure definitions and differentiations simply as emphasizing that in clinical encounters we should not be too swift to assume that we understand what we are hearing. This might be due to the speaker having their own subjective version of what they are saying: crucial nuances or associations between signifiers (words) that the clinician is not yet privy to. More radically, in cases of psychosis, elements of language may have taken on their own individual meanings for the speaker, and these can only be understood relative to their wider belief system or fantasies. In Lacan's view, working with the idiosyncratic potential of the signifier meant opening up further possibilities of meaningful engagement with a patient, not merely through their speech, but also through their symptomology, behaviours or general clinical presentation, including personal writings or artistic productions.

In Lacan's third seminar, 'The Psychoses' (Lacan 1993), he developed a number of ideas related to the diagnosis and treatment of psychosis. Central to Lacan's concerns was a single question: What distinguishes how a psychotic person uses language compared to the non-psychotic person? Lacan had observed in his clinical work that one thing that characterized the speech of the psychotic individuals in his practice was a peculiar 'concrete' relationship to words. This manifested itself in a difficulty in engaging with the vagaries of language (metaphors, metonyms and homonyms, for example) together with a certainty in which particular ideas or beliefs were held, even delusory ones. It was as if certain ideas or definitions *had* to be understood by the patient in their way, that they were axiomatic, providing structure in their world.

Searching for a theoretical mechanism to explain this phenomenon, Lacan concluded that the psychotic subject must have a specific lack in the inscription of language; he designated this lack a primary or foundational signifier, which he called the 'father'. This is not to be understood as a male figure in the unconscious, an internal object or a Jungian archetype, but as an original metaphor that asserts the primacy of the signifier over the sign and places the subject within the social order.

What does this mean? Essentially that the assimilation of an original 'paternal' metaphor within language was seen to affect a person's ability to engage with reality, both social and linguistic. The psychotic person's separation from this – the absence of the foundational signifier – would have a direct effect on their grasp of reality and would be discernible via their use of language. Hence Lacan's claim that psychosis can only be determined when the symptomatic presentation includes some evidence of disturbances at the linguistic level (Lacan 1993). Classically, this disturbance would entail the subject's inability to distinguish between what Freud (1915) had termed word-presentations and thing-presentations, that is language and reality. Hence a characteristic of psychosis is the slippage between word and thing, resulting in certainty about the real-world import of the psychotic subject's thoughts. This is in contrast to the incessant doubts typical of the neurotic subject.

Lacan's observations suggest the importance of diagnosis in clinical work with sexual offenders. But how can the Lacanian diagnostic be useful in work with sexual offending in the contemporary clinic, and how does it compare to psychiatric models such as the Diagnostic and Statistical Manual of Mental Disorders (DSM) and the World Health Organization's International Classification of Diseases (ICD)?

Diagnosis in Lacanian psychoanalysis focuses on a structural position in language. Whereas the DSM and ICD categories base diagnoses on clusters of symptoms, the key distinction in the Lacanian diagnostic is that symptoms are not necessarily related to a disorder, as the same symptom can relate to different psychic or clinical structures (Nobus 2000). In the case of a neurotic structure, word-presentations have not been separated from thing-presentations, but rather a word-presentation has been repressed and it is this repressed or unconscious word-presentation that determines the symptom. The clinician's task is to help recover and bring into awareness what has been repressed. In contrast, in a psychotic clinical structure, although symptoms are still determined by word-presentations, neither the word-presentation nor the thing-presentation has been repressed (Nobus 2000). There is no hidden unconscious. Symptoms are instead a 'subjective solution' (Sharon-Zisser 2018) to the psychotic subject's separation from the world of signification. In this regard, a Lacanian perspective is distinctly non-medicalized and eschews a diagnostic logic based solely on surface phenomena such as hallucination or behaviour. It is the subject's relationship to their symptomology, rather than the symptoms themselves, that points to the diagnosis and determines the direction of the treatment.

As an example of this, and one that looks ahead to the case study later in this chapter, let us take the signifying pair 'sexual offender'. This term may conjure up many different underlying concepts or images on the side of a clinical, legal or dictionary definition. However, for many, including often the patient themselves, this label might signify something else entirely: a moral pejorative, 'the worst person', or indeed an ego-syntonic (favourable to a person's self-image) inverse of this, a person beyond the law, the one who takes up a place of exception – a characteristic motif in psychosis, as Darian Leader has explored in a monograph (Leader 2011).

The point here is the difference between signification and definition. In both Lacanian psychoanalysis and art psychotherapy we are working on the subjective level of language and communication. Whether in the examples of speech or in the form of an artwork, the elements (signifiers) involved may constitute crucial supports of the psychotic subject's ability to take up a place in the world. The Lacanian clinician working with psychosis has to recognize the functionality of the signifiers the patient is using, and even potentially lend support to their delusion in order to help secure the patient's subjective position, their sense of who they are. The Lacanian approach works with what stabilizes the subject, not simply trying to align them with reality. This could be by privileging the associations of the client over the interpretations of the therapist, or it might be a more creative process, encouraging a particular narrative or safe point of identification.

Working in this way represents a standpoint in the ethics of clinical intervention. It also accentuates an alignment between art psychotherapy and Lacanian analysis, in the freeing up of the process of signification and the production of meaning through pictures or speech. In this regard, a Lacanian approach may not differ in practice from that of art therapists who attune themselves to their client's language and metaphors. Rather, what a Lacanian perspective offers is a slightly different language for conceptualizing the process and ethics of art therapy, and rigour on the question of diagnosis, which can help orientate the clinician's approach and understanding of the clinical material.

In the case that follows, we see how the patient constructs a safe point of identification in the character and narrative he develops, and how this identification functions in relation to recurrent signifiers and motifs. One example is the signifier 'losing face', which can be inferred from aspects of the patient's biography, sexual offending and later from his artwork, and which seems to serve a particular function for him in his relation to 'the other'.

In the case of a neurotic subject, interventions aimed at making the metaphoric value of this signifier 'losing face' resonate for the patient might bring into awareness a missing signifier or word-presentation, that of 'being humiliated' or 'being ashamed', along with certain thoughts and memories that begin to give the patient insight into their sexual offending, freeing them from the toxic symptomatic effects of the signifier. A neurotic patient may also be encouraged to reflect critically on identifying characters in the artwork and recognize the significations they contain of, for example, something they lack or something they desire.

By contrast, in the case of a psychotic subject, these identifications and signifiers have to be taken almost at face value. They give the patient a stable subjective position in the world, without which a more acute psychosis, a subjective experience of utter chaos, would prevail. Furthermore, given the psychotic subject's difficulty in engaging with metaphor in language, particularly metaphors that have personal resonance, any allusion or interpretation to the patient of a metaphoric signifier such as 'losing face' risks being destabilizing. Instead, the toxic or traumatic signifier is safer remaining as a benign inscription within the artwork.

It is in this regard that we should understand the later Lacanian concept of the *sinthome* (an old French spelling of symptom), a term increasingly discussed in art therapy theory (cf. Collins 2014; Biberman and Sharon-Zisser 2017) that designates a composite of the subject's modes of enjoyment or suffering contained within idiosyncratic forms of expression (including writings or art) beyond comprehension or interpretation by the therapist. The emphasis is on a model of clinical work that privileges the functionality of the patient's clinical material ahead of its translatability.

Having outlined some basic theoretical concepts that orient the direction of the treatment vis-à-vis diagnosis in the Lacanian clinic, I will present the case of Vincent from my practice.

Case vignette: Vincent

Reports described Vincent as having a relatively untroubled family upbringing with both his mother and father present. However, his childhood and adolescent years had been marked by rivalry with a younger sister, whom Vincent had perceived as favoured by their parents. This had led Vincent to turn away (or lose face), retreating into a world of isolation and fantasy, which became fixated on increasingly violent sexual assault. The subsequent victims of this were all females of a specific minority ethnic group in the UK (Vincent is of White British ethnicity). At the age of 17, Vincent was convicted of the murder and attempted sexual assault of a 12-year-old girl, whose face he had covered during the assault. The victim was of the previously fantasized ethnic minority group. Vincent had left his bus pass at the scene and was subsequently arrested. He later confessed to numerous other sexual assaults of teenage girls in the years prior to the offence mentioned above.

When I began working with Vincent in group art psychotherapy, he had spent over 20 years in prisons and special hospitals. He continued to experience residual symptoms of psychosis in the form of auditory hallucinations. Despite these, he had a calm and composed demeanour and participated in the group, working in silence, or at times pausing to invite interaction with other group members with a comment. In one of the first groups, for example, he asked: 'Do trees have souls? Are they called the tree of knowledge because of all the books and paper that come from them?' This was a characteristic remark of Vincent, reflective of a concretization in thinking. Stated as matter-of-fact questions, his remarks are in contrast to the figurative language of metaphor found in poetry, for example.

In some of the early groups, Vincent worked in abstract style. He produced a swirling circular image in black, red and blue, which he said represented a rock, blood and water. When asked about the shapes around the edge he said he thought they were 'overkill' and that he had 'gone too far'. He then requested to leave the room. Vincent often asked to go to the toilet during discussion of the imagery or responded to questions about elements in his image with 'It's just a picture'. Using the Lacanian distinction above, we might understand Vincent's reactions here as reflecting his need literally to separate himself from the signifiers in his artwork by leaving the room or, in his verbal response 'It's just a picture', to reduce them to the level of mere sign.

Vincent's artwork often consisted of portraits, which might be seen as images of masculinity. Figure 8.1 depicts a muscular male flexing his bicep. When asked how he felt about his drawing, Vincent, who had been holding the picture up, immediately put it down commenting, without humour: 'This is getting heavy now.' Again, Vincent's reaction could be heard relative to a difficulty in separating the metaphoric and literal meaning of 'heavy'.

Figure 8.1: Hero

Vincent developed his drawings of strong males to a specific character from a comic book series, a helmeted superhero who protected civilians from criminals. The eyes and top half of the face of this man – or man-like being – were always covered.

During debrief with the assistant psychologist who ran the group with me, we reflected on our feelings towards Vincent. I experienced Vincent as enigmatic but sensitive, his masculine depictions a counterpoint to his own apparent vulnerabilities. By contrast, my colleague found him strangely empty. Although our thoughts seemed to be marked by contrasting countertransferences, they shared Vincent's inability to engage with his artwork at the level of the signifier, in that he could not make links between his subjective experience and the elements in his drawings. This was reinforced by the covered eyes of the superhero.

At one point Vincent began to review and draw together certain images he had produced in group art psychotherapy to form a comic strip. The group witnessed the emergent narrative, which Vincent spoke about over a period of several weeks. This centred around the idea of an 'impossible choice' to be made by Vincent's helmeted superhero following a clairvoyant's vision of tragedy. He would need to crash a bus into an acid factory, killing the passengers and possibly himself, to save the world.

The central image of the story's main protagonist showed him pulling several ropes around the bus, drawn in perspective, which appeared to accentuate the outstretched lines. Vincent's association to the picture was that it was a 'necessary evil'. I felt it was important to encourage the project to reach its conclusion before making an intervention or comment. However, I mirrored the posture of the main protagonist, to encourage Vincent to reflect on how this pull might be embodied, and the impossible strain involved in pulling a bus. My own (unvoiced) associations to the story were on the apparent horror and the choice of acid, which, as perhaps suggested in Figure 8.2, takes away the face of the victim (a recurrence of 'losing face').

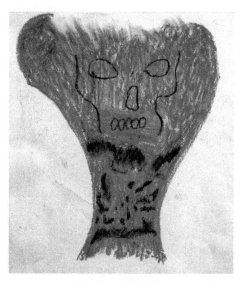

Figure 8.2: Explosion (see colour section)

At the end of these few weeks, Vincent produced the image in Figure 8.2. He began outlining the large red shape in oil pastel, and at one point I noticed him move the image so that it became slightly obscured from my line of sight behind several pots of paint, so that the image appeared to me to be a large red heart. At the end of the session, when Vincent showed the picture to the group, I was surprised by what he revealed. His associations were that the picture was an explosion and that the skull drawn on it represented death. I decided to bring out my own associations and commented that I had thought it was a love heart. He said, 'No, it's an explosion'. 'Maybe love is explosive,' I suggested. Vincent responded with an emphatic 'Yeah!'

In the weeks that followed, Vincent's artwork began to look more benign. He worked on an image entitled 'Genesis' using glitter, which he said was a 'starry start'. He then worked on an abstract image reminding him of a cinema screen. He recalled going to the cinema as a child to see *Star Trek II: The Wrath of Khan* (a film set around a fictional planet called Genesis) and being moved to tears by the alien character Spock's act of self-sacrifice, associated with the line: 'The needs of the many outweigh the needs of the few'.

After several weeks working in abstract style, Vincent returned to portraits and figurative comic-book characters. He made a picture of 'Nemesis' who he said was an 'alien fighting for human rights'. My own (unvoiced) associations were of human rights as being apparently alien to Vincent due to the nature of his offence. But it was clear that his identification with these figures was a way of situating himself as a tragic hero, the one who takes up the place of exception by choosing the logical rather than human path. These alien(ated) points of identification seemed to involve the question about what it was to be human. However, this was not elaborated by Vincent in any conscious way.

The following week, Vincent returned to a previous portrait of his superhero, this time adding bright colours – red, blue and yellow – and making the skin tone darker. Vincent himself identified the ethnicity, adding a remark about the previous skin tone that 'pink was too girly'. The identified ethnicity on his renewed image of the superhero was now the same as the victim of his index offence. Vincent's remark also suggests a further signification of ethnicity for him (which goes beyond the question of difference formulated below) in relation to gender and sexual identity as possible aspects of his psychosis and sexual offending. An exploration of this is beyond the scope of the current chapter.

A theme in Vincent's childhood was a sense of being ignored, or absent from the gaze of his parents, a 'losing face' in relation to the other, a factor that led to later self-isolation. His private fantasies seemed to have the function of producing a non-desiring sexual object of absolute difference through ethnic difference and sexual assault. The motif of covering over the face of the sexual assault victim, a signifier of 'losing face', was copied into the image of the helmeted superhero. Vincent's

Figure 1.1: Flap closed – 'Do Not Open'

Figure 1.2: Flap open – 'Evil Girl Pudsey'

Figure 3.4: Geisha

Figure 5.4: What is empathy? Part 2

I FEEL ~~BO~~ BEAUTIFUL

I AM A FEMALE

I LIKE THE CLOTHS I WEAR

I LIKE TO WEAR SKIRTS AND DRESSES

I LIKE SILKY, CHIFFON AND SATIN.

I USED TO PLAY WITH DOLLS STARTED AT 10 ONWARDS

I LIKE TO BE TREATED AS A WOMAN BEING PAMPERED PASSIVE

I LOVE SHOPPING FOR CLOTHES

I HAD A LOT OF UNIFORMS WHICH I WORE.

I WANT OTHER PEOPLE TO TREAT ME AS A
WOMAN FELT CONFIDENT DID NOT MIND WHAT OTHER PEOPLE THOUGHT

I LIKE SEXY UNDERWEAR.

MY NAME IS CHRISTINE. I CHOOSE THIS NAME
I CHANGED THIS BY DEED POLL

I LIKE TO HAVE SEX WHEN I AM DRESSED
UP.

MY FAVOURITE UNIFORM IS AIR STEWARDESS, NURSES

I ENJOY OTHER MALES PICKING ME UP AT
NIGHT WHEN I AM DRESSED.

I ENJOYED WEARING WEDDING DRESSES AND
UNDERSKIRTS.

I LIKED OTHER PEOPLE BEING TRUTHFUL WITH ME.
I EXPRESSED MYSELF FREE MYSELF
BEING DISGUISED ANONYMOUS

I HAVE CHILDREN   BEING FOUND OUT BY
                          RELATIVES

Figure 6.4: Being a female

Figure 7.4: 'I fucking matter'

Figure 8.2: Explosion

Figure 10.1: Honey Bee on Courtyard Sunflower

Figure 11.6: The JCB!

Figure 13.2: The corridor

Figure 14.1: Response image

Figure 15.4: Life in secure services as a theatre stage

Figure 17.3: George's felt-tip image

renditions of this image and others could be seen as significations of his initial offence. Again, this was not interpreted or alluded to verbally.

The 'bus crash' in Vincent's narrative can also be seen as related to the bus pass left at the scene of his index offence. Vincent seemingly recapitulated his incrimination as an 'impossible choice' tied to questions of ethics and morality. However, if we interpret the bus full of civilians as signifying community or humanity, the ropes connecting his superhero to the bus may hold particular significance in terms of Vincent's pull to the human factor, as well as the strain of taking up the place of exception in the logical position he tried to uphold.

Clearly there are limitations of working with Vincent in a group art therapy context. In individual therapy, there is scope for a more directly interventionist/interpretation-oriented approach, and transferential dynamics are more to the fore given the relationship-based nature of one-to-one work. However, this case highlights the emotional challenges of working with an insular, psychotic man who has killed and molested children. Neither my own countertransference, nor the apparent interpretability of the material, should necessarily be assumed as the dominant variables in assessing and treating this case. Rather, the clinical priority was the stabilizing of a disturbed man, with delusions and fantasies around violence and death. This was important both for the functioning of the group but primarily for Vincent himself. We will consider the question of the differences between these two considerations in more detail below.

From a Lacanian psychoanalytic perspective of this case, we may note the familiar motifs of certainty and concretizations in the use of language, as well as the taking up of the place of exception, as supporting the diagnosis of psychosis. But I hope I have shown that it is the psychotic subject's own clinical material (delusions and fantasies included), that indicates what gives equilibrium in their life. In Vincent's case, working with the stabilizing effects of identifying with an alien saviour of mankind is more clinically justified than an interpretation-led stance that aims for 'objective' rather than 'subjective' truths.

Ethics and morality in clinical practice

In the last part of this chapter I want to briefly consider Lacan's views on ethics in clinical practice and the consequences for working with sexual offenders. Aulich (1994), writing on issues of countertransference in art therapy with sexual offenders, poses the question of therapeutic neutrality and a basic assumption of unconditional love in the therapist–client relationship.

Lacan, in his 'Ethics of Psychoanalysis' seminar (Lacan 1992), reframes this challenge via a proposed distinction between morality in its relation to *the good* and ethics in its relation to *desire*. As we have seen, the hallmark of a Lacanian approach consists in a consideration of the signifier. Lacan develops his theory of morality through the signifier *good* in two key registers: the first as a sign, which he relates to the Freudian notion of the pleasure principle; and the second as a notion of the good in its value as a product. Here Lacan draws on Marx's theory of the relation of an individual to the object of production.

> The long historical problem of the nature of the good is in the end centred on how goods are created, insofar as they are organized not on the basis of so-called natural and predetermined needs, but insofar as they furnish the material of a distribution; and it is in relation to this that the dialectic of the good is articulated to the degree that it takes on effective meaning for man. (Lacan 1992, pp.228–229)

So, in this sense, the good also exists within a dialectical or symbolic register, one that draws the good out of its existence as pure sign, and opens up a possibility of different underlying meanings, which separate out the good from being a pure or natural good to one that obtains weight in an economic sense.

Under consideration here is the differentiation of the good within the register of morality and the good in terms of its utilitarian or functional value. In clinical terms, the latter concept relates to its social effect. In Vincent's case we might pose the question thus: Is the clinical goal simply for the good of the patient, or for the functioning of the group of which he is a member, as a microcosm of the broader social context and Vincent's difficulties existing within it?

There are no easy answers to the potential ethical tensions between our responsibility to the patient and our responsibility to society in forensic work. In Vincent's case, evolving narratives, including the bus-crash fantasy, might be instinctively deemed inappropriate to encourage. However, in Vincent's fantasy of the hero, he saw himself in a position of moral exception, which may have enabled him to justify actions that overrode the desires of the victim, resulting in his sexual offences. But Vincent's work in his therapy sessions may be alternatively understood as localizing his fantasies and delusions within artistic productions. Vincent's art can be understood as offering him stabilizing identifications and narratives that situate him in the social order, not as a mere exception, but as someone who has a place.

Conclusion

In this chapter I have tried to describe what a Lacanian psychoanalytic perspective might offer art psychotherapy in the field of sexual offending, regarding both the patient's diagnosis and the clinician's ethics of treatment.

Swales (2012) considers the potential difficulty in sex-offender treatment programmes of one-size-fits-all models based on the presupposition of a neurotic structure. She notes a deficit in the forensic literature on how to treat sexual offenders with a psychotic structure differently. A Lacanian psychoanalytic perspective, privileging diagnostic considerations, offers a way of working with patients' identifications that eschews an interpretation-based approach often used with neurosis. In Vincent's case of psychosis, the most appropriate mode of clinical engagement has recognized the stabilizing logic of Vincent's belief system and worked to support his attempts to prop up a fundamentally absent symbolic law.

Both Sharon-Zisser (2018) and Cohen (2017) argue that a Lacanian approach to art psychotherapy with psychosis can support the creation of a *sinthomatic* solution, the symptom functioning in writing or art not as a message to be analysed or interpreted, but as supplement to the missing signifier of the symbolic father (Lacan 2016). Vincent's art was his *sinthome*, a subjective solution comprising a series of identifications and narratives posing questions around ethical reflection and empathy for the other.

The hope in terms of broader forensic treatment goals is that Vincent finds a consistent and stabilizing signification for who he is in the world. From his compulsion during adolescence to establish an identity through radical difference via his sexual assaults, the clinical aim of his art therapy could be stated as the search for an alternative identificatory paradigm – to establish subjectivity by means of the relationship to others rather than through their objectification. The aim to promote solution-focused work through the production value of the *sinthome* can be contrasted with an interpretative approach that would privilege reality testing and disavow the fundamental ethical question of the patient's desire, namely, *what works for him*, in favour of what is assumed as a good.

I will conclude with the words of an artist and sexual offender, quoted in a *New York Times* article 20 years ago:

> I'm a work in progress, and that is why art is so important. It becomes you. Our first responsibility is rehabilitation. Being a sex offender is not my totality. I need to replace this thing. (Nash 2000)

References

Aulich, L. (1994) 'Fear and Loathing: Art Therapy, Sex Offenders, and Gender.' In M. Liebmann (ed.) *Art Therapy with Offenders*. London: Jessica Kingsley Publishers.

Biberman, E. and Sharon-Zisser, S. (2017) *Art, Death and Lacanian Psychoanalysis*. London: Routledge.

Cohen, R. (2017) 'A Lacanian Perspective on Art Therapy with Psychotic Patients.' In K. Killick (ed.) *Art Therapy for Psychosis*. London: Routledge.

Collins, L. (2014) *Making Sense: Art Practice and Transformative Therapeutics*. London: Bloomsbury.

Freud, S. (1915) 'The Unconscious.' In S. Freud (1986) *The Essentials of Psychoanalysis*. London: Penguin.

Lacan, J. (1981) *The Four Fundamental Concepts of Psychoanalysis. The Seminar of Jacques Lacan. Book XI* (ed. J-A. Miller, trans. A. Sheridan). London: W.W. Norton.

Lacan, J. (1992 [1959–1960]) *The Ethics of Psychoanalysis. The Seminar of Jacques Lacan. Book VII* (ed. J-A. Miller, trans. D. Porter). London: Routledge.

Lacan, J. (1993 [1955–1956]) *The Psychoses. The Seminar of Jacques Lacan. Book III* (ed. J-A. Miller, trans. R. Grigg).London: Routledge.

Lacan, J. (2016) *The Sinthome. The Seminar of Jacques Lacan. Book XXIII*. Cambridge: Polity Press.

Leader, D. (2011) *What Is Madness?* London: Penguin Books.

Nash, M. (2000, 25 June) 'Art: Art as treatment and expression for sex offenders.' *New York Times*. Accessed on 02/07/19 at www.nytimes.com/2000/06/25/nyregion/art-art-as-treatment-and-expression-for-sex-offenders

Nobus, D. (2000) *Jacques Lacan and the Freudian Practice of Psychoanalysis*. London: Routledge.

Sharon-Zisser, S. (2018) 'Art as subjective solution: A Lacanian theory of art therapy.' *International Journal of Art Therapy: Inscape 23*, 1, 2–13.

Swales, S. (2012) *Perversion: A Lacanian Psychoanalytic Approach to the Subject*. London: Routledge.

Music Therapy with Juvenile Sex Offenders with Social, Emotional and Mental Health Needs

STEVE COBBETT, MUSIC THERAPIST

Introduction

I am a music therapist and systemic/family psychotherapist and have worked since 2004 with young people with the special educational needs category of social, emotional and mental health difficulties (SEMH) in urban educational settings. They are almost always children who have experienced what is increasingly being termed developmental or complex trauma (Stolbach *et al.* 2000). This describes children who have experiences of both insecure attachment to caregivers and sustained periods of trauma, both of which interact developmentally in complex ways. They have been excluded or referred from mainstream schools because those schools have been unable to meet their needs, usually because of challenging or violent behaviours. They are a population of young people who are generally from socially disadvantaged backgrounds with experiences of social exclusion and poverty. Many young people with SEMH are involved in criminal activity and a proportion commit sexual offences.

In this chapter I will outline the advantages of music therapy (and arts therapies generally) with juvenile sex offenders (JSOs)[1] and suggest reasons for those advantages with reference to addressing specific risk factors and encouraging engagement in a therapeutic process. I will use a case study to illustrate how arts therapies can be used clinically with JSOs and also to discuss some practice issues that may arise. I will also advocate the use of an integrative theoretical approach.

Current trends in the understanding and treatment of juvenile sex offenders

There is increasingly an understanding that JSOs have complex needs that are different to those of adult sex offenders (ASOs) and require a correspondingly complex treatment approach (Fortune 2013; Letourneau and Minor 2005). Research has revealed a number of psychosocial factors linked to juvenile sex offending and has also highlighted the benefits of interventions that address them. These factors include family difficulties, attachment difficulties, loneliness, poor peer relationships and general social skills, issues of identity, emotional regulation difficulties, experience of trauma, including abuse, impulsivity, low self-esteem, cognitive distortions and conduct difficulties (Fortune 2013; Hunter 1999; Marshall, Hudson and Hodkinson 1993; McMackin *et al.* 2002; van Wijk *et al.* 2005). The treatments purported to have the best evidence base are two talking therapies: multisystemic therapy and cognitive behavioural therapy (Faniff and Becker 2006). However, many authors (e.g. Littel 2005) have questioned the validity of the research base for these treatments, which rarely include long-term recidivism data or figures for attrition (dropout) and refusal at point of offer. Underwood, von Dresner and Phillips (2006) also question the heterogeneity of research sample populations that have not represented the true heterogeneity of JSOs as a whole and in which, in particular, ethnic minorities and young people with mental health difficulties have been under-represented. The Youth Justice Board (2008) summarized the evidence for treatments with the

---

1   Throughout this chapter I will use the term juvenile sex offender (JSO). However, this is used for purposes of linguistic simplicity and should be seen as shorthand for 'young people who have committed a sexual offence', which I feel more accurately reflects the relationship between offending behaviour and identity.

conclusion that there is little significant evidence to suggest that any one treatment is better than others but that young people who have some kind of treatment are less likely to re-offend than those that do not.

There are a few examples of the use of arts therapies with JSOs in the literature (e.g. Gerber 1994; Skaggs 1997). I could find no evidence for the effectiveness of arts therapies with JSOs, but there is some evidence of their effectiveness with ASOs (e.g. Smeijsters and Cleven 2006; Watson 2002). There is, however, evidence that arts therapies can be effective with some of the previously identified risk factors for juvenile sex offending including self-esteem in previously sexually abused adolescents (Clendenon-Wallen 1991), trauma symptoms in sexually abused children and adolescents (Pifalo 2006), social skills in children and adolescents (Gooding 2011) and impulsivity in adolescents (Rickson 2006). I have also shown in my own research that arts therapies lead to positive outcomes for young people with SEMH in a study that included a control group (Cobbett 2016b). This is relevant as young people with SEMH typically experience the complex mix of difficulties identified as risk factors for JSOs.

Suitability of arts therapies for juvenile sex offenders with SEMH

Young people with SEMH, although a large population (estimated at 150,000 in 2009: Abrams 2010), tend to fall through the net when it comes to therapeutic support, and there is clear evidence that they are more likely to refuse treatment or drop out prematurely (Johnson, Mellor and Brann 2008). The reasons for this can include social factors such as stigma and cultural difference. Also, their psychological and behavioural difficulties mean that, ironically, they are often unable to engage with therapies aimed at treating those difficulties. These difficulties relate to regulating emotions, hyperactivity and reflecting verbally on feelings, thoughts and experiences. Research shows recidivism is associated with psychosocial factors that are prevalent for young people with SEMH, including impulsivity (Miner 2002), poor social skills (Långström and Grann 2000), general criminality (McCann and Lussier 2008) and conduct disorder symptoms (Långström 2002). Research also indicates that young people with SEMH are more likely to commit sexual offences in the first place with about 50 percent of all JSOs having already experienced persistent conduct difficulties by the time of their first offence (McCann and Lussier 2008). Therefore, it is important that suitable therapeutic interventions are offered for JSOs with SEMH.

From my own work with several JSOs with SEMH, I believe the arts therapies are particularly well suited as psychological interventions and will discuss reasons for this at the end of the chapter. Therapeutic interventions with JSOs are also more likely to be successful if based on an integrative theoretical and multi-format approach that enables practitioners to work holistically with their complex needs (Rich 2009). My own integrative theoretical framework includes elements of psychodynamic, person-centred, systemic, cognitive-behavioural and attachment approaches and the clinical work can include individual, group and family sessions (Cobbett 2016a).

Case study[2]

Kane was 14 when he was referred for music therapy. He was of mixed White British and Black Jamaican British heritage and lived with his mother Lisa and two brothers. He had been excluded from a number of mainstream schools because of challenging aggressive behaviour. He had experienced domestic violence (from father to mother) and physical abuse as a younger child, and also a horrific trauma in the form of discovering the body of his father who committed suicide by hanging. Their mother had suffered from depression but was committed to her children and engaged well with the school. Kane had been offered trauma-focused cognitive behavioural therapy through Child and Adolescent Mental Health Services but refused to engage. He was impulsive, found it hard to empathize, see other perspectives or take responsibility for his actions. He often presented as being highly emotional and aggressive. He was involved in criminal gang activity and was serving a youth offending order for persistent robbery offences. In terms of sexual offending, he had coerced a younger boy to perform oral sex a year previously but had not committed any known further sexual offences at the time of referral. He had also been referred to a specialist mental health unit for young people with problematic sexual behaviours but had not engaged. In refusing to engage with two talking

---

2   Names in the case study have been changed to protect confidentiality.

therapies offered to him, he was typical of the many JSOs with SEMH who fall through the net and end up being labelled as 'hard to reach'.

When I initially approached Kane about starting music therapy, he was very reluctant. I helped to deconstruct some of the ideas he had about therapy and outlined the various options available, including the use of music and other arts/play, highlighting the collaborative nature of my approach. In the first session, I suggested we play cards, and I initiated some safe conversation about various aspects of his life while we played, focusing initially on positive aspects. During the initial sessions, Carl Rogers's (1973) person-centred approach was important to help Kane engage, using humour and being warm and non-judgemental. It also involved using an appropriate degree of self-disclosure in order to model talking about feelings and help establish a genuine human relationship. I asked if he wanted to listen to some music on YouTube, and he agreed.

His choice of music was revealing. There was some rap glorifying violence and treating females as sexual objects, but there were also some songs about struggling through painful times. As the sessions progressed, we discussed emotional themes in the music, which led to direct conversation about his life experiences, for example conflict with his mother at home. In these conversations, I skewed the balance of my responses in favour of empathizing with his emotional experience with just a small amount of challenge to his thinking. I had in mind the importance of Kane developing empathy and the necessity for him to experience empathy first before he would be able to develop that capacity himself (Rich 2009).

During another discussion prompted by listening to a violent rap, we thought about how difficult it can be living in urban environments and the pressures on boys to act in certain ways, such as gaining respect through violence and avoiding expressing vulnerable emotions. I used systemic techniques to see if there was any room for flexibility in some of his beliefs about masculinity. This included raising awareness of the restrictive effect of some of those beliefs and exploring whether he could be influenced by other beliefs held by people he respected in his life. It transpired that his one-to-one teaching assistant was helpfully modelling different beliefs about masculinity.

We thought about his peer relationships generally, and I tried to help him think about values that were important to him regarding friendship. He identified that the key aspect for him was that a friend had a 'good heart'. My intent in these discussions was informed by some of those key risk factors for JSOs including peer relationships, identity and systemic pressures. I used narrative therapy techniques (White and Epston 1990) that are designed to help people question unhelpful narratives that might be influencing their behaviours and co-create new narratives. This also involves helping people to rediscover and nurture subjugated narratives dominated by the problem narratives.

In one session we were discussing the lyrics of a song he played me in which the artist spoke of struggling without a father and not knowing how to be a man as a result. At this point it felt necessary to acknowledge I was aware of what had happened to Kane's father and was sorry Kane had to experience such a traumatic loss. I asked a couple of questions, but it was clear from his body language that Kane did not want to talk about this yet. The conversation gradually stopped, and we continued playing cards. I felt unsure what he needed in that moment. In the end, he found his own solution and he initiated some musical improvisation, which he had never done before. He started playing a hang drum (a tuned metal instrument with a soft sustained tone). I moved slowly over to a piano, and gradually started supporting his playing using sparse sustained chords to accompany his melody and attempted to contain and reflect what he was expressing in his music. The improvisation continued for about ten minutes and he appeared totally absorbed in the music, which seemed melancholic and thoughtful. He clearly noticed my musical responses and adapted his music reflexively, so our music-making was a shared experience. Afterwards I thanked him and acknowledged it felt like he had just expressed something important, which helped me understand him. It felt important to ensure he experienced this as positive in the context of the narratives he had about males not expressing vulnerable emotions. This improvisation felt like the only way at the time he could express something of his trauma experience and for us to have some kind of dialogue about it.

There were tricky moments connected to boundary issues, which is a common theme with JSOs (Woods 1997). For example, I stipulated a boundary that he could not play any YouTube content that was sexually explicit or promoted violence. A number of times he threatened me with violence when I insisted on that boundary. I responded by remaining empathically connected to his feelings of frustration and emphasizing that I trusted he would not act out on those threats. There appeared to be an element of transference in some of these dynamics, and his experience of my not acting out on the countertransference was probably important for him. Gradually these boundary challenges stopped occurring.

After occasional prompts, Kane started creating his own raps. Initially they were freestyle raps; that is, improvised in the moment rather than using pre-prepared lyrics. His raps expressed a confusing mix of violent acts, expressions of love for his mum and brother, the appeal of being a drug dealer, hopes of becoming a mechanic, finding school boring but knowing it was important and explicit descriptions of sexual acts. They also included reference to domestic violence, his father's death and Kane discovering his body and surviving without a father. I explored with him some of the issues raised in his raps. This enabled us to address a wide range of his needs and difficulties, including processing trauma, building self-esteem, thinking about identity and exploring relationships. Music was clearly becoming a tool he could use to emotionally self-regulate. This initial success at emotional regulation led to us thinking of other ways he could use to regulate himself. There was a cognitive behavioural therapy element to this in terms of helping him notice how his thoughts in certain situations triggered emotional reactions, which in turn triggered unhelpful behaviours.

I was mindful of how improvised musical interaction between us could potentially be useful therapeutically, mimicking early attachment interactions. Kane was not much interested in free improvisation using instruments though, so I would musically support his rapping by playing either a synthesizer, bass guitar or electronic drum kit. I used my musical response to attune to the rhythm and emotional timbre of his voice and the emotional quality of the lyrical content. Sometimes I would be containing his emotional expression, sometimes offering a contrast (for example, picking up on the sadness behind the anger he expressed). My musical support would be in addition to whatever instrumental backing track he chose from YouTube, and I would also adapt my music to fit with the style of the track, which was generally of the genre termed 'drill music'. I saw this as showing respect for his culture, trying to work within the remit of his musical culture.

The work seemed to be progressing well. He was becoming more confident, and we seemed to be finding ways that could help him process his trauma, think about emotions and develop new narratives about himself. About four months into the work though, there was a major setback in the form of another sexual offence. He tried to rape a younger boy in his community and was violently attacked by the boy's relatives. As a result, the school decided he would be taught offsite because of safeguarding concerns with regard to other children. I was shocked and found myself questioning my approach; perhaps I should have been more challenging or directive. In hindsight I know that projected guilt is a major feature of work with JSOs, and I appreciate the necessarily long-term nature of the work. I decided it was important for Kane's therapy to continue, so I made arrangements to provide his sessions at the Youth Offending Service (YOS) centre. It was difficult, for many practical reasons, but we persevered.

In a sense, the challenge to the therapeutic relationship ultimately strengthened the attachment side of our work, in that he continued to experience me as a consistent secure base despite that challenge. It also helped to deconstruct some of the narratives he had about people giving up on him in relation to the multiple school exclusions he had experienced. I developed a good working relationship with his YOS worker. Joined-up care around Kane was an important aspect of the work generally, helping him to feel contained and reducing his tendency to split and divide people in an unhealthy way. This involved a degree of consented information-sharing from his therapy, which had the bonus of helping other people support him more effectively. I also, with Kane's consent, took a proactive advocacy role in terms of providing information to the courts about his needs and how they might relate to his offending behaviours.

Seeking Kane's consent for sharing this information involved being open with him about my hypotheses about the relationship between his needs and his behaviours; that is, the impact of trauma and insecure attachment neurologically and the psychological and behavioural consequences emerging from that neurology. Explaining this to him was challenging and involved a degree of psychoeducation about trauma and attachment. I believe though that psychoeducation can be an important part of work with JSOs in terms of helping them understand themselves and also understanding how change is possible through neuroplasticity, linking that to the good work they are doing in therapy.

In sessions immediately after the offence, Kane was overwhelmed with shame at being thought of as a paedophile or as being gay, both of which he denied. I felt it was important to help him distinguish between self-disgust, which was unhelpful, and guilt for his actions, which might lead to something useful. In terms of being gay, I was unsure if his denial of being gay was true or untrue and related to a fear of homophobic reactions. Despite his resistance, I felt it important to explore what being gay meant to him and helped him contemplate different narratives about being gay that could balance negative narratives he had been exposed to. This normalizing of being gay felt important in that if he was gay, perhaps his violent homosexual acts were related to self-disgust and an inability to contemplate being in a loving relationship with another boy. They could also have been a sexualized acting out of his own abusive experiences, and I was mindful of the importance of continuing the trauma-processing aspect of our work.

Talking around these issues was hard for Kane but was aided significantly by the musical aspect of our work. In raps, he managed to express thoughts and feelings about what had happened at a level that was not possible for him otherwise. He expressed guilt at what had happened and revealed the complex relationship with the boy he assaulted, describing him as his 'yungah', a street term for a younger boy who is mentored in gang activities by his 'older'. Some of his raps clearly expressed his love for the boy and the pain of the consequences of what he did. He also continued to rap about the trauma he experienced and his complex feelings about his father, how he missed him, and how maybe he would be a better father in the future. The lyrics below are from one of the first raps he did during this period at the YOS centre and show clearly the different feelings he was experiencing:

I'll be by your side, by your side
Didn't want it, didn't have to do it
Gonna earn the Ps[3] and we'll have to do the hustle
Don't want anyone in this life to treat you like a prick
So I'm gonna get a girl to suck your dick
You might be young but you might as well be my yungah
Don't let anyone treat you like a dickhead

---

3   Ps = money

Don't have to hate
Bare people[4] hate us because you're my yungah
I'm by your side, gonna ride or die
This boy had to lie
He ran home to his mum and dad
Cos he was feeling sad
How about that?
Cos we're gonna live our lives to the fullest
I'm gonna prove that I can be a better older
Don't wanna bully you, I'm not fucking trying
I swear down N, please forgive me for anything I've done
Cos I'll be by your side
You're a skinny little black boy but you're not my fucking toy
You're a superstar, you're my little superstar
Please forgive me for what I've done
Don't be sad
Please don't let anything get in the way of our good friendship
Please N, I'll be by your side, I'll do this for you every day
By your side
For N, my yungah, rest in peace

Denial is an important aspect of work with JSOs, and rap was a useful way for Kane to explore safely the painful truths and denied feelings. We reflected together that in reality he could not see N any more (there was a court order preventing this) and how that was a painful loss.

I asked Kane about doing some family sessions, and he agreed it would be a good idea. This was informed by my awareness of ongoing family relational difficulties being a risk factor for JSOs. I supplemented his individual sessions with family therapy sessions involving his mother, brothers and occasionally grandmother, uncle and mother's friend. These family sessions were informed mainly by the systemic approach used by family therapists in the UK. This involved helping the family think about how they interacted with each other and identify any unhelpful patterns, linking these to beliefs, aspects of difference such as gender, and the meaning they ascribed to each other's behaviours. We then collaboratively worked on developing new patterns through

4   Bare people = Many people

deconstructing meanings and thinking about beliefs. For example, there was a pattern of Kane being seen as the 'bad' brother and being treated critically and punitively, and I helped the family reframe some of his behaviours in the context of his needs and difficulties so they could interpret his behaviours differently and relate to him differently as a result.

There was also an aspect of trauma processing for the whole family, and I did some sessions with just Kane and his mother, Lisa, to help her support Kane's individual recovery from his trauma. The family sessions also involved music and this aspect was important. The family preferred to use improvisation on instruments in contrast to Kane's predominant use of rap in his individual sessions. These musical interactions were useful in a number of ways, one being that they helped Lisa develop more secure attachments with her sons through facilitating playful interactions where emotions could be safely expressed and she could attune to their needs. I coached Lisa on some basic music therapy techniques, such as mirroring to support her with this, informed by the well-established and evidence-based intervention 'theraplay' (Booth and Jernberg 2009), which uses play activities in a similar way.

In his individual sessions, I encouraged Kane to try writing some lyrics to augment his freestyle rapping as I thought this could offer him a different therapeutic experience. We also started recording and producing his raps so that we could work on a piece over a period of a few weeks, and he became excited by the different creative possibilities. This new kind of music-making involved a higher degree of cognitive functioning, for example the ability to plan ahead and make thoughtful choices. This more thoughtful way of working also helped to augment the trauma-processing side of our work, and over a period of about two months he wrote a long and very moving rap called 'My Life vs. Your Life' in which he essentially wrote a narrative about his father, his relationship to him and his bereavement.

The court eventually decided a custodial sentence would not be in his or society's interests and he was given a community sentence. The family were moved to a different area because of continual threats and actual acts of violence. His school place was restored, although with careful restrictions regarding unsupervised contact with other children. Our work ended when he eventually left the school aged 16 after a period of two years of therapy. If Kane had been at the school for longer,

I would have asked him to consider joining an arts therapy group at the school, a useful additional intervention for JSOs in terms of developing social skills and healthier peer relationships. Unfortunately, this was not possible. He went on to do a mechanics course at college, and I heard later he was given a special award at the end of his first year for his achievements. In the feedback form completed at the end of therapy he wrote that music therapy 'helped me be a better person'.

Discussion and conclusions

This case illustrates the usefulness of an integrative theoretical approach and the therapeutic use of the arts with JSOs. I believe that no one approach has all the answers when it comes to the complex needs of JSOs, and each of these elements meets important needs related to risk factors. The combination of the arts and talking is important, each modality offering different therapeutic qualities.

Arts therapies may offer particular advantages therapeutically in terms of engagement for JSOs with SEMH, which as discussed previously are likely to be the majority of JSOs. Availability of the arts in therapy enables young people with SEMH to communicate emotionally difficult themes in a way that might feel safer than talking. Arts-based communication relies less on neurological competencies not yet fully developed because of their SEMH (Cobbett 2016b). In addition, the arts can act as tools young people can use to self-regulate, helping them stay safe in sessions, supporting their continued engagement as well as providing them with resources to use in their lives outside of therapy. Use of the arts as well as talking provides a therapeutic environment that feels safe enough for JSOs but also offers enough challenge for therapeutic change to take place. This is what Cozolino (2010) calls optimal stress, the conditions under which neuroplasticity and neural integration take place.

Improvised musical interaction in particular can mimic early attachment interactions vital for young people to develop social and emotional competencies linked to reducing offending. Arts therapies are particularly well suited to facilitating young people's processing of, and recovery from, trauma. The arts may offer an accessible way for JSOs to begin processing trauma non-verbally before words can be involved, later in therapy, through creating lyrics or talking.

Finally, artistic creations in therapy sessions are often seen as real achievements by young people and can help to address low self-esteem, another key psychological aspect of juvenile sex offending.

The arts therapies offer robust, evidence-based and, most importantly, accessible therapeutic interventions for JSOs with SEMH offering hope to some of the hardest-to-reach young people, whose needs are often not met by traditional talking therapies. The argument for using arts therapies with this client group is particularly cogent considering the lack of robust evidence for talking therapies. This is a high-risk group of offenders, and it is important that the range of therapeutic interventions on offer to JSOs includes those particularly tailored to their needs.

References

Abrams, F. (2010, 9 March) 'No problem pupils in my backyard.' *The Guardian*.

Booth, P.B. and Jernberg, A.M. (2009) *Theraplay: Helping Parents and Children Build Better Relationships Through Attachment-Based Play*. Hoboken, NJ: John Wiley & Sons.

Clendenon-Wallen, J. (1991) 'The use of music therapy to influence the self-confidence and self-esteem of adolescents who are sexually abused.' *Music Therapy Perspectives 9*, 1, 73–81.

Cobbett, S. (2016a) 'Context and relationships: Using the systemic approach with music therapy in work with children, adolescents and their families.' *British Journal of Music Therapy 30*, 2, 65–73.

Cobbett, S. (2016b) 'Reaching the hard to reach: Quantitative and qualitative evaluation of school-based arts therapies with young people with social, emotional and behavioural difficulties.' *Emotional and Behavioural Difficulties 21*, 4, 403–415.

Cozolino, L. (2010) *The Neuroscience of Psychotherapy: Healing the Social Brain*. New York, NY: W.W. Norton.

Fanniff, A M. and Becker, J.V. (2006) 'Specialized assessment and treatment of adolescent sex offenders.' *Aggression and Violent Behavior 11*, 3, 265–282.

Fortune, C.A. (2013) 'Youth who sexually abuse: Characteristics, treatment outcomes and practice implications.' *Practice: The New Zealand Corrections Journal 1*, 2, 10–13.

Gerber, J. (1994) 'The use of art therapy in juvenile sex offender specific treatment.' *The Arts in Psychotherapy 21*, 367–374.

Gooding, L.F. (2011) 'The effect of a music therapy social skills training program on improving social competence in children and adolescents with social skills deficits.' *Journal of Music Therapy 48*, 4, 440–462.

Hunter, J.A. (1999) 'Understanding juvenile sex offenders: Research findings and guidelines for effective management and treatment.' *Developments in Mental Health Law 19*, 18–28.

Johnson, E., Mellor, D. and Brann, P. (2008) 'Differences in dropout between diagnoses in child and adolescent mental health services.' *Clinical Child Psychology and Psychiatry 13*, 4, 515–530.

Långström, N. (2002) 'Long-term follow-up of criminal recidivism in young sex offenders: Temporal patterns and risk factors.' *Psychology, Crime and Law 8*, 1, 41–58.

Långström, N. and Grann, M. (2000) 'Risk for criminal recidivism among young sex offenders.' *Journal of Interpersonal Violence 15*, 8, 855–871.

Letourneau, E.J. and Miner, M H. (2005) 'Juvenile sex offenders: A case against the legal and clinical status quo.' *Sexual Abuse: A Journal of Research and Treatment 17*, 3, 293–312.

Littell, J.H. (2005) 'Lessons from a systematic review of effects of multisystemic therapy.' *Children and Youth Services Review 27*, 4, 445–463.

Marshall, W.L., Hudson, S.M. and Hodkinson, S. (1993) 'The Importance of Attachment Bonds in the Development of Juvenile Sex Offending.' In H.E. Barbaree, W.L. Marshall and S.M. Hudson (eds) *The Juvenile Sex Offender*. New York, NY: Guilford Press.

McCann, K. and Lussier, P. (2008) 'Antisociality, sexual deviance, and sexual reoffending in juvenile sex offenders: A meta-analytical investigation.' *Youth Violence and Juvenile Justice* 6, 4, 363–385.

McMackin, R.A., Leisen, M.B., Cusack, J.F., LaFratta, J. and Litwin, P. (2002) 'The relationship of trauma exposure to sex offending behaviour among male juvenile offenders.' *Journal of Child Sexual Abuse 11*, 2, 25–40.

Miner, M.H. (2002) 'Factors associated with recidivism in juveniles: An analysis of serious juvenile sex offenders.' *Journal of Research in Crime and Delinquency 39*, 4, 421-436.

Pifalo, T. (2006) 'Art therapy with sexually abused children and adolescents: Extended research study.' *Art Therapy 23*, 4, 181–185.

Rickson, D.J. (2006) 'Instructional and improvisational models of music therapy with adolescents who have attention deficit hyperactivity disorder (ADHD): A comparison of the effects on motor impulsivity.' *Journal of Music Therapy 43*, 1, 39–62.

Rich, P. (2009) 'Understanding the complexities and needs of adolescent sex offenders.' In A.R. Beech, L.A. Craig and K.D. Browne (eds) *Assessment and Treatment of Sex Offenders: A Handbook* (pp.431–435). Hoboken, NJ: John Wiley & Sons.

Rogers, C.R. (1973) *On Becoming a Person: A Therapist's View of Psychotherapy*. London: Constable.

Skaggs, R. (1997) 'Music-centred creative arts in a sex offender treatment program for male juveniles.' *Music Therapy Perspectives 15*, 2, 73–78.

Smeijsters, H. and Cleven, G. (2006) 'The treatment of aggression using arts therapies in forensic psychiatry: Results of a qualitative inquiry.' *The Arts in Psychotherapy 33*, 37–58.

Stolbach, B.C., Minshew, R., Rompala, V., Dominguez, R.Z. *et al.* (2000) 'Complex trauma exposure and symptoms in urban traumatized children: A preliminary test of proposed criteria for developmental trauma disorder.' *Journal of Traumatic Stress 26*, 4, 483–491.

Underwood, L.A., von Dresner, K. S. and Phillips, A.L. (2006) 'Community treatment programs for juveniles: A best-evidence summary.' *International Journal of Behavioral Consultation and Therapy 2*, 2, 286–304.

van Wijk, A., van Horn, J., Bullens, R., Bijleveld, C. and Doreleijers, T. (2005) 'Juvenile sex offenders: A group on its own?' *International Journal of Offender Therapy and Comparative Criminology 49*, 1, 25–36.

Watson, D.M. (2002) 'Drumming and improvisation with adult male sexual offenders.' *Music Therapy Perspectives 20*, 2, 105–111.

White, M. and Epston, D. (1990) *Narrative Means to Therapeutic Ends*. New York, NY: W.W. Norton.

Woods, J. (1997) 'Breaking the cycle of abuse and abusing: Individual psychotherapy for juvenile sex offenders.' *Clinical Child Psychology and Psychiatry 2*, 3, 379–392.

Youth Justice Board for England and Wales (2008) *Key Effective Practice Points: Young People who Sexually Abuse*. London: Youth Justice Board for England and Wales.

CHAPTER 10

Beads, Bees, Glitter and Perversion

Forensic Art Therapy with Older Adults

RONALD P.M.H. LAY, ART THERAPIST

Introduction

This chapter aims to seamlessly support this book's global objective of seeking to highlight the contribution the arts therapies make in developing good clinical practice and outcomes in the context of national efforts to enlist sex offenders in meaningful therapeutic engagement. The text draws upon an extensive forensic mental health art therapy practice with older adults mandated for treatment, within a secured inpatient residential setting in Northern California. It is a consolidated and retrospective discourse from a practitioner-based perspective and is nuanced with insights from my current position as an academic within higher education in Southeast Asia.

Although having a rich reservoir of individual narratives from practice, I have purposefully resisted the temptation to focus on one case study alone and, instead, have opted to provide an overarching review of my experience. Examples of arts projects, both individual and group, will be highlighted to acknowledge the inherent challenges and resistance involved in working with this particular population, while also acknowledging the hope and successes that were witnessed, observed and experienced. My intent is to share my observations and experiences from an informed, self-reflective and practitioner-based stance.

This chapter is structured into three sections: Naivety to nuanced; Beleaguered to boundaried; Restraints to recovery. Although a linear narrative might seem logical, I thought it best to illustrate my learnings, my understanding and my direct experience of working and engaging with sexual offenders into these three sections using select examples from practice, further linking the deliberate and provocative keywords and concepts of this chapter. Working with sexual offenders challenges therapists to consider both their professional and personal understanding, perceptions and limits, as well as their intentions, motives and practice.

Oftentimes, sexual offenders are calculating men who have committed crimes against others that have long-lasting and devastating effects on their victims and the community. Unlike most client populations that purposefully seek out therapy to address areas of concern and/or to enhance their overall quality of life, convicted sexual offenders are mandated for treatment and rehabilitation through the justice system (Bach and Demuth 2018). This poses its own set of challenges, given the commonly held belief that in order for change or for personal transformation to take place, one must want to change; being mandated to treatment does not necessarily guarantee that one has the intention to change.

In order to be effective, therapists must acknowledge and understand this peculiarity, and keep this in mind as they plan, implement and evaluate treatment and progress. Therapists must be aware of their own emotional and psychological reaction(s) to those they provide services to in order to remain ethical, safe and consciously aware of the complex dynamics and processes involved in this type of work (Bergman and Hewish 2003; Walker *et al.* 2018). Through team guidance and support, through individual and group supervision and through my own reflective artmaking, I was also able to navigate and negotiate some very difficult and unexpected dilemmas that are sometimes unavoidable while working with offenders.

Naivety to nuanced
This section seeks to highlight the critical need for self-awareness, the development of core skill sets, such as open and transparent communication between multidisciplinary team members, and the

development of an art therapy practice that is relevant within the context that it is applied. Naturally, an art therapist must continue to develop and refine their skills to truly meet the needs of those they provide services to. My first position as a qualified art therapist was under the auspices of Rehabilitation Therapy in a large-scale forensic mental health facility, and this expedited a steep learning curve. I needed to learn and understand context-specific vocabulary and concepts such as, for example, gerontophilia, paraphilia, phallometric assessment, posturing, gassing and psychogenic polydipsia.

The majority of the 1000+ inpatients were mandated for treatment, all had a clinical diagnosis, and their crimes ranged from murder to lewd and lascivious acts to theft to terrorist threats to name a few (Lay 2016). Fortunately, I was assigned to an experienced, functioning and welcoming multidisciplinary team that was also client centric, matching my own philosophical stance. This dedicated and compassionate team was essentially responsible for nurturing my professional development, understanding and approach to working with vulnerable groups of people, primarily older adults from age 50 onward, and for instilling a strong commitment to treating the patient. Based on a residential unit for older men, I also provided individual and group art therapy as well as open art studio to both male and female adult clients from around the facility.

Forensic mental health is just as multilayered and complex as the shifting paradigms that guide the treatment and rehabilitation of sexual offenders. The recovery model is one that has been integrated within forensic mental health, given its strengths-based and hope-driven principles (Anthony 1993; Roberts *et al.* 2006). Through this model, the client becomes a contributing member of the multidisciplinary treatment team wherein their input essentially directs their own treatment. Clients are invited to share their life goals and these are considered throughout the treatment planning, implementation and evaluative processes. This has been seen as a clinical cultural shift, especially when this multidisciplinary model is based on individual choice and preference rather than a perceived expert opinion as in a medical model approach.

Part of the therapist's role is to encourage the client to gain insight, to maintain hope and to assist with balancing emotions, expression and related behavior (Cordess and Cox 1996); oftentimes, this is achieved by the therapist modeling their own emotional expression and behavior. Safety, trust and boundaries are paramount, and the clinician needs to consistently address these. Similarly, this extends to the wellbeing and safety of the therapist, wherein the structure and culture of the setting itself has its impact (Bach and Demuth 2018) and wherein the therapist must stay grounded in terms of their purpose and expertise (Guarnieri and Klugman 2016). One of many factors that impede reintegration into the community is the stigma associated with mental illness, criminal behavior and incarceration (Peterson and Etter 2017). The complete removal and/or isolation of offenders may be a temporary solution to maintaining order within the community; however, at some point the offender may return to the community. Thus, addressing the offending behavior as well as the related stigma becomes paramount.

Where I worked there was a trend to utilize 12-week pre-planned and goal-oriented treatment. Prior to being implemented with clients, these written session plans were reviewed and approved by a multidisciplinary team of mental health specialists. This was effective in providing evidenced-based treatment to larger groups and served to record and document client progress. Such session plans were adapted to art therapy groups that addressed anger management, coping skills, communication skills, reality orientation and substance recovery. These allowed the therapist to conceptualize the intended treatment outcomes, to address areas for change and to provide learning opportunities through the arts. Although some therapists may argue this dilutes the spontaneity of group therapy, there are obvious advantages of using prepared session plans: they provide organization, defined expectations and a level of predictability.

Contributing additional layers to the complexities of providing therapeutic services to sexual offenders are those associated with an aging population (Farmer and Yancu 2018; Lay 2016). My multidisciplinary team proactively sought to uphold the dignity and humanity of the clients and endeavored to develop meaningful relationships with each client regardless of any personality changes, aggressive behavior and decline in mental and/or physical functioning (Cipriani *et al.* 2017). There were two streams of older adults, those with lifelong relationships with offending behavior and legal systems, and those who were first-time offenders in later life. The unit I was assigned to was designated for older male adults, and this was the first of its kind within the forensic section of the facility. Organizing the unit in this manner was advantageous on many levels (Cipriani *et al.* 2017; Farmer and Yancu 2018). Increasingly, we needed a ward that catered for an aging population and was accessible for more wheelchairs, and needed loudspeakers, more space and nursing care facilities. We experienced many firsts, including how to integrate hospice care, compassionate leave, and so on.

Disillusioned and perhaps traumatized by the internalized crime of an older gentleman describing his artwork at the beginning of my career at this facility, I acknowledged that I needed to dramatically alter my forensic art therapy interventions. After years of residing within multiple forensic mental health settings, this particular individual seemed to have lost a genuine sense of self and without hesitation introduced himself as his crime. Although intrigued by the complexity of the various interrelationships between forensics, mental health and rehabilitation, I quickly realized I needed to somehow have my clients reconnect with themselves on an individualized manner in order for sustained change and/or insights to occur. Keeping the above in mind, my art therapy directives, interventions and overall way of working with older adults centered on building trust and relationships, with an overarching aim of transforming their own self-narratives and engagement with others.

Trust is an underlying component of our relationships, decisions and, indeed, our behavior. It develops, evolves and becomes more sophisticated as we gain more experience and mastery in the world. At times, however, there are ongoing impairments, conditions and maladaptive behavior that seriously erode the ability to build meaningful and sustaining relationships. Within the forensic setting it is understandable and almost predictable that trust will be difficult to develop given the inherent characteristics and vulnerability within such a setting. However, sexual offenders do have opportunities to address these primarily through the conscious and deliberate development of a therapeutic relationship.

This relationship provides a focused opportunity to explore various elements of trust whether directly, symbolically or metaphorically, as well as to promote the development of skills that will improve the client's overall mental health and wellbeing. As such, trust should guide the work for both the client(s) and the art therapist (Guarnieri and

Klugman 2016). In line with this, trust amongst co-workers and the setting must be prioritized and actively developed. This speaks directly to safety and boundary concerns as well as the need for one to have the environment suitably safe and secure. Developing such a relationship is difficult at best, given the reality of the client's connection with the legal system, their past experiences and the symptoms of their mental illness. However, the therapeutic alliance must be skillfully constructed to effectively address the identified changes and maladaptive behaviors demonstrated by the client. Within a recovery-based paradigm, relationships are at the core of the client's recovery, and trust is an underlying concept that guides these relationships. The concept of trust is not stagnant, linear or restricted to one circumstance or one relationship.

Granted, it does take time. This can be achieved through ongoing professional development and a concerted effort for the therapist to develop the necessary stamina and wherewithal. It is imperative that the therapist confront their own perceptions and perhaps prejudices of working with people who have seriously impacted the lives of others through destructive and criminal means. This is needed to consistently establish and re-establish the necessary limits and boundaries that aim to ensure the physical, emotional and psychological safety of themselves, the community and the sexual offender. Combined, these lead to a sustained sense of hope for transformative change in the behavior, actions and decisions of the sexual offender that active engagement in their own treatment and rehabilitation aims to achieve (Lay 2016).

The benefits of active engagement in structured art activities played a significant role in enhancing the client's personal awareness, transformation, and improving their overall quality of life. Refining these naturally led to their increased reality orientation, ownership of feelings and behaviors, and a willingness to re-integrate with society, whether realistically or on a metaphorical level. These were my observations from several different art therapy projects and individual encounters over my 12-year tenure. Some of these individuals naturally gravitate to the arts and may even have an art practice of their own, however, the majority have not engaged with the arts since grade school. Trust needed to be carefully constructed with this population, while balancing the objectives and expectations of the facility with creativity and self-expression (Lay 2016).

Creating artwork provided a range of experiences for the clients, with many extending beyond the therapeutic encounter. With their consent, artwork was installed in tamper-proof and sometimes theme-oriented bulletin boards throughout the residential unit, leading to a sense of ownership as well as providing a personalized and stimulating environment. Prior to installation, the content of the bulletin boards was carefully reviewed and screened for any potential symbols, metaphors or underlying messages that may be perceived as threatening, offensive and/or gang-related. This allowed for transparent discussions, and sometimes debates, with the clients in regard to concepts of private and public, and how decisions impact others.

Art therapists in forensic settings have a significant responsibility in ensuring, maintaining and even modeling consistent limits and boundaries as well as the emotional, psychological and physical safety of others. Left unchecked, the art therapist may inadvertently compromise these critical pillars. It was essential for me to develop systems to monitor the art materials accessed during art therapy sessions, ensuring that all art materials that left their marked containers were returned at the end of the session. Also, I was aware that any potentially threatening symbols, metaphors and even verbal associations associated with the artwork were acknowledged and attended to, including suicidal ideation and/or intent to harm others (Lay 2016). Depending upon the situation, I would have had to address these in session, in team meetings, in clinical supervision and through documentation.

I came to learn that in a supportive and structured therapeutic milieu, clients within the forensic mental health setting have opportunities to transition from a self-absorbed and potentially violent state(s) to gentlemen who are consciously aware and sensitive to community. Although working with sexual offenders can be shocking and horrifying for the novice as well as the seasoned professional, there are also instances of gratification and pleasure derived from this line of work (Walker *et al.* 2018). Regardless, clinical supervision is a must in order to remain effective, focused and therapeutic.

Beleaguered to boundaried
This section provides a transparent reflective account of my own learning curve wherein my skill sets and understanding of the complexities of

forensic mental health with offenders transitioned from novice to more seasoned. In acknowledging my struggles, learning and understanding through ongoing experience, I was able to more effectively design and implement therapeutic art interventions that were relevant to offenders and to the overarching directives of the facility. The aim of this section, therefore, is to provide the reader with a more realistic sense of what this work entails, while still championing art therapy as a key catalyst for change.

A fear I had, while working within this environment full-time and long-term, was that I would become desensitized, given the realities of the culture, systems, attitudes and circumstances that brought those I worked with to this setting. Even though I developed an emotional and psychological sensitivity to those I worked with, it was still very difficult to come to terms with, and to try to make sense of, the victims and how their lives had been changed for ever by those that I provided my services to. I quickly came to appreciate that my job was to provide meaningful therapeutic engagement through the arts, and that it was outside of my role to judge, punish or discipline.

While working with a range of male clients throughout my tenure, I found it remarkable how many of them ended up growing a goatee similar to mine. Although I was flattered at times I also understood and appreciated the multitude of potential associations, meanings and even infatuations that this might instigate. For a good majority, I simply accredited this to the development of a positive working relationship and of a *relating to* aspect; however, for a couple of clients I wondered about a sexual transference and how this might have been manifested. Increasingly, I became more comfortable with this complicated concept and with how I, sometimes, became a sexualized object to some of my clients. Granted, this did provide for rich material to be worked through in clinical supervision and my own artwork.

While working with one older male client who remained quiet, emotionally distant, reserved and socially awkward, I felt truly uncomfortable and unnerved by his long-term preoccupation with cutting and re-cutting of paper into rather fine pieces. Over several weeks he assembled and glued these into a thick and wild goatee. The final paper collage developed into a devil-like figure with a thick goatee. I thought that it had an uncanny resemblance to me and wondered how he might be perceiving our therapeutic relationship and/or if he may have perceived that I had somehow infringed on his personal space when I inquired about various aspects of his artmaking. I carefully observed his process, being mindful of my safety given his crime wherein he almost succeeded in decapitating the head of a man he believed was making sexual advances toward him. My wonderings were neither confirmed nor denied as this client typically remained nonverbal throughout his artmaking which involved detailed cut-out collages of multiple eyes, teeth, mouths and hands. This experience was early in my career, when I believed I needed to regularly inquire about the client's process and about their artwork. Reflecting further, I can now see how this may have been intrusive and have since allowed the process and artwork breathing space.

Setting limits and maintaining these is another challenge that must be openly discussed and reinforced. After installing bulletin boards throughout the unit and filling each with client artwork, poetry and unit-based photographs of our courtyard garden, arts projects and the pet therapy dogs, one client submitted several poems to be included. Upon review, it was determined that all of the poems were laden with sexual innuendos and metaphors and were therefore deemed inappropriate for public viewing by means of the bulletin boards. Although invited to submit poems that were not as blatantly sexual in nature, the client loudly accused me of being more perverted than him. He proceeded to leer at me and make suggestive gestures during groups and in the hallway as I passed by.

I embarrass easily and my face flushes red, giving a distinct visual indication that I am uncomfortable. I needed to learn to not take such directed behavior personally and to professionally hold my ground in ways that did not denigrate him or other similar clients. Such techniques were raised in clinical supervision and needed to be practiced and rehearsed ahead of time in those supported sessions. In time, my own confidence grew, and I was able to fully assert what was going on in ways that maintained the dignity and safety of all. In time, the client ceased this behavior and provided me with poems that were much more acceptable, and that could then be installed with the rest of the client displays.

My increasing level of experience and confidence shifted my way of working, and this involved several significant learning points that, eventually, led to a more informed practice. I found it necessary to not simply dismiss a client's actions but to seriously look beyond the obvious and try to understand the motivation behind behaviors, perceptions and attitudes. Building a thick skin, so to speak, being able to overcome challenges and difficulties, and having faith in decisions throughout the therapeutic encounter, is part of effective work with sexual offenders (Guarnieri and Klugman 2016). Notwithstanding, clinical supervision is a definite must, to ensure we do not over-personalize the dynamics and/or dialogue that transpires with sexual offenders.

Restraints to recovery

This section captures some pivotal art therapy interventions and projects that culminated in a further enriched and cohesive community, evidencing the benefits of art therapy and active engagement. Given the potency of the outcomes, this rich material has not only informed further interventions and projects but has also formed the basis of many of my national and international presentations and workshops. Aligned to the principles of wellness and recovery, clients often provided input into what was to be shared and discussed with the outside world, and the majority provided consent to include their case material. I believe that their consent attests to the high level of trust established within art therapy and that it serves as a function of reciprocity.

Working within a recovery model afforded the opportunity to consider novel ways of working with clients, and this extended to alternative spaces. In such instances, it is imperative that trusting relationships are developed. One example is when I introduced a multi-pronged participatory intervention with a client who had a long-standing assaultive and aggressive history with his peers and who was sexually intrusive with female staff. His peers often threatened him, given his lack of boundaries, his intrusiveness and his preoccupation with making and trying to sell beaded jewelry. Together, the client and I created a personalized, trifold color brochure that contained images of his artwork, his sayings and slogans, his strengths, phrases that he could use while proactively engaging with others, females in particular, and some positive affirmations. We then would go off-unit and sit on a bench practicing effective and intended social skills and interaction with those that passed by. This proved invaluable as it not only enhanced positive interaction but also promoted social skills, communication and self-esteem.

Establishing a long-term relationship with this particular client was essential in also working through a range of transferential material. There was a marked shift in our complex relationship and his associations to me variously as punitive father, sexual competitor, and perhaps sexual object, brother, comrade and artist. His humor was carefully integrated within the therapeutic encounter, he was provided with strategic opportunities to be at the center of attention, and his peers increasingly began to tolerate him with some even becoming his friend. The impact of this long-term therapeutic relationship and the positive impact of the arts in his life were also evidenced through his self-appointed nickname that was a combination of both his name and a world-renowned artist.

The integration of technology within a group context presented itself when the setting introduced a facility-wide gardening beautification competition, wherein residential units were encouraged to improve their courtyard and environment. This was especially beneficial for those clients that tend to become isolative and who may not attend cognitive or psychoeducational-type treatment groups. Several of these clients attended courtyard breaks and others chose to attend gardening groups. The art therapist photo-documented the progress of the garden, and this stimulated further interest, discussions and a sense of community between staff and clients. To enhance the gardening project during the second year, the art therapist selected three close-up photographs of flowers from the previous year's garden to serve as inspiration for the mural project. This promoted further ownership of the project and of the residential living unit's outdoor courtyard. It also allowed for a sense of reality orientation and consistency in one's involvement with a sustaining project.

Living legacy projects were another area wherein technology was utilized to chronicle a client's collection of artwork, poetry and voice recordings. This is a more individualized approach to documenting a client's body of artwork or creative expression. These projects relate more to an art studio approach wherein the client is viewed as an artist. Creating these living legacy projects has resulted in long-overdue validation for the client that they are in fact more than their criminal history and their clinical diagnosis. They are able to hold tangible objects of their own creation and have opportunities to share these with others. Photo-documentation and maintaining a digital art portfolio had several advantages. A digital art portfolio validates and promotes the clients' investment with their visual expressions, it can be viewed and shared with the treatment team, the client and with family members, and it serves as a practical storage file.

Figure 10.1: Honey Bee on Courtyard Sunflower (see colour section)

In addition to using technology to create and document art therapy projects and to stimulate interest in the potential of technology, it can be used to augment current projects. A digital camera was used to photo-document the growth and progress of the residential unit's courtyard garden. While reviewing these digital photographs, it was observed that special visitors were enjoying the fruits of our labor (Figure 10.1). Observing honeybees on the sunflowers that were planted stimulated the idea to engage in 'The Great Sunflower Project'. This is a project wherein the public was encouraged to plant sunflowers, register their garden online and document the number of bees that were observed on their flowers over the growing season. Although the art therapist's clients resided in a locked and secured environment, they were able to plant sunflowers and take an active part in this project.

Clients were able to learn more about a sustainable project, learn more about their environment and how they have an impact on it. Some clients planted the seeds, others assisted with observing the bees, and others tended to the garden itself. A local beekeeper provided two kinds of honey for sampling as well as facts about bees and bee behavior. At the end of the summer, photographs of the bees were provided to the clients and a garden party was held to celebrate everyone's efforts. This project allowed a forensic mental health population to become connected with the outside world and allowed them to participate in an international activity.

Increasingly, we became more attuned to the implications of how the aging process impacted sexual offenders and perhaps even exacerbated their capacity for sound judgment, decision-making and safe behavior (Cipriani *et al.* 2017). Working on a unit for older men, which included aging sexual offenders, also brought with it the realities of life, such as progressive disease, medical decline and, ultimately, death. Honoring humanity, we purposefully held memorial services and were sometimes involved in final plans with their families.

For one client that I had worked with for over six years, I was able to visit him at an outside medical hospital. I met his elderly sisters, who informed me of their dilemma regarding how best to honor his life. As we conversed, they revealed that after every art therapy session their brother would describe his session, what he learnt about himself, and the sometimes struggles he had with me and my so-called revelations about his artwork, and that they were grateful for my long-term dedication and commitment to him. They acknowledged their own difficulties with him since the commission of his crime and the impact that this, as well as aggressive and destructive behaviors over five decades, had had on them and their family. They appreciated the coffee table books that we had made with his artwork during the final year of his life. They revealed that the family was surprised at his artistic ability and that from this gift they were able to make new and renewed connections with him as a *human being*. This affirmed my work and reminded me that all of the hard work and struggles are well worth it in the long run given the far-reaching benefits.

Engaging in one's own art practice, a potent tool of the art therapist, allows difficult material to be expunged into the open enabling it to be acknowledged, examined and reflected upon. This was a proactive measure to consciously address the inherent demands of this line of work and the inevitable stress that certainly affects the therapist as well (Bach and Demuth 2018). I created a great deal of artwork while working with this population, partly because clients invited me to do so while they were creating and partly because I had an inherent compulsion to do so myself either to ease my own anxiety, release my own range of confusing emotions or simply to co-create with another while consciously enjoying the pleasure of the resulting synergy with my client(s).

Figure 10.2: Exposed

Rifling through my collection of artworks created during that time, I came across an image that surfaced memories linked to my work with sexual offenders (Figure 10.2). I recalled being surprisingly comfortable with the chaotic mess of the materials and recounted how there was still a sense of balance and boundary within the artwork. The antique photograph of the male figure is one that I have used in my artmaking since my undergraduate studies and the repetition of his photograph is reminiscent of the same old story being told to me. Looking at this image now, I am reminded of the clients I encountered, their individual stories and their own responses to the artwork they created. I am reminded of their struggles and their triumphs, and how artmaking allowed them to experience a new way of being with themselves and with others.

Summary
By entering the complicated discourse on art therapy and sexual offending through the consolidation of this chapter, I aimed to articulate good clinical practice that evidenced meaningful therapeutic engagement. The therapeutic relationship was a pivotal impetus for

changes in behavior and attitudes, and this relationship served as a starting point to build, reinforce and model a sense of community. Integrating art therapy services and open art studio with theme-oriented projects also allowed a sense of community to be established within the setting and reinforced positive qualities of those that participated (Peterson and Etter 2017).

Projects that build upon trust, relationships, legacy, insight and communication not only have a lasting positive impact on the client or group of clients, but also on the community and society at large. Perceptions of the professional staff migrated away from strictly diagnosis-based understandings of their clients to more of a well-rounded understanding, which further impacted a shift in how they interacted with their clients; staff can and do find satisfaction in this line of work (Lay 2016; Walker *et al.* 2018). Shifts in sexual offender identities and perception of their own abilities and potential as surfaced through direct interaction with the arts can be achieved (Peterson and Etter 2017). Art therapy within forensic mental health is one clinical treatment modality that can be effectively implemented as part of one's overall rehabilitation.

References

Anthony, W.A. (1993) 'Recovery from mental illness: The guiding vision of the mental health service system in the 1990s.' *Psychosocial Rehabilitation Journal 16*, 4, 11–23.

Bach, M.H. and Demuth, C. (2018) 'Therapists' experiences in their work with sex offenders and people with pedophilia: A literature review.' *Europe's Journal of Psychology 14*, 2, 498–514.

Bergman, J. and Hewish, S. (2003) *Challenging Experience: An Experiential Approach to the Treatment of Serious Offenders.* Oklahoma City, OK: Wood 'N' Barnes.

Cipriani, G., Danti, S., Carlesi, C. and Di Fiorino, M. (2017) 'Old and dangerous: Prison and dementia.' *Journal of Forensic and Legal Medicine 51*, 40–44.

Cordess, C. and Cox, M. (eds) (1996) *Forensic Psychotherapy: Crime, Psychodynamics and the Offender Patient.* Philadelphia, PA: Jessica Kingsley Publishers.

Farmer, D.F. and Yancu, C.N. (2018) 'Aging inmates: Issues surrounding health care, end-of-life and dying in prison.' *Palliative Medicine and Hospice Care 4*, 2, 3–5.

Guarnieri, M. and Klugman, S. (2016) 'Trust in a Forensic Setting.' In K. Rothwell (ed.) *Forensic Arts Therapies: Anthology of Practice and Research.* London: Free Association Books.

Lay, R. (2016) 'Practitioner-based Reflections and Creative Engagement.' In S. Yau and C.Y. Mok (eds) *Documentation: Taiwan, Hong Kong and Singapore Creative Arts Therapy Exchange: Symposium and Workshops Towards Health on Body, Mind and Spirit Symposium.* Hong Kong: Centre for Community Cultural Development and New Life Psychiatric Rehabilitation Association.

Peterson, J. and Etter, A. (2017) 'Creating community and shattering stigma: Collaborative arts interventions for the forensic population.' *Canadian Art Therapy Association Journal 30*, 2, 78–87.

Roberts, G., Davenport, S., Holloway, F. and Tattan, T. (eds) (2006) *Enabling Recovery: The Principles and Practice of Rehabilitation Psychiatry.* London: Royal College of Psychiatrists.

Walker, E.J., Egan, H.H., Jackson, C.A. and Tonkin, M. (2018) 'Work-life and well-being in U.K. therapeutic prison officers: A thematic analysis.' *International Journal of Offender Therapy and Comparative Criminology 62,* 14, 4528–4544.

CHAPTER 11

Attachment, Trauma and Art Therapy in the Treatment of Sexual Offending

THEMIS KYRIAKIDOU, ART THERAPIST

Introduction

A few years ago, I was in the fortunate position of working as a Specialist Child and Adolescent Mental Health Practitioner in a youth offending team (YOT), and as an art therapist in a low-secure unit treating adults with learning disabilities.

In my role at the YOT, I received specialist training in working with young people who displayed sexually problematic behaviour, whilst simultaneously completing an MSc in Forensic Psychology and Criminology. At the same time, in the low-secure unit, I worked with numerous adults with learning disabilities whose index offences were of a sexual nature. Through my specialist training, my clinical experience and my postgraduate studies, I was able to develop a formulation of the usefulness of art therapy and a comprehensive approach towards sexually problematic behaviour.

Trauma and attachment with sex offenders

It is no surprise that trauma becomes a noticeable and repetitive theme, whilst working with an offending population (Anda *et al.* 2010). There is a lot of research that recognizes the positive correlation between trauma and sexual offending (Reavis *et al.* 2013), as well as research that identifies trauma and abuse as antecedents of sexually harmful behaviour (Levenson, Willis and Prescott 2016; McMackin *et al.* 2002). Basto-Pereira *et al.* (2016) suggest that childhood sexual abuse is the most significant developmental factor in predicting future crime amongst juvenile offenders, whilst Grady, Yoder and Brown (2018) suggest that trauma has both 'direct and indirect relationships with all risk factors associated with criminal behaviour' (p.25).

Hanson and Morton-Bourgon (2005) suggest that abuse and trauma often lead to mistrust, hostility and an insecure attachment. These in turn may contribute to emotional and behavioural difficulties, feelings of social rejection, loneliness and offending behaviour (Grady *et al.* 2018). Personal relationships may be perceived as threatening, and the need for love, comfort and companionship is considered as the cause of distress, fear and pain (Marshall and Barbaree 1989). This idea is compatible with Marshall's (1989) theory, where intimacy deficits and emotional loneliness contribute to sexual offending.

In such cases, a treatment plan that incorporates work on trauma, relationships and interpersonal skills is necessary (Hanson and Morton-Bourgon 2005; Marshall *et al.* 1983). By treating the trauma, there is a decrease in behavioural and emotional difficulties, an increase in empathic responses (Bratton, Landreth and Lin 2010; Cohen *et al.* 2016) and a better chance for healthier relationships, without the need for further offending. Through the use of therapy, offenders may be able to identify patterns of behaviour and gain an understanding of the emotional reasons behind their actions and triggers.

Creeden (2009) suggests that healing can take place through the positive therapeutic experience between therapist and offender, to provide trust and safety. The therapist acts as an emotional container, developing a narrative through storytelling, which can help individuals process feelings associated with their trauma experience and may make further offending unnecessary.

This suggests that interventions such as art therapy can enable individuals to process their trauma and repair the responses associated with an insecure attachment. Through an art therapy intervention, offenders can overcome their interpersonal difficulties and reduce their risk of re-offending.

Case study
Introducing Steven
Steven was a 35-year-old male offender with a mild learning disability.
He was detained under the Mental Health Act 1983, Section 3, due to
multiple episodes of indecent assault and sexualized behaviour.

Steven's offending behaviour was formulaic and repetitive; he often
masturbated hidden behind a fence, calling passing women to 'show
him their knickers'; belittling them whilst exposing himself. He had
never formed a close personal relationship and, even though he had
paid for sex, he had not experienced a consensual relationship.

Steven's behaviour had attracted many criminal charges, such as
cautions, warnings and orders with the youth offending team and the
probation service prior to his admission to the low-secure unit. When
he was 28, and still offending, the Crown Prosecution Service decided
that, due to his learning disability, an adapted sexual offender treatment
programme (SOTP) in a hospital was better suited to his needs than a
prison sentence.

I was working as an art therapist in the unit when Steven arrived,
but he was not referred for art therapy. He always said hello politely
and told me how well he was doing. He was the 'ideal' patient, never
a 'management problem', always compliant, always working hard and
always displaying a significant desire for change. After Steven started
his SOTP treatment, he said to me, 'I don't need to work with you, do
I? I am doing SOTP, I don't need art therapy'. I smiled politely and said,
'Probably not'.

I thought of his comments as his need to reassure himself, to mark
his progress and to manage his anxiety in relation to his treatment
and to his eventual discharge. I did not notice the ambivalence he felt;
rejecting support, when in fact he was struggling on a deeper level, a
level that his SOTP treatment had not touched. I was too busy to notice.
I did not have any capacity to work with him and my long waiting
list sadly made me reticent to talk to him about the benefits of my
intervention.

Art therapy sessions
One day, many months later, Steven saw me from the window of the
games room. He ran out to meet me in the corridor and asked me,

almost out of breath, if I could do 'family reunited work', whilst bringing his hands into an X-shape. I was amused by this action, which resembled some sort of 'X factor' activity. I asked him if he meant 'family work' and he nodded positively.

Steven explained that he wanted to work with me to help him negotiate and understand the relationships with his family. I recognized how difficult it was for him to express vulnerability and to admit that his successful SOTP had not been fully sufficient for his emotional needs. Steven hadn't spoken to his named nurse about this, but he spoke directly to me, and I felt that he had already trusted me enough to reveal some of his ambivalence towards his treatment. Of course, thoughts of grooming crossed my mind, but my countertransference was telling me that there was no sexualized motive towards me, more one of a 'frightened ego', which I was able to appreciate over time.

Steven was at the end of his stay at the hospital and a discharge pathway had been agreed. After all, he had completed his SOTP successfully and there were never any problems with his treatment. I wondered about the validity of starting a short-term intervention, when his treatment pathway was nearly completed. Nevertheless, my curiosity about his intensions prompted me to work with him for a short period of time.

During the first session, Steven talked about the beginning of his problematic behaviour and criminal journey. I wondered whether this was an easy starting point for him, as he had just accessed this material through his group SOTP treatment. Steven told me that he had now completed his SOTP and he had got his certificate of achievement. Therapy outcomes had shown that his risk of re-offending had reduced; nevertheless, he explained that he was still troubled by the story of his little sister.

Steven narrated the story of the day when he lost control of his thoughts. He was 16 and was looking after his baby sister who was one year old. He went upstairs to change the baby's nappy, and as he was cleaning her, he started getting aroused. He looked at and touched her genitals, and various sexual acts passed through his mind, but he didn't do any of them. He was scared, realizing that his thoughts were fundamentally wrong, so he spoke to his mother about his sexualized desire, requesting help.

However, he did not receive the reassurance and support he wanted and needed. He said his mother informed social services, asking them to remove him from the family home. She saw him as a threat towards her daughter, which planted the seed in Steven's self-perception of his being a threat to all women. Although no formal offence had been committed, social services prohibited any contact between Steven and his sister until she was 18. This experience was very traumatic for Steven. He not only had to confront his own guilt and shame, but he also experienced the rejection and 'disgust' of his family. Feelings of shame and disappointment accompanied his emotional development throughout his childhood, triggered by his sexual arousal.

Steven talked about feeling alone and uncared for. He was confused, but also disgusted for allowing himself to feel sexually aroused by his baby sister. In his mind, his sexualized feelings had cost him his family, so he saw any sexualized thoughts as dangerous and forbidden. His identity had started to form, as a dangerous individual with uncontrollable sexual needs who needed supervision and management to prevent further harm. I reflected on Steven's experience of losing contact with his mother and wondered whether he needed to make sure that he was safe with me, or whether I would reject him as his mother had done.

Steven had not had any contact with his sister since the occasion when he had sexualized thoughts, and he had grown up with this burden. Nevertheless, now that his sister was over 18, he was aware that he could approach her to re-establish their relationship, and this was his intention. Steven wanted to become emotionally stronger, to find the courage to get in touch with his sister. He thought that by doing so he could perhaps 'forgive himself' and move on, as he was trapped by his own actions and feelings of guilt.

Steven was emotional and cried in his first session. He then completed his first picture with great skill, creating what he called his 'self-portrait' (Figure 11.1). His pencil drawing did not reveal the tears and the emotional pain expressed earlier. Instead, with a cigarette between his lips, Steven masked his true feelings and appeared superficially happy. This resembled his general attitude, that of an individual who was happy and doing well but hiding his internal struggles.

Figure 11.1: Self-portrait

Nevertheless, I felt it was a positive start. The emotional containment (Bion 1962), our relationship replicating feelings of a mother and child, our emotional attunement and the therapeutic 'holding' (Winnicott 1945) might be able to facilitate some emotional healing. I felt that I could help Steven discover a different narrative about himself and achieve further emotional development as well as a sense of self-worth.

In the second session Steven talked about all his offences, up to the point he was admitted to the low-secure unit. He talked about his need to fulfil his sexualized urges and his inability to stop offending. He talked with pride and confidence about his SOTP group, explaining that this group had made him feel stronger and that he had been offered the opportunity to see himself from a different perspective.

Steven then talked about his sister again, the current circumstances between them, as well as the sexualized thoughts and feelings he had experienced towards her. This time, more meaning and context was attributed to this incident. As a young boy with mild learning disabilities, Steven hadn't been looked after properly. He spent lots of time at home on his own, away from parental warmth and affection. His mother worked a lot and his father was frequently out. Steven's school attendance was sporadic; nobody really motivated him to attend and nobody cared.

Furthermore, Steven had been exposed from a young age to hardcore pornography. He talked about watching porn alongside his father on a regular basis. He recalled women not only being engaged in sexual activities, but also being degraded and mistreated, often with their hands tied and their mouths covered whilst enduring violence.

All these factors – the graphic pornographic imagery; the lack of parental input, supervision, care and warmth; the premature and abusive sexual arousal; and Steven's cognitive and emotional limitations – contributed to the creation of a distorted mind, with confused ideas about women, relationships and sexual satisfaction. In Steven's mind, love, comfort and companionship were replaced by violence, degradation and pain. As a result, Steven was unable to love the way other people did. The constant conflict between pleasure and abuse was a reminder of his abusive upbringing.

Over 40 percent of adult sexual offenders are believed to have distorted cognitive ideas and sexual arousal, limited sexual knowledge, impaired social skills and low self-esteem (Cauffman *et al.* 1998). Steven was clearly part of this percentage. I wondered if Steven often looked after his baby sister, and why his parents were unable to care for their children. I wondered about my role as a female therapist; one of support but also of professional power and relational authority. I voiced my own reflections with the hope of eliciting Steven's views. I reframed the role of the female, as a supportive person who cared, so that Steven's own storyline could perhaps begin to change.

My questions were not answered; perhaps these were too intense. Instead, Steven talked about a pleasant experience with his father, perhaps as an attempt to 'cover up' his emotional suffering. Perhaps this was how he coped with his feelings of shame and worthlessness; avoiding them, denying them and replacing them by positive imagery. Steven spoke about going fishing with his father, and as he grew older on his own. He remembered finding this therapeutic and a place of retreat, where he could relax and think of nothing. He decided to do a picture of this, again choosing to complete an image away from his painful subject.

Steven chose a green felt tip for his image and proceeded with his drawing (Figure 11.2). Again, it did not reflect the emotional weight of the session. When the picture was finished and we looked at it together, I noticed the obvious phallic reference. I thought his image looked like a female with a penis, and spontaneously laughed a little. However, Steven did not, he gazed at me nervously.

Figure 11.2: Fishing

Although Steven's image was spontaneous, I thought a lot of effort had previously gone into masking the sexualized thoughts of our earlier conversation. These problematic thoughts seemed to have found a way to surface, despite Steven's attempts to hide them. I wondered whether I would have noticed the embodied sexual reference if Steven did not have any recorded sexual offences, and I concluded that it was so obvious that I would. Steven seemed to be embarrassed and anxious and was unable to smile back at me. We were unable to reflect together, and I did not ask any questions about the image.

Over the following three sessions Steven talked about some of his more ordinary experiences. He spoke about his Christmas at the family home, which he used to really enjoy as both his parents were present (Figure 11.3). He spoke about his first girlfriend and their first date in the park (Figure 11.4) and buying her a bunch of tulips (Figure 11.5) for Valentine's Day. Interestingly, he did not include his girlfriend in his picture in the park.

Figure 11.3: Christmas

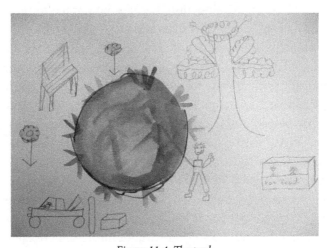

Figure 11.4: The park

Figure 11.5: Romantic memory

A degree of playfulness started to make its way through, and new emotional material started to appear. Perhaps Steven was trying to find a sense of normality and innocence within his family context and his personal relationships. Maybe he wanted to tell me that he was not 'all bad' and that, once upon a time, he had experienced fragments of normal development, perhaps forgotten and lost within his experiences of repeated abuse and dysfunction. Perhaps he wanted to re-write his story, starting from a 'healthier beginning'.

Whatever his motives, I felt that Steven had moved on from stating the offences and was now making attempts to use the space therapeutically, finding space for some positive experiences and feelings. It was clear that the artmaking enabled Steven to relax and, more importantly, helped him to create a positive relationship with a female therapist. During the sessions, he made references to his mother and sister, wondering what they were doing and imagining what it would be like to meet them again. He rehearsed hypothetical scenarios of visiting his family home. However, when his anxiety become unbearable, he changed his mind, saying that it would be better if he did not contact them, and that they were better off without him. I did not take part in this decision-making, but I was there to help him explore his feelings of ambivalence, insecurity, avoidance and anxiety about his options.

In a later session, Steven arrived looking slightly quieter than usual. He looked at me straight in the eyes, but the words could not come out. He looked down and said he was 'sorry'. I asked him what for and he said that he had hidden behind the bushes whilst on Section 17 leave, and he had shouted to a woman to show him her panties. Steven's idea of being treated successfully was shattered, and his belief that he was able to control his urges was now in doubt. He was afraid of the consequences of his actions and questioned whether he would be discharged into the stepped-down unit. His named nurse was unaware of this event, and in fact nobody had seen him re-offending. He could have just kept quiet, but instead he chose to speak up. This reminded me of the episode with his sister, when he could have just kept his thoughts to himself, but instead chose to confess them to his mother.

I felt the emotional pressure and the significance of my response, the conflict between truth and honesty and the fear of hopelessness. Using the trust and safety created between the two of us, I chose to praise Steven for being honest and for talking about his emotional struggle. I praised him for trying to make sense of his feelings and for seeking help, and for being able to recognize that he was feeling anxious about his imminent discharge. Within the session, while working with playdough, Steven was able to verbalize, with my help, that he had felt really worried about being discharged to a less secure environment. He talked about the paradox of being unable to deal with 'the pressure of having more freedom'. When I reassured Steven that he did well for talking to me, and that even though he needed further support everything would be okay, Steven looked me in my eyes with disbelief. His attachment, which I believe had become more secure, seemed to have activated previous defences of mistrust.

We worked together to inform the multi-disciplinary team, and his discharge continued as planned. Nevertheless, I made sure that Steven realized that, at times of stress and anxiety, he had very few skills. It was also clear that his sexual gratification served many emotional needs, not only those of direct sexual satisfaction.

Steven continued coming to our sessions and, interestingly, the conversation shifted once again. This time I did not feel that he wanted to hide any sexual thoughts, but that he had now managed to link his emotional state with his inner feelings, and this had offered him a new dimension to his emotional development. Steven explained how he was always fascinated by diggers, and these started appearing in our sessions (Figure 11.6). Heavy duty machinery, suggestive of something penetrating and 'dominant', was now the focus of the sessions.

Figure 11.6: The JCB! (see colour section)

Surprisingly, I felt very nurturing feelings towards Steven's enthusiasm about this unusual topic. I wondered if I had adopted a maternal role, whilst Steven was exhibiting a 'toddler' interest in the 'diggers'. His colouring ability with felt tip pens reminded me of school drawings, and his excitement resembled a sense of innocence and playfulness of a school-age child. In psychodynamic thinking, perhaps he was allowing himself to be young again, and through the playfulness of our relationship he was able to heal his trauma.

I felt that Steven was now beginning to trust me, and through this was able to look for forgiveness, not necessarily from me, but from himself. As our conversations grew, I was more curious to hear about his perception of women, bearing in mind his relationships with his mother, sister and victims. In one session, he drew a picture in pencil of a woman with long hair, a square body, wearing a pair of shorts and having a somewhat 'evil' smile.

I voiced my aesthetically driven reflections, that this woman did not look very 'womanly'. In response, Steven drew, very nervously, a pair of breasts to make his depicted figure looking more feminine (Figure 11.7). I added that Steven's woman looked scary and unfriendly. This opened up a new dimension in our conversation, and Steven admitted for the first time how terrified he was of women. For the first time I saw him shaking, perhaps as he realized that I was a woman too, but he did not stop talking. He talked about his inability to have a casual conversation with a woman, his inability to order a cup of coffee if the waitress was female, his inability to be served if the cashier was a woman, and so on.

Figure 11.7: A woman

Steven's social anxiety around women was very profound, but this emotional need had never been identified. The mask that Steven had so often used to hide his emotions had stopped others from realizing his inability to form relationships with women. Despite his hospital admission, his individual meetings with his male named nurse, his SOTP and the art therapy intervention, it was the first time that such feelings were disclosed. I felt that we were entering new therapeutic territory, of vital significance for Steven's treatment. He needed to function, form relationships and fully integrate in a world full of females.

Steven concluded his work with me on this topic and together we explored his fear and hyper-vigilance associated with females. He spoke about some of his fears: being on a bus and sitting next to a woman, wondering how he could manage to stay seated, without entering negative and dangerous emotional states (see Figure 11.8). As he drew this picture, I observed Steven going through some sort of aesthetic paralysis and emotional numbness, losing his artistic skill in the process. Fortunately, he recovered his skill and drew many more coloured pictures with diggers.

Figure 11.8: On the bus

Through therapy, Steven was able to recognize and perhaps accept that he was not the sole contributor to his offending behaviour. He was a person who had suffered abuse at a young age, and whose sexual offending had many contributing factors that had been beyond his control. Steven was beginning to forgive himself and was making progress, building on new social experiences. We celebrated when Steven successfully bought a loaf of bread from a female baker on his own; his sense of achievement was palpable.

Endings

The time for Steven's discharge had come and art therapy was no longer available to him. I was certain that Steven needed further support to tackle his social anxiety, his core beliefs about women, as well as his intimacy deficits and emotional loneliness. Nevertheless, I was confident that, even though we only had three months of art therapy, our work had been meaningful and beneficial to him and to the system around him.

Steven's experience of art therapy was not typical as he joined art therapy after he had undertaken the SOTP. I am not in a position to comment on Steven's reduction of risk through his SOTP treatment. But I am confident in saying that through our therapeutic engagement and the artmaking, Steven was able to connect his feelings to his early experiences and open up a dialogue about the dysfunction and abuse he had experienced when younger. He was able to make some sense of his emotions, understand some of his actions and process the shame he carried throughout his life. This made a massive difference to his sense of self; and, at our last session, he spoke about his future in a very hopeful way.

Conclusion

Treatment programmes such as relapse prevention (Laws, Hudson and Ward 2000) and the Good Life model (Willis *et al.* 2012) are amongst the most common treatment approaches. Nevertheless, current research suggests that trauma-informed approaches in the treatment of sex offenders enhances clinical effectiveness and public safety (McMackin *et al.* 2002) and are important factors in the reduction of re-offending and in the healing process (Levenson *et al.* 2016). Furthermore, Reavis *et al.* (2013), suggest addressing the early experiences and attachment processes in sex offending treatment. This enables offenders to experience an honest relationship with a therapist, opens new opportunities for advancing the offender's intimacy skills and reduces the risk of further offending (Levenson 2014).

Perhaps this approach does not fit every sex offender. Nevertheless, when offenders have experienced abuse and trauma and the effects have contributed to their offending behaviour, a trauma-informed treatment is needed. I suggest that such work is completed prior to any behavioural or cognitive approaches to treatment, to lay the foundations for deeper emotional change.

References

Anda, R.F., Butchart, A., Felitti, V.J. and Brown, D.W. (2010) 'Building a framework for global surveillance of the public health implications of adverse childhood experiences.' *American Journal of Preventive Medicine 39*, 93–98.

Basto-Pereira, M., Miranda, A., Ribeiro, S. and Maia, A. (2016) 'Growing up with adversity: From juvenile justice involvement to criminal persistence and psychosocial problems in young adulthood.' *Child Abuse and Neglect 62*, 63–75.

Bion, W.R. (1962) *Learning from Experience*. London: Karnac.

Bratton, S., Landreth, G. and Lin, Y.D. (2010) 'What the research shows about Child Parent Relationship Therapy (CPRT): A review of controlled outcome research.' In J. Baggerly, J. Ray, J. and S. Bratton (eds) *Child-centered Play Therapy Research: The Evidence-Base for Effective Practice*. Hoboken, NJ: Wiley.

Cauffman, E., Feldman, S., Waterman, J. and Steiner, H. (1998) 'Posttraumatic stress disorder among female juvenile offenders.' *Journal of the American Academy of Child and Adolescent Psychiatry 37*, 11, 1209–1216.

Cohen, J.A., Mannarino, A.P., Jankowski, K., Rosenberg, S. *et al.* (2016) 'A randomized implementation study of trauma-focused cognitive behavioral therapy for adjudicated teens in residential treatment facilities.' *Child Maltreatment 21*, 156–167.

Creeden, K. (2009) 'How trauma and attachment can impact neurodevelopment: Informing our understanding and treatment of sexual behaviour problems.' *Journal of Sexual Aggression 15*, 261–273.

Grady, M.D., Yoder, J. and Brown, A. (2018) 'Childhood maltreatment experiences, attachment, sexual offending: Testing a theory.' *Journal of Interpersonal Violence 25*, 1–35.

Hanson, R.K. and Morton-Bourgon, K. (2005) 'The characteristics of persistent sexual offenders: A meta-analysis of recidivism studies.' *Journal of Consulting and Clinical Psychology 73*, 1154–1163.

Laws, D.R., Hudson, S.M. and Ward, T. (2000) *Remaking Relapse Prevention with Sex Offenders: A Sourcebook*. Thousand Oaks, CA: Sage.

Levenson, J. (2014) 'Incorporating trauma-informed care into evidence-based sex offender treatment.' *Journal of Sexual Aggression 20*, 1, 9–22.

Levenson, J.S., Willis, G.M. and Prescott, D.S. (2016) Adverse childhood experiences in the lives of male sex offenders: Implications for trauma informed care.' *Sexual Abuse: A Journal of Research and Treatment 28*, 4, 340–359.

Marshall, W.L. (1989) 'Invited essay: Intimacy, loneliness and sexual offenders.' *Behaviour Research and Therapy 27*, 5, 491–503.

Marshall, W.L. and Barbaree, H.E. (1989) 'Sexual Violence.' In K. Howells and C. Hollin (eds) *Clinical Approaches to Aggression and Violence*. New York, NY: Wiley.

Marshall, W.L., Earls, C.M., Segal, Z. and Darke, J. (1983) 'A Behavioral Program for the Assessment and Treatment of Sexual Aggressors.' In K. Craig and R. McMahon (eds) *Advances in Clinical Behavior Therapy*. New York, NY: Brunner/Mazel.

McMackin, R.A., Leisen, M.B., Cusack J.F., LaFratta, J. and Litwin, P. (2002) 'The relationship of trauma exposure to sex offending behavior among male juvenile offenders.' *Journal of Child Sexual Abuse 11*, 2, 25–40.

Reavis, J., Looman, J., Franco, K. and Rojas, B. (2013) 'Adverse childhood experiences and adult criminality: How long must we live before we possess our own lives?' *The Permanente Journal 17*, 44–48.

Willis, G.M., Yates, P.M., Gannon, T.A. and Ward, T. (2012) 'How to integrate the Good Lives model into treatment programs for sexual offending: An introduction and overview'. *Sexual Abuse: A Journal of Research and Treatment 25*, 2, 123–142.

Winnicott, D.W. (1945) *Getting to Know Your Baby*. London: Heinemann.

CHAPTER 12

Finding Paul

Dramatherapy with a Man Whose Denial Rendered
Him 'Stuck' in the Criminal Justice System

KATIE GREENWOOD, DRAMATHERAPIST

Introduction

Paul[1] has a conviction of rape for which he is serving an indeterminate
sentence. Originally detained in a prison, Paul was transferred to a
medium-secure hospital when his mental health deteriorated. To
be discharged back into the community, Ministry of Justice (MOJ)
stipulations require Paul to demonstrate he has lowered his risk to
the public by addressing his offending. For Paul, the prospect of this
is unthinkable; like 30 percent of men convicted of a sexual offence
(Craissati 2015), Paul denies his conviction, which renders him 'stuck'
in the system and facing a lifetime of imprisonment.

Paul had been in hospital for several years before I met him. Under
his section (47/49[2]), he could return to prison once his mental health
stabilized, but his multi-disciplinary team (MDT) believed this would
be hugely detrimental for Paul and wanted to explore other options.
However, Paul's engagement remained superficial and compliant. The
dramatherapy referral was deemed the last hope before returning
Paul to prison; paradoxically, the referral itself felt hopeless. His MDT
had reached an impasse, stuck between the MOJ's requirements and
Paul's denial. Paul too, recognized the hopelessness of his situation, a

---

1   A pseudonym.
2   Transfer of prisoners to hospital under the Mental Health Act, with a Restriction Order.

feeling that permeated our first meeting. I was struck by how lost Paul seemed, demonstrated by the fluidity with which he played the role of a convicted offender, as if this was expected of him. I wondered who 'Paul' was and whether he knew himself. I considered the meaning of his denial, and whether his fragile sense of self meant that engaging with treatment – thereby accepting the sex offender label – felt even more terrifying than life imprisonment.

This chapter illustrates how dramatherapy helped Paul to rediscover his sense of self, which became a key factor in his treatment. I outline the importance of assisting Paul's MDT to unpick their countertransference and adopt a different way of working with him. The chapter also explores denial: its function, its relevance to treatment, and how it needn't encumber progress. Instead, a holistic approach demonstrates positive outcomes.

Paul's story describes how 'hope' and 'movement' can be found from a place that appears 'hopeless' and 'stuck'. Paul consented to my sharing his case because he hopes it will help patients in a similar position. I hope Paul's story assists professionals on how to work with patients like him.

Denial in the context of sexual offending

Thirty percent of offenders convicted of a sexual offence are in total denial; others sit on a continuum between categorical denial and admittance (Craissati 2015). Historically, denial was seen as a cognitive distortion and, thus, a causal factor in offending, a thinking process that disinhibits the offender, permitting an offence through rationalizing or minimizing their actions and the resulting harm (Deacon *et al.* 1999). However, further thinking emphasizes that denial that follows an offence is not causal, it is 'excuse making' (Maruna and Mann 2006), a normal human process that shifts the cause away from being central to a person's sense of self. This allows a person to uphold a stable personal narrative and retain their core self (Blagden *et al.* 2014). Removing this protective armour risks immersing a person in stigmatizing shame, which may lead to further offending (Maruna and Mann 2006).

The stigma of being labelled a 'sex offender', whether rightly or wrongly convicted, is substantial and impacts on a person's identity and their social system (Evans and Cubellis 2014). As psychological protection, denial relates to 'adaptive characteristics, such as capacity for shame, distaste for the behaviour, and attachment to social networks whose opinion of the offender matters to him' (Craissati 2015, p.402). Denial may suggest that, on some level, a person accepts their behaviour was wrong. Conversely, denial may also indicate a person's innocence.

Debate surrounds whether treatment should focus on denial, and whether someone in denial should access treatment at all. Generally, admission onto prison treatment programmes hinges on whether the individual accepts any responsibility for their offence; 'categorical deniers' are therefore excluded (Blagden *et al.* 2014). For offenders in denial, progress through the justice system depends on their meaningful engagement with treatment (Marshall *et al.* 2001), which is deemed essential for gaining insight into behaviour and lowering a person's risk to the public. However, research suggests no consistent correlation between denial and recidivism (Blagden *et al.* 2014; Craissati 2015; Ware and Harkins 2015). Furthermore, treatment outcomes demonstrate positive changes in areas relating to sexual offending, such as self-esteem and cognitive distortions, regardless of whether a person is in denial (Beckett *et al.* 1994).

Paul's denial prevented him from accessing treatment, or, accessing it in a way that would be considered meaningful. However, treatment can take a holistic approach by addressing a person's sense of self and their view of the world (Blagden *et al.* 2014; Craissati 2015) rather than focusing on risk reduction and tackling denial. Treatment can also explore factors surrounding an offence, such as problems in relationships, low self-esteem, and maladaptive coping strategies, or address how someone might have put themselves in a position to be accused of an offence (Marshall *et al.* 2001; Ware and Harkins 2015). Essentially, denial should not obstruct treatment, and those in denial who have committed an offence and remain untreated will continue to pose a risk (Marshall *et al.* 2001). Unfortunately, opportunities to work on the self within forensic settings are limited. Programmes tend to be manualized, leaving little room for individualized treatment. Therefore, the person's need for denial as a protective function continues (Blagden *et al.* 2014) as their sense of self remains fractured and elusive.

Dramatherapy – in search of 'Paul'
The 'last hope'

Paul's MDT referred him for dramatherapy following his recent, positive, engagement with art therapy, sessions that ended when the therapist left; dramatherapy was seen as the 'last hope'. Historically, Paul had shown minimal response to treatment and had a fractured relationship with his team. He vehemently denied his offence and was unremittent in his anger at being detained. Paul attended therapeutic sessions but with an invisible barrier, as if he viewed all psychological treatment as attempts by the system to break down his denial. The team were at an impasse and questioned the therapeutic value for Paul remaining in hospital. Their only alternative was a return prison transfer, but this meant sending him to prison to stay. They hoped the creative nature and distanced approach of dramatherapy might encourage Paul to explore his personal material, with it perhaps being easier to view things through the eyes of the drama than talk about directly.

Yet despite being the last hope, the seeming futility of the referral was palpable. I suspected the referral was, in fact, the team's way of finding some breathing space by passing on their stuckness and hopelessness; I felt a weight being passed to me. I felt isolated, concerned that I would be left holding everyone's failure if Paul returned to prison. Tentatively, I agreed to meet him.

'How can you help me?'

Paul was calm and polite but seemed suspicious of me and angry about life. Like his MDT, Paul was stuck and felt hopeless about his future. He was acutely aware of time, how fast or slowly time passed, his time lost in institutions. Time is a recurrent theme in forensic settings. It almost ceases to exist as something that offers measurement and structure to one's life. Managing time becomes an art form; people copiously fill time or block it out altogether. Gersie (1993) relates 'time-distortion' to inner turbulence: 'Feeling cooped up by the turmoil of their inner world, oppressed by the past and hemmed in by seeing impossibilities, the person does not relate to time as something that involves possibility and choice' (p.3). Paul believed nothing and no one could help him and spoke as if he felt powerless about his future – not surprising given the indeterminate sentence ahead of him. My dramatherapy offer suddenly sounded immaterial.

Paul described his time in prison and hospital, his innocence, and feeling affronted by a 'system that wants to lock me up and keep me here'. Paul seemed mistrusting of the criminal justice system and everyone in it. His speech was intense, uninterrupted and repetitive; it was difficult to create a dialogue. I felt imposed upon by his monologue and wondered whether this reflected how imposed upon he felt by the system; perhaps this was his only way to make space for himself. Paul spoke about his conviction, acutely aware of how convicted sex offenders are viewed, describing how people see 'them' as 'evil'. Repulsed by the label he maintained 'That isn't me'. He recited stories about his bodily functions and illnesses in a way that seemed crude and repulsive. I wondered if he was trying to repulse me, push me away, and whether keeping people at a distance was a protective strategy – clearly effective given that his team were discussing his prison transfer. Perhaps Paul wanted to test whether I would be repulsed by him, a convicted sex offender, as he feared others would be.

I observed the fluidity with which Paul played a stereotypical 'offender' role – his manner, his language, his stories. I wondered how often he felt drawn into this role, and how conscious this was. My experience of forensic and secure settings is that roles synonymous with these environments, such as 'offender' and 'patient', overshadow other roles in a person's repertoire. Treatment should therefore offer people opportunities to strengthen and develop a more rounded sense of self. I wondered who else Paul was and asked him to tell me about himself unrelated to his conviction. Paul looked surprised, as if he expected I only wanted to hear about 'Paul the offender'. Paul told me stories about his family, caring for his siblings, school days, his friend's death and his love of writing songs. As Paul spoke, something changed – he became animated and energized, invested in these stories. He identified with roles other than 'offender' – 'bereaved friend', 'brother', 'son', 'pupil'. This was hopeful.

Paul asked, 'How can you help me?' adding that other professionals 'didn't help'. His tone was hopeless. In the 1994 film *The Shawshank Redemption*, the character Red believes, 'Hope is a dangerous thing. Hope can drive a man insane. It's got no use on the inside. You'd better get used to that idea.' For me, this connected with Paul; facing an indeterminate sentence, perhaps it felt easier to be without hope than to have some and it be taken away. Yet hope is a key therapeutic factor and sets a milieu for change. Therapists' hope for their clients directly effects progress (Bartholomew *et al.* 2019). I did not want to give Paul false hope but, equally, it needed to exist somewhere for him. Perhaps *I* needed to hold Paul's hope until he could hold his own. I agreed that dramatherapy isn't a magic wand but could offer him space for himself – a space for self-expression and to process his experiences. Paul gave me a fist bump and told me I 'seemed a nice lady'. The following week, he agreed to dramatherapy.

The MDT agreed that dramatherapy sessions should be Paul's space, not cluttered with offence-focused work. Therapy should be led by him and allow room for stories and roles – other than 'offender' – to breathe and develop. I also wanted to explore the interpersonal dynamics between Paul and his MDT, and whether this reflected Paul's internal world. Kirtchuk, Reiss and Gordon (2008) emphasize that, once a person's internal dynamics are formulated, an intervention can be developed and implemented. Simply an understanding of the dynamics is often enough to facilitate more integrated working between staff and patient. I shared my observation of the similarities between Paul and his team – how stuck and hopeless everyone seemed – and my own feelings towards being 'the last hope', a label that carried feelings of isolation and projected failure. In forensic settings, projective identification is common. Feelings are difficult so patients avoid emotions that seem overwhelming or dangerous. Instead, the feeling parts of self are projected outwards, often landing with staff who introject it and identify with it as their own. It seemed that Paul's isolation, stuckness, perceived failure and hopelessness had landed with his team, blocking them from seeing Paul with clarity. Consequently, they felt an urge to distance themselves from him both physically and psychologically. Processing these experiences through reflective practice would assist our understanding of Paul's internal world, and thus avoid acting this out.

'Where's Paul?'

During early sessions, Paul spoke of professionals' 'lies' about him – in reports, ward rounds and in court. Paul referred to himself by many names: 'Paul', 'Mr S', 'Paul Star', 'P' and 'Mr Star'. He explained that he introduces himself differently to people – with professionals, for example, his uses 'Mr Star'; I recalled his psychiatrist telling me he could 'never get beyond Mr Star'. We laid his different names out and Paul placed image cards under each to depict that persona. Unsurprisingly, 'Mr Star', Paul's 'offender' role, was vivid – dark, bleak images that painted him as bad. 'Paul Star' was who he could have been were it not for his conviction. His different selves seemed hugely fragmented. Pausing, Paul noticed there were no images under 'Paul'. 'Where's Paul?' he commented. 'There's no Paul!' We discussed how 'Paul' may have become lost, perhaps entangled within the roles of 'patient' and 'offender'. He reflected it would be 'good to find "Paul" again'.

Evans and Cubellis (2014) discuss the substantial impact of a sexual offence conviction, further compounded if someone lacks robust coping strategies and social support. Even when innocent, a person risks losing family, friends and their identity, thereby becoming lost in the label and seeing themselves only as a 'sex offender'. Was this true for Paul? Was his sense of self so lost that engaging in treatment – thereby accepting the sex offender label – meant this is all he would be? Paul was acutely aware of the stigma surrounding his conviction, and admitting responsibility could mean losing his family. With so much at stake, perhaps incarceration felt the lesser of two evils. It was also unclear when and where 'Paul' had become lost – Prison? Hospital? Before? Reflecting on this, I was also mindful that Paul grew up with nine siblings, and I wondered what it might have been like to find one's own individual identity in a context where the group has such prominence. Whatever the meaning of Paul's denial, and wherever 'Paul' had got lost, finding 'Paul' was essential and became the focus of therapy.

The importance of stories

Stories were fundamental in our work; 'storyteller' was a role Paul enjoyed. His demeanour changed – he became animated and emotionally expressive. The story of Paul's conviction and, as he described, 'being set up' remained a central feature for a long time. Paul repeated it using the same words and embittered tone. It was not surprising that the 'offender' role was repeated given his impoverished role repertoire (Hall in Guarnieri 2012). It was difficult to sit with and left me feeling powerless and suffocated. Yet this story needed space; it was Paul's truth, how he saw the world and himself in it. If denial was a protective function, then this story was Paul's armour; I couldn't take it away from him without offering a better replacement (Yalom 1991). Gradually, his conviction story consumed less space and made room for others and his 'offender' role stepped back, making way for new ones.

Stories are often used in dramatherapy. They invite us to project aspects of ourselves and our life onto them to see it differently, opening up an imaginative 'what if' world to see life as it is and how we would like it to be (Gersie 1992, 1993). I find people are often drawn towards particular stories without knowing why; perhaps this has to do with the metaphorical nature of story. Wilkinson (2010) describes how metaphor and imagery act as a bridge between implicit and explicit memory, giving the example of dreams as unconscious material emerging into conscious form. As a metaphor, story permits safe access to previously buried material, allowing personal connections to surface to help people process their experiences. Metaphor also emerges from factual narratives. For example, Paul's conviction story was his truth but may have also held metaphorical meaning – an unconscious communication of his internal world, perhaps one that felt powerless and suffocated.

Metaphor is multi-faceted and can hold many layers of meaning. For example, a monster in a story may represent 'the perpetrator', 'anger', 'the inner critic' or all of these simultaneously. Making explicit the meaning(s) of the metaphor is not always necessary. It can be useful to allow multiple possibilities of meaning, letting it permeate both conscious and unconscious levels. I find clients often uncover hidden depths of meaning over time. Rushing this may jeopardize the therapeutic process by concretizing something prematurely or bringing into conscious awareness something that a person is not ready for. Story offered Paul a safe platform to step onto and re-examine his perception of the world, to acknowledge and express things he otherwise couldn't. I trusted that Paul was making links at both conscious and unconscious levels. It often seemed as though aspects of the metaphor were discussed explicitly whilst others – too difficult for words – were processed in the background, demonstrated through subtle changes.

Paul's confidence in therapy grew, and he attended because he wanted to rather than through compliance. He accepted feedback that challenged his perception of the world and acknowledged emotions other than anger, considering the possibility that anger might offer a safe channel for expressing other emotions; he once reflected that sadness and anger 'felt the same'. Story offered a container for Paul's feelings and a language to express them. The themes we explored varied but were all pertinent.

VIGNETTE 1

I observed the unremitting anger with which Paul spoke about his conviction and wondered what else, metaphorically, this story might be communicating. Perhaps there were other things Paul was angry about but couldn't articulate, therefore his conviction became the object onto which his anger was directed. I introduced Shakespeare's *King Lear*, believing certain themes would resonate with Paul's internal world. Paul did not fully understand the language, but he made sense of the emotional content immediately. 'He's cussing his daughters,' he said, 'like I used to cuss people as a teenager.' I invited Paul to re-write the monologue in his own words. Paul did so, using imagery and rhyme to express feelings of 'emptiness' and 'betrayal'.

VIGNETTE 2

Paul brought up the biblical story of Joseph, who is sold into slavery by his brothers because they are jealous of him for being their father's favourite (Genesis 37). Paul initially stated that Joseph's brothers were 'bad' (Paul often categorized people as 'good' or 'bad'). In role as Joseph's brother Jonah, Paul noted how rejected Jonah felt by his father. His actions towards Joseph were simply an expression of this. Paul considered that perhaps Jonah wasn't bad – that it was difficult to categorize him as good or bad. Together, we considered that doing bad things does not make someone a bad person.

The story of the kings

Paul brought up the story of 'The Evil King of Syria' (Daniel 11:21–45 Good News Bible). The Syrian King believes he is the greatest and gains power through deception. He attacks the Egyptian King whose attempts to fight back are unsuccessful. The two Kings have dinner together, but their motives are malevolent, and they lie to one another. The Syrian King, again, attacks Egypt but is met with opposition from the Romans.

He continues to fight and defend his position, killing thousands and looting Egypt's riches. The Syrian King eventually dies alone with no one to help him. Paul believed the story was about 'people who don't get on because of power'. Keen to explore this, he devised the following scene:

> Each King has a Worker who tells his King that the other is planning to kill him; this is a lie and a ploy by the Workers to get money from the Kings in return for their safety. The Kings meet for dinner and lie to each other. They are suspicious of one another but suggest a trading deal. The Egyptian King asks the Syrian King to trade him some horses, food and wine for a party he is holding. The Syrian King makes an unreasonable offer in return, which is refused. The Egyptian King reveals that he knows the other is plotting to kill him. The Egyptian King proposes this is a lie and that both have been tricked by their Workers. The Syrian King is proud. He disbelieves this as it would make him a fool for believing his trusted Worker. Eventually, the Egyptian King agrees to a lesser trading deal so he can, at least, have his party.

Paul played the Syrian King. He commented on the Kings' suspicion of each other, demonstrated by their fixed eye contact. He described their vigilance, fearful that the other might 'make a move'. To me, this echoed the fight/flight response, our automatic mechanism that responds instinctively to threats of danger. Something about this scene was threatening and dangerous, and I wondered how this resonated with Paul. He reflected on how 'stuck' the characters were because neither would shift their position. Paul felt the Workers were also unlikely to shift, as admitting their lies would carry consequences. We discussed the Kings' 'stuckness' and their impossible situation. Paul felt that pride and fear kept them stuck, even if this meant their eventual demise.

The story of the Kings was discussed in Paul's ward round. Story had become a common language between Paul and his MDT. It allowed everyone to communicate and united the therapy space with the outside world. Paul recognized the similarities with his own position, stating, 'I could have got out by now, but I stuck to my story... so I'm stuck.' The team explained their impasse. Paul's psychiatrist fed back his position of feeling stuck between Paul's denial and the MOJ's requirements. He explained if Paul engaged in offence-focused work, the MOJ might shift their position. Paul responded, 'Nobody gets out of this place... I won't gain anything. I'll be a loser.' I observed this meeting of the Kings: Paul and his psychiatrist. Neither in a position to negotiate. Stuck. Paul's body language echoed the Kings' vigilance, perhaps indicating how threatening ward rounds felt for him, thus activating his fight/flight response, which meant bearing his 'offender' armour.

Yet something about the Kings' story resonated with Paul. He had made a personal link with the metaphor, one that questioned his perspective and resulted in a shift. Weeks later, Paul said, 'I want to admit I done the thing... to move on, so I ain't in the same position.'

'Paul' emerges

A year after our initial meeting, we revisited the exercise of exploring Paul's many selves. Again, Paul's different names were laid out and he placed images under each. He created the following:

> 'Mr Star' has never seen an ostrich or been on a boat. He tells jokes.
>
> 'Mr S' buys nice clothes, wants a holiday, and will be able to see things one day. He likes riding bikes.
>
> 'Paul' needs a holiday. He needs fruit for vitamins, wears slippers in his room, and likes sweets. He wants to learn to look at the stars.
>
> 'Paul Star' walks his dog, has money, could've been a vet or a gardener, and will have old hands when he is 60.
>
> 'P' is sweet. He likes a bath and taking pictures. He is strong.

I noted there were now images for 'Paul' – he laughed and said this felt good. I observed similarities between the selves where, previously, there weren't, as if Paul was less fragmented and more integrated. I also noted his description of someone who, 'will be able to see things one day'. Although Paul did not express this explicitly, his comment suggests he has hope for his future.

Update

Paul continues to grapple with his denial and maintains that his admission was purely to shift positions; outwardly, he still denies his offence. It would be easy to deduce that Paul is playing the system, but neither I nor his team believe this. In the decade Paul spent in prison and hospital he never contemplated this option. Shifting from 'I'll deny my offence whatever the cost' to 'something has to change' is a huge step, and enables a position that offers leverage, a way to engage, meaningfully, in the work the MOJ requires of him without risking his identity and social network. The team feel Paul was initially testing the water, perhaps gauging reactions to his admission. I believe Paul needed space to find himself before he could consider anything else. Previously, the 'convicted sex offender' label felt all-consuming, but now it doesn't define him as he is constructing a more rounded sense of self.

Paul currently engages meaningfully with offence-focused work and has a strong therapeutic relationship with his psychologist. They are using the Good Lives model (Ward, Mann and Gannon 2007), an approach that emphasizes the construct of a meaningful and fulfilling personal identity. As a convicted sex offender, Paul acknowledges the obstacles he faces but appears better equipped to manage these. Positively, the MOJ have granted Paul community leave for the first time. He now visits his family. Paul's MDT are planning his referral to low-secure and are hopeful that he will, one day, be released.

Discussion and conclusion

Significant to Paul's progress were three things:

- space to find himself
- using metaphor via story
- exploring the dynamics between him and his team.

First, through years of detainment, never had the *meaning* of Paul's denial for him been fully formulated. Instead, perhaps due to external pressures from the MOJ, denial was deemed as something that needed challenging to reduce his risk level. My sense is that denial kept him safe in a place where 'Paul' was lost; without denial he would simply become a 'sex offender'. Finding 'Paul' gave space to rebuild his narrative, thus the 'sex offender' label became less consuming.

Second, using metaphor via story allowed Paul to work with personal material from a distance. With Paul, we did not need to make everything explicit by analysing every detail. Distance created a buffer, allowing Paul to safely delve deeper into his personal material; given Paul's level of defences and mistrust in professionals and the system, this was crucial. Some things Paul talked openly about, such as how stuck he and the Kings were. Other things remained implicit, yet with a felt sense that something in Paul's infrastructure was shifting. This was demonstrated through changes in him – acknowledging his feelings, accepting feedback, exploring different perspectives, trusting our therapeutic relationship and, ultimately, changing his position. Sometimes it is important to simply trust the process and believe that the client will use the material as they need to.

Third and finally, we come to the work with Paul's team through addressing their countertransference. In therapy, I saw significant changes, yet some staff maintained he was, 'the same old Paul'. Their observations monitored the presence or absence of risk behaviour, which contradicted the holistic approach we'd established. Dramatherapy offered Paul space to experiment with multiple roles, letting him play with *who he wanted to be* to make the reality of this more tangible. In contrast, the ward offered two roles: 'patient' and 'offender'. Focusing on risk reduction as a progress indicator perpetuated this. At that time, Paul's process of self-discovery was tentative; the reality of who he wanted to be seemed intangible. Perhaps this process was paralleled by staff, changes were there but were too elusive to capture. Or perhaps, like Paul, it felt safer for staff to hold on to 'Paul the offender' than to step into the unknown of who else Paul might be. Raising staff's awareness of this through reflective practice was necessary to support Paul's process. Subsequently, observations of progress were assessed holistically, noting subtle changes, such as how Paul's interactions with them felt (e.g. warmer). Staff modelled the changes we wanted to see from Paul, such as instigating conversation. This wasn't simply about modelling social skills. A therapist's hope for their client correlates with stronger therapeutic alliances and progress in therapy (Bartholomew *et al.* 2019). Demonstrating hope for Paul through reflecting back his desired self, fostered Paul's own hope for who he could be. Gradually, staff's observations of Paul became more congruent with the person I saw in therapy. His doctor said, 'You [Katie] have brought Paul to centre stage... so we can see the human being.' This encapsulates how differently people feel about Paul, and perhaps how differently he feels about himself.

I worked with Paul for over two years. In our final session, Paul entered the room and I was struck by his size. He filled the space in a way he had not done before; 'Paul' had arrived and was finally owning his space.

I conclude with words from Paul and his psychiatrist and their thoughts on this process. Both highlight the importance of a holistic approach rather than a risk-reduction one. They acknowledge the significance of finding 'Paul' and how this, subsequently, impacted on his relationship with the team and his progress, allowing him to become unstuck.

Psychiatrist: 'I recall a sense of hopelessness and resignation of having to send somebody back to prison when it wasn't in their best interest. I remember feeling totally despondent, then feeling some relief when he engaged with art therapy. I remember feeling hopeful about dramatherapy, and it feeling important that this wasn't about risk reduction – it was just his space. I remember feeling hope, relief, happiness when there was movement. I don't think I appreciated how much the denial defined him to the extent that he had no idea of himself. I feel pleased that there has been progress. I feel proud of him.'

Paul: '[Dramatherapy is] about thinking about myself and what I wanna gain. You asked me where 'Paul' is… Dramatherapy helps you to find out who you are, and you need to know who you are before you can do any of the other stuff.'

My thanks to Paul and his psychiatrist for their contributions, to Paul for allowing his story to be told, and to Clark Baim for his endless support and wisdom.

References

Bartholomew, T.T., Gundel, B.E., Li, H., Joy, E.E. *et al.* (2019) 'The meaning of therapists' hope for their clients: A phenomenological study.' *Journal of Counseling Psychology 66*, 4, 496–507.

Beckett, R., Beech, A., Fisher, D. and Fordham, A.S. (1994) *Community-Based Treatment of Sex Offenders: An Evaluation of Seven Treatment Programs.* Home Office Occasional Paper. London: Home Office.

Blagden, N., Winder, B., Gregson, M. and Thorne, K. (2014) 'Making sense of denial in sexual offenders: A qualitative phenomenological and repertory grid analysis.' *Journal of Interpersonal Violence 29*, 9, 1698–1731.

Craissati, J. (2015) 'Should we worry about sex offenders who deny their offences?' *Probation Journal 62*, 4, 395–405.

Deacon, L., Gocke, B., Baim, C. and Grant, D. (1999) *Understanding Perpetrators, Protecting Children*. England: Whiting and Birch.

Evans, D.N. and Cubellis, M.A. (2014) 'Coping with stigma: How registered sex offenders manage their public identities.' *American Journal of Criminal Justice 40*, 593–619.

Gersie, A. (1992) *Earthtales: Storytelling in Times of Change*. London: Green Print.

Gersie, A. (1993) 'On being both author and actor: Reflections on therapeutic storytelling.' *Dramatherapy 15*, 3, 2–11.

Guarnieri, M. (2012) 'Moving with the Patient: Boundary Phenomena in Forensic Dramatherapy.' In A. Aiyegbusi and G. Kelly (eds) *Professional and Therapeutic Boundaries in Forensic Mental Health Practice*. London: Jessica Kingsley Publishers.

Kirtchuk, G., Reiss, D. and Gordon, J. (2008) 'Interpersonal Dynamics in the Everyday Practice of a Forensic Unit.' In J. Gordon and G. Kirtchuk (eds) *Psychic Assaults and Frightened Clinicians: Countertransference in Forensic Settings*. London: Karnac.

Marshall, W.L., Thornton, D., Marshall, L.E., Fernandez, Y.M. and Mann, R. (2001) 'Treatment of sexual offenders who are in categorical denial: A pilot project.' *Sexual Abuse: A Journal of Research and Treatment 13*, 3, 205–215.

Maruna, S. and Mann, R. (2006) 'A fundamental attribution error? Rethinking cognitive distortions.' *Legal and Criminal Psychology 11*, 155–177.

Ward, T., Mann, R. and Gannon, T. (2007) 'The Good Lives model of offender rehabilitation: Clinical implications.' *Aggression and Violent Behaviour 12*, 87–107.

Ware, J. and Harkins, L. (2015) 'Addressing Denial.' In D.T. Wilcox, T. Garrett and L. Harkins (eds) *Sex Offender Treatment: A Case Study Approach to Issues and Interventions*. Chichester: John Wiley & Sons.

Wilkinson, M. (2010) *Changing Minds in Therapy: Emotion, Attachment, Trauma and Neurobiology*. London and New York: W.W. Norton.

Yalom, I.D. (1991) *Love's Executioner and Other Tales of Psychotherapy*. London: Penguin.

Expressing the Crime for a Young Sex Offender Using Art Therapy in a Forensic Psychiatric Hospital in the Netherlands

THIJS DE MOOR, ART PSYCHOTHERAPIST

Introduction

This case study centres around an art therapy process with a patient I have called Philip, with whom I worked for almost two years. The sessions took place in my art therapy studio in a forensic psychiatric hospital (hereafter called the clinic) in the Netherlands, where I have worked since 1997. Because of Philip's age (19 years old when sent to art therapy treatment) and the fact he still was in development, the full diagnosis of borderline personality disorder (BPD) couldn't be confirmed; therefore, one of the aims of art therapy was to prevent the full development of BPD.

Philip was convicted for a sexual crime when he was 17 years old and placed in adult forensic treatment. This was decided by the judge because of the risk of re-offending. Philip had violently harassed an older woman on the street. He was also diagnosed with attachment disorder. In an earlier conviction, when he was aged 16, he seriously harmed the privacy of a family by sexually assaulting an 11-year-old girl (inappropriate touching). At that time, Philip was sent to a treatment programme for adolescents for a period of three months. Within three months after leaving the programme he re-offended, and he was sentenced to follow the adult therapy programme for sexual offenders in the clinic.

For confidentiality reasons the images shown in this chapter are artistic impressions and reproductions.

Art therapy and sexual offending
The role of treatment for sexual offender patients in the Netherlands

Participation in the treatment programme aims to rehabilitate the patient to the extent where they can return safely into society. The number of different programmes to establish this goal is enormous, varying from cognitive-behavioural approaches to psychodynamic and psychotherapeutic programmes. Overviews of treatment programmes and scientific investigations of them are presented by Keulen-de Vos (2013), Hodgins and Muller-Isberner (2000), and Cordess and Cox (1996). A final goal in the treatment of sexual offender patients in the Netherlands is to prevent recidivism. We believe treatment is a better option for reaching that goal than a prison term. As well as the final or long-term goal, each treatment programme should have a within-treatment goal. However, the lack of insight into their own behaviour interferes with goals the therapist has in mind (Hellinga 1997). Moreover, many sexual offenders are good talkers. They often use verbal skills to lie to the therapist, use their verbal charm to mislead them, to express themselves abusively and aggressively or to act out a macho type.

The pre-problem

Van de Gaag and van der Plas (1997) describe these patients as people with a 'pre-problem'. A pre-problem occurs because of a patient's ambiguity regarding the goals to be reached in therapy. The patient may express the desire to change, but they are unable to put their problem into words and cannot formulate the goals of the therapy. The sexual nature of their problem merely contributes to, or even complicates, the pre-problem. They often are too embarrassed to talk about the offence. Forcing them to elaborate on their sexual crime or their sexual experiences usually only adds to their distress (Donisch-Seidel 1996; Keulen-de Vos 2013; Schnabel and Sorbi 1993). In sum, patients with a pre-problem are unable to engage in the therapeutic alliance, a necessary condition for successful participation in psychotherapy (Smeijsters 2007; van der Gaag and van der Plas 1997; van Marle 1995).

The large number of patients with a pre-problem is due to the majority suffering from developmental disorders, visible, for example, when learning, in their non-verbal and verbal communication, and in antisocial behaviour. Most of these patients are not able to explain or verbalize how their problem came about, as aberrant behaviour developed in early childhood. The absence of healthy interaction structures hinders or even precludes effective participation in traditional psychotherapy.

Art therapy in forensic psychiatry

Despite their differences, all arts therapists believe the very act of creating is healing and the majority of approaches aim to provide a safe non-verbal creative space that usually is combined with a verbal psychotherapeutic use of the artwork (Haeyen 2018b; Lusebrink 1990; Smeijsters 2008). Artwork stimulates the patient to verbalize, to become more conscious and to apply new skills. To be able to benefit from art therapy in a psychodynamic and/or verbally inclined approach, the patient needs to have the healthy interaction structures of a cognitive-functioning five-year old (Keulen-de Vos 2013). Many people suffering from underdeveloped or disturbed interaction structures, including most sexual offenders, function below this developmental level (Smeijsters *et al.* 2011). They often lack the capacity to discuss and set the goals for therapy when they are expected to undergo therapeutic treatment (Hinz 2009; Lusebrink 1990; Smeijsters 2008). I believe art therapy for patients with underdeveloped or disturbed interaction structures contains aspects that are rather valuable. Personal expression has a certain quality, which Stern (1985) called vitality affect: a quality of experience, which arises directly from our interactions with others, distinct from categorical affects such as, angry, sad or happy. They are best characterized in dynamic terms, such as, bursting, explosive and fading away.

Impulsive and aggressive behaviour can be defined by uncontrolled and unconscious emotional eruptions, leading to extreme acting out (Liebmann 2008; Smeijsters and Cleven 2006). Art therapy makes problematic behaviour visible by giving opportunities for creating and reflecting. This opportunity might not be present in other forms of therapeutic intervention where the focus is in the narrative.

Visualizing and expressing emotional states

Working with art materials appeals to sensory experiences and recalls emotional experiences. By becoming conscious of and gaining sensitivity for emotional experiences through artmaking, the patient is able, according to Hass-Cohen and Carr (2008), to get better insight into emotional states and, in particular, angry eruptions. Sexual offenders with uncontrolled impulsive behaviour problems often get aggressive as a result of experiencing failure during their artmaking process. This failure is often due to their impulsive behaviour. Through the art therapy process the patient can learn to attain clear art forms with personal structures and interactions. By making physical contact with the art materials, the patient learns to develop more healthy actions (Haeyen 2018a; Muijen and Marissing 2011).

Providing a secure base

Most of the clients referred to the clinic suffered disruptive primary relationships, lacked affection and experienced complex trauma. The consequences of these experiences are intimately connected with severe difficulties in bonding. It was hoped that providing a secure base (Bowlby 1988), in addition to the quality of the continuity and framework, would result in a renegotiation of trust. The materials in the art studio acting as a vehicle for dialogue would allow access to both conscious and unconscious content in a holding environment, supporting a re-organization of attachment wounds. Winnicott (1971) located a space between the baby and the mother and called it the transitional space. The environment of the clinic can be visualized as a transitional space between the inner and outside world.

By offering this transitional space between the in and out in art therapy, forensic psychiatric treatment gives good results, especially with patients who still have skills and possibilities for changing and developing, like in Philip's case. These are the patients who will probably return to an independent life in society. These patients in general do not have a long history of crime, do not have the burden of severe psychiatric disorders and have a relatively high level of intelligence and education. Within this group of patients, neurotic development patterns are partly contributing to the offence (de Moor 2016).

Case study
Referral
In the beginning of the art therapy process, my aims and interventions are mainly focused on patients' behaviour with the material, and on increasing the intensity of the artmaking process. Interventions relating to form, shape and symbolism will be directed later in the process. I strive to allow patients, within the safe environment, to have as much control as possible in their therapy processes. Philip was referred by the treatment coordinator to follow an art therapy programme, which is standard procedure when a patient arrives for treatment. During the first six weeks in the forensic unit, patients are obliged to follow the assessment programme.

Prior to the first session I had to pick Philip up from his room at the unit where he stays. Observing him, it was clear Philip was scared and lonely in his new environment. He was, however, immediately interested in art therapy, as he told me when we walked together to the art therapy studio. When starting the first session, I talked to Philip about art therapy, explaining that we work with goals in the treatment and that both he and I should agree and find commitment about these aims. Philip was pleased he could have input regarding what he wanted to work on in therapy. We set the following goals: exploring possibilities for art therapy, especially on expressing emotions, as well as exploring impulsive behaviour and ambivalent thinking.

First sessions
During the introductory session, Philip was able to put into words what he needed to work on, saying: 'I have the tendency to suppress feelings and emotions. That's what makes me vulnerable. This happens

when I have more tension. I am very sensitive and scared to get hurt. I am also an 'all-or-nothing' thinker and I can get disturbed when there are interpretations about my being.' Philip told me he had almost no experience in working with art and wanted to be given assignments for the first sessions. His first assignment was to try to work intensively within the given time, to make an art piece, by using lines and squares. I couldn't persuade Philip to work with paint. He only wanted to work with pencil on a small piece of paper. I was not insistent, allowing Philip to have these materials. Philip showed resistance regarding the material choices. However, he accepted the squares and lines. Rather than confronting him about conditions within the art therapy, I wanted to build up a reliable and trustful therapeutic relationship.

At the second session, Philip worked on an assignment, taking circles as a starting point. He told me he had a good art therapy session and liked the working process. However, on the same day, Philip had a urine control problem in the morning and was very upset about this. When I reflected on this with him and asked him to have some understanding for his treatment, he reacted in a verbally aggressive manner. He didn't want to be interrupted. In the evaluation it became clear he interpreted my intervention and intention differently. Philip labelled the incident (urine control) in a negative way (mistrust) and became impulsive and aggressive. I recognized the narrow thinking, which also related to his sexual offences. Philip's ambivalent thinking, where he felt rejected by women, took place over a long time and led in the end to his acting without any sense of reality.

Reflecting on Philip's working process, it showed Philip was very creative, able to combine visual data and benefit from art therapy. Philip preferred working rationally in his artwork. The treatment team in the clinic accepted my recommendations for ongoing art therapy.

Building a therapeutic work alliance

Philip and I agreed to connect his needs to work with line, form and composition. He had a preference to combine shape and form in his artwork. When he begun an art piece, he took time to think first. During the working process, he made jokes and tried to seduce me by extolling the benefits of art therapy, watching me while he worked. He seemed to be in a trance, then he smiled with a naughty expression. At the end of the session, he was happy with his work and reported with pride that he made his first production in colour.

In the tenth session, Philip's assignment was to make a composition with curved lines. I observed that he first worked out a landscape composed out of straight lines and squares. He was not following the instructions. I chose not to react to this because I saw he was really focused and engaging with the material. At the end of the session, I asked why he worked on the assignment in this way (see Figure 13.1). Philip replied that he had this idea already in his mind before I gave the assignment. We spoke about this behaviour, concluding that Philip was holding tight to his intention but was also open to my external influences, even though the assignment and therapeutic agreement were different.

Figure 13.1: Painting with squares

Evaluation and conclusion after 12 weeks of art therapy

At the end of the first three months we had a review. We looked at all his artwork in chronological order, starting from session one. I invited Philip to verbalize what he observed when looking at his art as if he did not make it himself. He said: 'Philip is creative, his choices for artistic problem-solving are not logical at first sight. He chooses contrast, shapes and forms.' Philip's urge for perfection related to his need for total control. He asked me to watch over him during moments in therapy when he got annoyed and irritated. He wanted me to give him feedback during these moments.

The aim for this period in art therapy was learning to work through Philip's impulsive and aggressive behaviour, with the possibility for him to recognize, accept and verbalize his actions, reducing ambivalent thinking. At the start of the session, Philip said he felt like shit and did not want to use examples out of a magazine. Philip wanted to change our agreement because aiming for perfection is difficult. I allowed him to work more freely. He was responding freely to the material and told me he would like to explore different materials. Philip worked with control and at the same time in a loose way. He wanted to transform it into a graffiti artwork and use spray.

I supported his need and Philip enjoyed the new material. Philip made a composition inspired by an image taken from a magazine. He was searching and looking, not focusing on artistic quality, working spontaneously and flexibly with the material (see Figure 13.2).

Figure 13.2: The corridor (see colour section)

From this moment he needed less support from me. It seemed Philip found his safe space in the art studio. By letting go he found trust. In the art therapy sessions thereafter, Philip experimented as much as he could with paint, gouache and graffiti. It seemed Philip accepted the art therapy as a whole: time, medium, context and me, trusting more on his creative skills and problem-solving abilities and felt safe in our therapeutic relationship.

Increasing intensity in artmaking

Philip entered a point in his therapeutic process where he could decide to work more expressively in an emotional way. At this point in his treatment, Philip spoke openly about his offence to the treatment team. The underlying themes in his offence were low self-esteem, fear of being rejected, feeling shameful about his sexual feelings, and his need for self-control. We agreed he would bring these themes into the session, and that I would give suggestions for materials. I wanted to give him materials with more possibilities for expressing feelings in different physical ways. The following session he brought up a theme relating to being in prison. I gave him acrylic paint and large brushes. Philip was interested in using an old cardboard panel. It had a strange angular and edgy shape. He titled his art piece 'Alleen!' (Alone!) (Figure 13.3). The expressiveness felt powerful. During the making process, I noticed Philip was restless. For the first time, Philip was able to shape his emotional experience in an artistic form.

Figure 13.3: Alleen!

Exploring the outside world

After four weeks of summer break we resumed therapy. When Philip entered the art studio, he looked restless and irritated, he was feeling frustrated about his situation at the forensic unit. He had acted verbally aggressively to his mentor during the summer, feeling the need to get out. At the same time he was happy because he might finish his high school diploma that year while he was in the unit. We agreed he should try to explore his feelings in the artwork. Before starting, Philip told me that he had an idea that didn't fit with the agreement we made before. He seemed insecure.

My suggestion was to drop the agreement and start expressing and playing, by suggesting I could be next to him and embrace the unknown. He put the paint firmly on the canvas. The painting was powerful, symbolic, and a bit dark, with a lively structure (Figure 13.4).

Figure 13.4: Nobody fuckz with me

Philip's art piece had intense expression. He shared with me that he had been sexually harassed, around the age of six, by older boys. It was the first time in the treatment he shared this traumatic material with me. I receive the material as a form of intense countertransference. After digesting my own emotions in supervision, I concluded that Philip needed me as a father figure. The shared experience and symbolic language developed through the materials made Philip secure enough to explore the idea of the outside world (Winnicott 1971).

In the following sessions, Philip and I agreed to explore the feelings of shame, related to his background. I thought it was important to focus on his early traumatic events before starting to introduce the crime he committed. I give Philip a huge board to work on. His theme was holidays. Philip worked for three weeks on this piece. In a short evaluation, Philip explained what he experienced during the first sexual crime he committed when he was 16, with an 11-year-old girl. He was participating in a bush-craft camp and told people he was 18 and staying by himself. Everybody thought he was on holiday alone. People at the camp were very friendly with each other. Nobody had any idea of what emotional and confused state he was in. Philip used the session to represent the last days before the offence.

The composition of the painting looked very empty, focusing on the horizon with himself sitting on a horse. The piece depicted a deep and dark loneliness. Philip shared with me that he felt moments of loneliness and became fascinated by, and attracted to, young girls. He wanted to explore if he really had those kinds of feelings. He was feeling trapped, lost all sight of reality and could not overlook the consequences of his actions. He was not able to overlook his obsessive and controlled thinking and behaving. After making this piece, Philip was sad and emotionally empty. However, he was able to get back into the here-and-now.

In the following three sessions Philip wanted to explore fewer heavy themes. He made an artwork about happy memories; sun, summer and happiness. As the image progressed over time, it revealed an important theme. The final art piece (Figure 13.5) was very expressive and turned out to be a self-portrait.

Figure 13.5: Self-portrait

Philip was content with the emerging function of the art piece. He started the process in a relaxed way, making connections with both the shape and the content of the artwork. He told me he felt the need to project himself into the painting. The physical contact with the paint, brushes and canvas gave him the association of his position in life. Philip felt the same loneliness as he felt when he was looking for emotional contact at the time of his last offence. In this offence he forced a woman in her late thirties to tongue kiss him.

Review after 45 sessions

Just before the Christmas break, we had a review. We hung up all his art pieces to evaluate them. Philip felt very proud of what he had made, commenting: 'It's so diverse that it could be made by several people. The compositions were built up by different visual elements.' Some pieces gave a sinister and aggressive impression, especially with the use of a palette knife and large brushes, used to expresses Philip's potency. Sometimes the brush or the palette knife made cuts in the canvas or paper.

Philip worked extremely very hard during the next three months. He made artwork with themes about his school days, his youth, holidays, and later focused more on the moments around his offences. Philip was discovering a free and playful way of using the materials. The use of brushes and palette knives were his preferred choice. In some of the work his aggression is visible and sensible. At this stage, Philip achieved a lot by expressing emotions and controlling his actions with others, and by regulating his aggression. During the last months, content and shape were emerging simultaneously. Philip was able to stay in the process allowing him to reflect upon his offence and give it place in his life.

Expressing the crime (sessions 46–58)

After the Christmas break, we had a long conversation about trust. Philip shared with me his fear when he forms an attachment to another person. In the meantime, we were looking together at the artworks Philip had made before. The self-portrait especially motivated him. Philip said: 'I want to share myself.' I experienced this as a next step in trust and growth in his identity development. I suggested to him to do a 'trust-exercise'.

We started by making a plaster mask of Philip's face. For that he had to give himself, literally, into my hands. Philip stood still for almost a whole hour while I put plaster gently on his face. He was able to breathe only through his nose for 30 minutes. During this process, I noticed his intense physical reactions: shivering and trembling. When the plaster was dry enough, we took off the mask. Philip was disorientated for a few minutes, after a while he started to cry slightly, and he was looking very lonely. I addressed my observations to him about his emotional state, which helped Philip to get back in the here-and-now.

In the following sessions, Philip chose to work with plaster and clay. Philip was able to reflect more about what the making, touching and feeling of the materials were evoking in him, resulting in increasing confidence and capacity to express his emotional states. Philip engaged in a theme around identity, creating several sculptures and masks (see Figure 13.6 for an example). According to Philip, these pieces represented meaningful stages in his development.

Figure 13.6: Mask

After a few weeks, Philip started a session by taking a lot of clay. In the beginning he was calm and focused, but after 15 minutes he became restless. Philip decided to make a mask (Figure 13.7). Throughout the process Philip was both emotional and restless but able to work. The face he made appears to be his own face, and the tongue is hanging out of his mouth. Philip was able to express his last offence.

Figure 13.7: Clay mask

We took an extra hour to evaluate the art piece. Philip said he worked well and was able to combine shape and content. Philip shared the facts related to the offence and was able to be emotional at the same time. He told me of how he prepared himself the evening of the crime and was seeking contact with a girl. Struggling with his words, he outlined how he made the plan and randomly decided where it should happen. That evening he was out with some friends. They drank beer and smoked joints. When he approached a girl in the bar, his group of friends joked about how he was acting. Philip felt loneliness again and ran out to the street. He passed a supermarket and saw a woman standing next to the entrance. Philip impulsively decided to hit her in her face and jumped on her. When the victim started screaming, he wanted to kiss her. Philip was able to put his tongue in her mouth by using his physical strength. I asked for clarity during his story at various points and at the end of the session encouraged Philip to close this experience emotionally. He was back in reality and able to leave the therapy session.

During the last five sessions, Philip wanted to work with a theme relating to things that were keeping him busy. I advised him to follow the impulses he gets during the artmaking. Philip took some art pieces he made before and decided to transform them into new art. Philip worked on subjects that were present for him, such as finishing high school, social events at the forensic unit, and his treatment in general. In the meantime, Philip was getting a permit to go outside to finish high school. Leave was granted according to progress made in treatment in general. As a result of having this special leave, Philip was having more distance from the other patients, reflecting that many of them were negative in their interactions and behaviour towards others.

Final review after 58 sessions

Philip and I had a final two-hour evaluation. In the aims Philip worked on for himself, he was able to deal with his disruptions during the process and could express himself better emotionally. In his way of engaging with the materials there was a shift. Elements and forms were less rational, and materials were used more playfully and with more expressive strength. Philip was able to look at things together with me, and at the same time became able to make his own decisions. In the direct contact during the working process, there was less verbal interaction between us; the interaction took place between Philip and the materials. Philip was able to trust himself throughout the process. It was positive that Philip gained insight into how his moods could be influenced by external events. When feeling overwhelmed, it was important for Philip to take time to process events through his art and the art materials.

Evaluating the specific themes and aims within the individual art therapy, we concluded that Philip was ready to end the individual therapy. Philip was attending high school four days a week. Philip was able to participate in an open studio group. Artmaking in the open studio group would give him support during his new stage in treatment. Philip was able to express himself through his artmaking, and the weekly space in the open studio gave him the continuity of exploring and developing.

Conclusions

The main aim in the treatment of forensic psychiatric patients is to reduce the offensive behaviour, but it is difficult to get through the thoughts and emotions around these behaviours. Adapted behaviour is very common within this group of patients, and that makes this population difficult to treat in general.

Patients like Philip seek stability in structure and rules, and as a result they are capable of showing doubt and emotions. In expressing and working in art materials, Philip was not only showing himself, he was also being himself. Art working is undisguised and it very often results, in the first instance, in many patients fearing this uncontrollable medium, and showing a great deal of resistance.

In Philip's process, he started with a pre-problem: suffering from developmental disturbances visualized in his antisocial personality development. Philip was not able to explain or verbalize how his (sexual) problems came about as a result of aberrant behaviour developed during his early childhood. The pre-problem seriously challenged the therapeutic process because Philip started with a lack of healthy interaction structures, which made the engagement in the therapeutic alliance very complex. Art therapy offered a way to trust the world around him, and by gaining trust he gained the ability to grow and develop.

Most treatment offered in forensic psychiatry is verbally orientated. Art therapy treatment in forensic psychiatry is a powerful form of therapy because it encourages the patient to act differently and offers new experiences in the present moment. These (artistic) processes and experiences are mainly outside the cognitive layer, and, as a result of that, art therapy has obtained a unique position in the treatment of sexual offenders. If the art therapist is able to foster the patient's work through the materials, things can be visible that otherwise would have stayed hidden. Even though the patient will take over control again during verbal review (like we observed in Philip's treatment) and will try to explain their acts, the experiences during the artmaking process and the product of the process will remain as visible clues for their thoughts, feelings and behaviour.

The forensic patient who is forced to change their behaviour needs contact with their thoughts, feelings and fantasies. Philip learned to trust himself and others by engaging in the artistic process. He connected to his vulnerable side and achieved insight on his offensive behaviour and crime; instead of developing unhealthy interaction patterns, Philip reversed the development of his personality problems in such a healthy and positive way that he was ready to re-integrate in society with enough trust in himself and the world around him.

Acknowledgements
Grateful thanks to my patient Philip, current and previous members of my team for the supportive discussions, my editors Simon Hastilow and Marian Liebmann for their feedback, and last but not least to my art therapy colleague Marcela Andrade del Corro for her support and critical comments on the early draft of this chapter.

References
Bowlby, J. (1988) *A Secure Base: Clinical Applications of Attachment Theory*. London: Routledge.
Cordess, C. and Cox, M. (eds) (1996) *Forensic Psychotherapy: Crime, Psychodynamics and the Offender Patient*. London: Jessica Kingsley Publishers.
de Moor, T. (2016) 'An Art-based Exploration in Forensic Treatment in The Netherlands'. In K. Rothwell (ed.) *Forensic Arts Therapies: Anthology of Practice and Research*. (pp.371–384). London: Free Association Books.
Donisch-Seidel, U. (1996) *Konzeptvorlage für Forensische Psychotherapie and Pädagogig*. Bedburg-Hau: Rheinische Kliniken Bedburg-Hau.
Haeyen, S. (2018a) *Art Therapy and Emotion Regulation Problems: Theory and Workbook*. London: Palgrave Macmillan.
Haeyen, S. (2018b) *Effects of Art Therapy: The Case of Personality Disorders cluster B/C.* (Dissertation manuscript). Radboud University, Nijmegen.
Hass-Cohen, N. and Carr, R. (2008) *Art Therapy and Clinical Neuroscience*. London: Jessica Kingsley Publishers.
Hellinga, G. (1997) *Lastige Lieden: Over de Grens tussen Psychiatrie en Psychotherapie*. Nijmegen: HAN/VDO.
Hinz, L.D. (2009) *Expressive Therapies Continuum: A Framework for Using Art in Therapy*. New York, NY: Routledge.
Hodgins, S. and Muller-Isberner, R. (2000) *Violence, Crime and Mentally Disordered Offenders*. Chichester: Wiley.
Keulen-de Vos (2013) *Emotional States and Violence*. Maastricht: University Press.
Liebmann, M. (2008) *Art Therapy and Anger*. London: Jessica Kingsley Publishers.
Lusebrink, V.B. (1990) *Imagery and Visual Expression in Therapy*. New York, NY: Plenum Press.
Muijen, H. and Marissing, L. (2011) *'Iets' maken*. (Making 'something'.) Antwerpen: Garant.
Schnabel, P. and Sorbi, K. (1993) 'Effect en process: Meer aandacht voor het einde van psychotherapie.' *Tijdschrift voor Psychotherapie 19*, 5, 271–284.
Smeijsters, H. and Cleven, G. (2006) 'The treatment of aggression using arts therapies in forensic psychiatry: Results of a qualitative inquiry.' *The Arts in Psychotherapy 33*, 37–58.
Smeijsters, H. (2007) *Agressieregulatie in de Forensische Psychiatrie*. Heerlen: KenVak.
Smeijsters, H. (2008) *Handboek Creatieve Therapie*. Bussum: Couthino.
Smeijsters, H., Kil, J., Kurtsjens, H., Welten, J. and Willemars, G. (2011) 'Arts therapies for young offenders in secure care – a practice-based research.' *The Arts in Psychotherapy 38*, 41–51.

Stern, D. (1985) *The Interpersonal World of the Infant.* New York, NY: Basic Books.

van der Gaag, M. and van der Plas, J. (1997) *Doelgericht Begeleiden van Psychiatrische Patienten.* (Effective Treatment of Psychiatric Patients.) Utrecht: De Tijdstroom.

van Marle, H. (1995) *Een Gesloten Systeem: Een Psychoanalytisch Kader voor de Verpleging en Behandeling van TBS-Gestelden.* (A Closed System: A Psychoanalytic Frame for the Care and Treatment of Forensic Patients.) Arnhem: Gouda Quint.

Winnicott, D.W. (1971) *Playing and Reality.* London: Routledge.

CHAPTER 14

Knowing Me, Knowing You

Bodies in Relationship, Working with Adolescents with
Learning Disabilities and Harmful Sexual Behaviours

KATE SNOWDEN, DANCE MOVEMENT PSYCHOTHERAPIST

Introduction

This chapter is informed by my clinical and managerial experiences as a dance movement psychotherapist working within a charity organization that works therapeutically with people with learning disabilities who have experiences of abuse and trauma. The organization's work is underpinned by attachment, psychodynamic theory, trauma and systemic models. The charity works with survivors of abuse, offenders of violence and sexual violence and individuals at risk of offending. The charity is placed within an urban area and works in a centrally located clinic and also within several schools including primary, secondary and special needs schools.

Creative arts therapists are working in this field because the arts allow for playful, indirect, non-verbal and spontaneous ways of working, which can often be more accessible to young people with learning disabilities (Upton 2009). Dance movement psychotherapy (DMP) recognizes bodily knowledge as central to therapeutic change within a creative and dynamic therapeutic relationship. DMP recognizes body movement as an implicit and expressive instrument of communication and expression. DMP is a relational process in which client and therapist engage in an empathic creative process using body movement and dance to assist the integration of emotional, cognitive, physical, social and spiritual aspects of the self.[1] When the body is located as central, there is an appreciation that we live and learn through our bodies, and our differences are honoured (Best 2005). Focusing on the body and engaging with my 'felt-sense' (Ghendlin 1996) seems crucial to me when working in this field, as the bodies and minds of people with learning disabilities in the wider society are often devalued, rejected and abused (Cottis 2009).

We learn-in-relation (Best 2005), yet opportunities for positive relationships for adolescents with learning disabilities can sometimes be limited or overly supervised. Curen states that 'the expression of [a healthy] sexuality relies on an understanding of our motivation and our desires' (Curen 2009, p.93). For people with learning disabilities, this can sometimes be disjointed or fragmented. It makes sense to me that to know one's own sexuality requires a connection to one's whole body and mind, and this supports working within a DMP approach. A DMP framework allows for opportunities to creatively express and explore how our bodies and experiences are shaped by and are shaping the therapeutic relationship. It is an opportunity for us both to learn about ourselves and the other (Best 2005).

In this chapter I intend to explore how, as a dance movement psychotherapist, I engage with my bodily knowledge in the moment-to-moment, live relational experiences with the client and also in DMP supervision, using models of interactional shaping and person positioning (Best 2003, 2008, 2010b). For me, this leads to multiple understandings and meaning-making of my bodily somatic information that supports communication between the different parts of myself: the unconscious and conscious, the personal and the professional, my historical, present and future experiences (Best 2010b). This I feel supports the integration and expression of the fragmented and denied parts of the self both in the therapist and in the client. The outcome of this leads to an increased awareness of our body-selves and our relational-selves. With this greater clarity and capacity to know ourselves in relationship we are able to acknowledge our differences and our impact on others, with the hope that feeling more leads to less acting out of harmful sexual behaviours.

---

1 See the website of the Association for Dance Movement Psychotherapy UK: www.admp.org.uk

Learning disability, trauma and vulnerability

A learning disability is defined by the Department of Health as a 'significant reduced ability to understand new or complex information, to learn new skills (impaired intelligence), with a reduced ability to cope independently (impaired social functioning), which started before adulthood' (Department of Health 2001, p.14).

Learning disabilities arise from abnormal brain development. Possible causes include an inherited condition, chromosome abnormalities, complications during birth resulting in a lack of oxygen to the brain, a very premature birth, an injury to the brain in early childhood as a result of an accident or physical abuse, and neglect due to deprived experiences of relating, or possibly multiple traumas.

Parents of a child with a learning disability are likely to hold mixed and complex feelings of shame, blame, anger and grief for the loss of the healthy hoped-for baby (Cottis 2009). If these feelings are left unprocessed, it can be damaging to the development of a secure attachment and the learning-disabled child may internalize this sense of shame, compounding feelings of loss and adding further trauma. Society can be cruel towards people with learning disabilities, acting in harmful, abusive, devaluing and rejecting ways, adding multiple experiences of trauma that the learning-disabled young person and their family has to face and process (Cottis 2009). The learning-disabled young person may further internalize this and develop a sense of self as bad (Alvarez 1992).

Of course, many young people with learning disabilities are very much loved by their families, and I am not saying that this is the experience of every learning-disabled young person. However, when we can begin to understand the level of trauma and abuse that a young person with a learning disability may encounter, we can begin to understand why feelings of rage, hurt, shame and confusion might be experienced, and finding safe ways to connect with others might become complicated.

Harmful sexual behaviour

There is no one agreed definition of harmful sexual behaviour (HSB). However, taken from the Barnardo's report to a parliamentary inquiry into support and sanctions for children who display harmful sexual behaviour, one helpful definition is:

> Harmful sexual behaviour is when children and young people (under 18) engage in sexual discussions or activities that are inappropriate for their age or stage of development, often with other individuals who they have power over by virtue of age, emotional maturity, gender, physical strength, or intellect and where the victim in this relationship has suffered a betrayal of trust. These activities can range from using sexually explicit words and phrases to full penetrative sex with other children or adults. …the term harmful sexual behaviour encompasses both sexually abusive behaviour – i.e. where one child manipulates or coerces another; and sexually problematic or concerning behaviour – where there is no victimisation, but where the behaviour negatively interferes with the child's development. (Ghani 2016, p.10)

This parliamentary inquiry found that there is no definitive data on the prevalence of HSB. Figures from police forces in England and Wales in 2013/14, showed that 4209 children and young people under 18 years of age were recorded as perpetrators of sexual offences against other children and young people. The report highlights that as the age of criminal responsibility in England and Wales is ten years old, HSB displayed by children under ten cannot be viewed as an offence and is therefore not recorded in the same way. The inquiry heard that research has generally indicated that around a third of incidents of sexual abuse involve children or adolescents as perpetrators, some studies suggest that this is as high as 65 percent.

The inquiry suggested factors that place some young people at risk of developing HSB. These factors include children who have experienced abuse and neglect, including sexual, physical and emotional abuse. This does not mean that all children who have been abused will go on to become perpetrators themselves, but in some cases the child's behaviour may be a direct consequence of their own experience of being sexualized through abuse (Ghani 2016). Therefore, we might view the harmful sexual behaviours as a communication of something of their experiences of abusive relationships and trauma, and a possible acting out of their internalized sense of shame and projection of their sense of self as bad (Corbett 2014).

Another factor identified in the inquiry was poor social competences and learning disabilities. It suggests that children who display HSB often have poor social skills, a lack of sexual knowledge and high levels of social anxiety. The report highlights that for some young people the combination of poor social ability, low self-esteem and emotional difficulties can lead to problems in establishing appropriate intimate relationships, and that they attempt to solve this through abusive relations with other children. However, research cautions against concluding that children and young people with learning disabilities and autism spectrum disorder are more likely to sexually abuse than their peers. This group may be over-represented in the data due to factors relating to their presentation, such as repeating the same patterns of offending, habitual selection of victims, the impulsiveness in their offending, and their naivety when challenged (Ghani 2016).

There is more to be researched in understanding the links between HSB and child sexual exploitation (CSE). However, we know from another Barnardo's report that young people with learning disabilities are particularly vulnerable to CSE because they tend to be overprotected from potential harm (Franklin, Raws and Smeaton 2015). Society struggles to view them as sexual beings, they experience higher levels of social isolation compared with their non-learning-disabled peers, there is a lack of specialist education on sex and relationships, and there is a lack of awareness among professionals about their vulnerability to sexual exploitation. This then contributes to a lack in multi-agency working and effective interventions, which consequently leaves young people with learning disabilities unprotected in relation to experiencing sexual harm, and/or becoming perpetrators of harm.

The Three Secrets of Disability

The Three Secrets of Disability, as described by Sheila Hollins (Hollins and Sinason 2000), is, I feel, a helpful framework to use when making sense of young people with learning disabilities who are engaging in harmful sexual behaviours. Hollins talks about *sex*, *dependency* and *death* being core themes in therapeutic work with people with learning disabilities, and all three issues are influenced by the presence of the disability.

Sex can be experienced by the parents and unconsciously by their child as something potentially destructive and harmful, rather than something as creative and life-giving. Parents may wish for the disability to end with their child, and as a consequence they may deny the presence of their child's sexuality and/or supress its development by avoiding conversations about sex and relationships and by restricting opportunities that may give space for sexual expression.

It is not uncommon for the child with a learning disability to retain a childlike dependency on their parents; this is co-constructed and shaped by the parents and the child. Continuing to maintain the level of dependency in the parent–child relationship may unconsciously be a way of supressing the development of the child's sexuality.

In my experience it can be difficult and painful for families to be able to express their feelings of grief, loss, blame and shame in relation to having a disabled child. In the wider society, disability can represent trauma and loss and individual responses to this are of course varied, but one way of managing these associated feelings might be to devalue the life of the person with a learning disability; to deny the possibility of a healthy sexuality and to respond in rejecting, harmful, abusive and dehumanizing ways (Cottis 2009).

From within this framework of the three secrets it is possible to say that, for the learning disabled young person, feelings of sexuality and desire may feel powerful, dangerous, potentially destructive and/or as something that needs to remain hidden. It may be these themes that are being expressed in acts of harmful sexual behaviours.

To feel more and act out less: Using a DMP approach

In dance movement psychotherapy (DMP) practice, the body is located centrally in the therapeutic process and in the meaning-making process in DMP supervision. My body is the starting point for living, learning and for understanding clients, understanding myself in relation to clients, and understanding the therapeutic relationship (Best 2005).

Corbett states that the 'therapist acts as an anchor that grounds the learning-disabled client in a sense of his own embodied presence' (Corbett 2009, p.49). This is possible by engaging with my own bodily responses, which supports me to stay present in the moment-to-moment interactions (Best 2010a). My body is the main tool I have for listening and for knowing. Through engaging with my somatic awareness, I have an enlivened sense of myself in-relation, and an awareness of how I am being impacted upon on a somatic level by the client. It is through engaging with pre-verbal and non-verbal ways of listening, and exploring through creative processes in supervision what my body holds about what it's like to be a particular client in this world, that I can understand the subjectivity of the adolescent with a learning disability presenting with harmful sexual behaviours (Best 2008; Frizell 2017). It is also vital for me to explore what my bodily responses are made up of, including my personal and professional selves, my unconscious and conscious, my beliefs and values, and past, present and future experiences.

Relationship is central in creating experiences (Best 2003), and in DMP the intersubjective bodies of the client and the therapist are in a continuous co-creative process (Allegranti 2011). I am curious about how my body narrative is shaped by my interactions with a client, and how I too may be shaping the client. The relational dance between sensing what is mine, what belongs to the client and what is shared allows for the co-construction of a map of feelings (Best 2005), and it is possible to reach multiple understandings of self-and-other in relationship (Best 2003). I feel strongly that I need to engage and experience my whole body when working with this complex client group, sometimes that doesn't even feel enough! I need an awareness of my inside and outside, my front and back, my up and down and the spaces in between.

One construct I have found helpful in holding this process is interactional shaping – a concept developed as a way to observe relationships and explore the relational shaping that takes place between the body of the client and the body of the therapist and the body of the supervisor (Best 2003, 2010). This mutual shaping is both active and passive and takes place unconsciously and consciously between individuals and their environments (Best 2003). The principles of interactional shaping are located within other theoretical perspectives, which I will name briefly here.

Winnicott described the importance of interactional synchrony and mutuality as essential for healthy communication in the mother–infant relationship, marked by the mother's adaptability and synchrony with her infant's heartbeat and breathing (Winnicott 1965). Stern (1985) coined the term 'intersubjective relatedness', which states the importance of the mother's use of shape when attuning with her infant. In terms of models of movement observation, Laban (1992) developed a system that describes movement in relation to the use of the body (actions), where the body moves (space) and how the body moves (qualities or efforts). In Laban's system, space relates to how the body moves in relation to the environment, objects and people, and between its own body parts.

Kestenberg developed these concepts in The Kestenberg Movement Profile (KMP), which is a developmental model that suggests that as we mature, our body-movement patterns evolve over time and psychological development can be observed through these movement patterns (Loman and Foley 1996). The KMP is made up of the Tension-Flow system which relates to the expression of our inner needs, and the Shape-Flow-Shaping system which relates to the development of an individual's relationships to people and their environment. The shape system follows a developmental sequence; the initial phase is Shape-Flow, in which the infant's body shrinks when repulsed and bulges when attracted. The middle phase is Shaping in Directions, where the infant connects with others and objects through pointing. The final phase is Shaping in Planes, in which the individual moulds to their environment and people; this includes using three dimensions, which supports advanced relational connectedness (Loman and Foley 1996). It is this moulding to find connection in the environment that I am curious about in making sense of my relational experiences when working with young people with learning disabilities.

Sinason (1992) writes about the handicapped smile that becomes a secondary handicap in the learning-disabled individual and their families and support networks. The smile can act as a defence against trauma and further abuse for the individual with a learning disability. In my experience individuals with learning disabilities are often described as happy and smiley, but this may be because they are often deprived of expressing negative emotion and are in need of finding ways to fit in and be accepted by others. I sense at times that the young person with a learning disability who is also presenting with harmful sexual behaviours may be shaping me and moulding the therapeutic relationship with a false happy self, perhaps in order to ensure that joy and happiness is mirrored back to them to 'cover the cracks of disappointment' and 'to keep depressed parents happy' (Sinason 1992, p.143). Kestenberg's shaping system relates to how safety is communicated and experienced in the environment (Loman and Merman 1999). I attune to and shape myself in relation to the handicapped smile in order to communicate safety, and for acceptance and validation to be felt in the relationship.

However, I must also find ways to not collude with this smile and to remain authentic to my whole-body experience. In my body, I find ways to hold and give expression to their complex internal feelings that remain hidden, deadened or disallowed, for I feel that an increased synchrony between the inside and outside will lead the client to feel more and act out less (Welldon 1984), and it is DMP supervision that supports me to do this.

The role of the body and the movement relationship in DMP supervision

In DMP supervision, the body and movement are central to exploring the complexities between the therapist-client, therapist-supervisor and the setting. The body is used as 'a receptive instrument for kinaesthetic empathy and imagination and to understand the somatic countertransference' (Payne 2008, p.4). In DMP supervision we are valuing the multiplicity of bodily experiences and knowledge, and the co-construction of meanings of the client material (Best 2010b). Interactional shaping widens the lens of the traditional narrative of transference to include the multiple moment-to-moment experiences of relating (Best 2003).

In DMP supervision, one model that supports me to make sense of the mutual ways we shape one another is Person Positioning. A brief explanation of this is: Position 1 – moving one's own felt sense; Position 2 – moving as the client as a way to explore more about how it feels to be the client; Position 3 – moving Positions 1 and 2 together, which is looking at the therapeutic relationship; and Position 4 – the helicopter view, as a way to create more distance from the therapeutic relationship. It's acknowledged that there are more positions, creating further distance and perspectives to include the social and political viewpoints (Best 2010b). As I move between person-positions working with my felt-sense (Ghendlin 1996) I begin to form a complex body map of feelings that are co-created and perhaps shared between therapist and client(s). By exploring points of overlap and separation I am taking responsibility for what I bring to the therapeutic relationship (Best 2008).

I will now explore various themes that are taken from several supervision sessions when working with a number of clients in this field.

Moving in Position 1: I notice tension in my jaw and tightening around my throat. I reach out with my arms to create circular motions as if welcoming, offering and holding. In relation to my own shape-flow I notice a retraction and shortening in my torso, a moving away from. A conflict in my body becomes apparent, it is both moving towards and away from the client. With this realization I feel somewhat confused, frustrated and guilty. As I move around the room I feel as though I am switching off, disappearing, emptying, an image of a 'no vacancy' sign comes to my mind.

Moving in Position 2: I am very aware of the front of my body – eyes wide, chin propped outwards and a broad smile. I move with my hands behind me, pulling each hand out in turn, opening up my palm as if to reveal something that's been hidden. I feel light-footed and airy, almost jester-like, but inside I feel heavy and sinking.

Moving in Position 3: I feel the need to make noise. I make sounds with my mouth, clap and stamp my feet; sounding out rhythms. I feel solid, enlivened and broad.

Stepping back into Position 4: The words *sounding, release, expression, rhythm* and *synchrony* come to mind.

I transition to image-making as a way to capture the movement experience and form a bridge to verbal reflection, as 'moving between modalities keeps alive the complexity of human experience and expression' (Best 2008, p.141).

When transitioning to verbal (written) reflection I am struck by my choice of colours, which I became aware of as I was drawing (See Figure 14.1). There are both similarities and differences between the therapist (Position 1) on the left of the page and the client (Position 2) on the right. Shades of blue and figures-of-eight shape how we are relating, moving towards but also away from. Perhaps we are practising in how to connect and also separate, playing with distance and safety. The central part of our bodies are the red block and the pink smile. The smile now appears to me more as a grimace with teeth; I question if this is an expression of aggression. I feel the smile is shaping me; it could be why I am relating by moving towards and also away from. I wonder if I am fearful or feeling the need to protect myself. I am curious about the red block in me. I ask myself, what is blocking me? It could be the disguised levels of aggression in the client and myself.

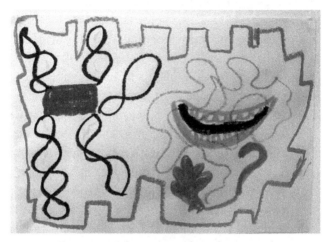

Figure 14.1: Response image (see colour section)

I feel frustrated by the blue hand and the game of 'now you see me, now you don't' which entered my mind as I drew the hand and question mark. I feel a pull to join the game, to seek and to see, but at the same time I feel I need to move away from the game, to manage my feelings of frustration, boredom and anger. I am struck by the theme of power play and how this may be shaping our relationship; this is not surprising, as Corbett (2014) states that the most common factor for forensic patients is that of extreme powerlessness. The blackened mouth links to my somatic internal sense of the client being heavy, which is somewhat masked by the handicapped pink smile. When drawing the blackness, I quickly became aware of themes of trauma, abuse and possible sexual abuse.

The orange line around the outside marks Position 3, the therapeutic relationship. I felt comfort and stability from finding an up-and-down rhythmic structure that I can share with the client, that will hold all of us together and allow for all of our parts to be expressed. I wonder if this may also represent the safe structures within which I work.

This way of working offers me rich information about what it is like to be, to communicate and to be in relationship with this particular client group. It is likely that they have had multiple relationships and experiences of others moving towards them and then also away from them. I feel I need to keep finding possibilities to keep seeing and being with, and to also give permission to my feelings of ambivalence and associated feelings of shame, guilt and judgement.

I need to find ways to create space for, and to allow for the expression of, feelings of aggression and frustration, and this also includes my historical relationship to such feelings in relationships, which could be contributing to the red block in me. I am curious about the smile and how I too am shaped and shape the therapeutic relationship by wanting to be valued and appreciated by the client and the systems within which I work. Holding and embodying empathy with the blackness through a creative, rhythmic and enlivened relationship is central to finding the way towards feeling more and acting out less.

When in supervision, through shifting perspectives playing with possibilities by working across creative modalities and paying attention to qualities of relating, I notice what I am attuned to, and what I am distant from. I am in an alive relationship with my multiple selves and that of the client (Best 2010b). Working in this way allows me to be curious about what I might become more attuned to and to find the space and attention within my body to allow for this. Giving permission for feelings of anger, aggression and the blackness allows for the awakening, enlivening and expression of the parts that have been denied, deadened and disabled in the client and myself. Feelings that can be felt/re-felt, expressed, experienced and integrated contribute to an increased sense of body self, moving towards an increased capacity for body synchrony, authenticity and reflection; to feel more and act out less (Welldon 1984). For being more body aware shapes how we can become more relationally aware. This contributes to an increased awareness of our similarities and differences, our desires and our boundaries, our histories and expectations. With an increased capacity to feel more, there is a development in the capacity to reflect; to speak the unspeakable, and to name experiences of trauma and abuse and how this may have shaped our bodies and our relationships.

Corbett (2009) suggests that, as therapists, we need to be able to stay present to our own experiences in order to be able to hold the hopelessness, dread, deadness and fear that can be overwhelming for our clients and consequently projected into the therapist. We are tasked with being able to allow these painful feelings to be acknowledged, felt and experienced more fully, so that the risk of acting out is reduced. In my experience the pathway to achieve this is through the body, which allows for the early non-verbal, pre-verbal experiences to become known (Corbett 2014).

Conclusion

When working therapeutically with young people with learning disabilities who are presenting as risky in terms of harmful sexual behaviours, I have found that being able to access pre-verbal and non-verbal ways of working supports a more authentic feeling-self and relational-self to develop. Using my own bodily knowledge, arising from being with clients and through movement supervision using models of interactional shaping and person positioning, I am able to attune to the parts of myself and the client that have been masked by the secondary handicap, as well as feelings that have been denied and disabled. Becoming more engaged with our bodies allows for an increased capacity to feel and to relate authentically. Over time, the development of feelingful thinking (Alvarez 2012) can lead to a greater capacity to reflect together on the impact of disability and being good-enough, sexuality and the desire for relationships, and the capacity to empathize with one's own experiences of abuse and personal victimhood (Curen 2009), thus leading to less acting out of harmful sexual behaviours.

Implications for the future

Responding appropriately to harmful sexual behaviours can help prevent young people becoming victims and/or perpetrators of child sexual exploitation.

When planning the appropriate interventions, it is important to balance the interplay between an individual's vulnerability and their level of potential risk. It is crucial that the young person receives the level of support that recognizes their lived experiences of having a disability and the impact of early and ongoing trauma. Interventions must also ensure the safety of others at the same time as upholding the human rights, and the possibility for growth and development, of the potential offender (Curen 2009).

Children displaying HSB are often supported either within the child protection system or the criminal justice system. It appears that our systems lack the services for early intervention in relation to HSB. I suggest that more support and multi-agency working needs to be established as a preventative approach within the community and schools. The Barnardo's reports highlight a need for more sex and relationship education, and for this to be specific for young people with learning disabilities. Recommendations for young people with learning disabilities include interventions that support the development of social skills, having increased opportunities to develop positive relationships and building self-esteem, and I suggest that this would contribute to reduced rates of HSB in this client group.

It is important to remember the role of the family and the impact that having children with learning disabilities who may also be displaying HSB has on the whole family, including feelings of fear, shock, denial, guilt, shame and self-blame. Therefore, offering therapeutic support for the family could support the whole family system to feel understood, safer and more contained, leading to a reduction in levels of HSB.

I suggest that more needs to be done at a political and societal level that will help shape all of us in ways of understanding the needs and experiences of people with learning disabilities, leading to increased acceptance and cohesion, which may well lead to decreased levels of harmful sexual behaviours being expressed in young people with learning disabilities.

References

Allegranti, B. (2011) *Embodied Performances: Sexuality, Gender, Bodies.* Basingstoke: Palgrave Macmillan.

Alvarez, A. (1992) *Live Company.* London: Routledge.

Alvarez, A. (2012) *The Thinking Heart: Three Levels of Psychoanalytic Therapy with Disturbed Children.* Hove: Routledge

Best, P. (2003) 'Interactional Shaping within therapeutic encounters: Three dimensional dialogues.' *USA Psychotherapy Journal 2,* 2, 26–44.

Best, P. (2005) 'Embodied choices and voices.' *E-motion XIV,* 12, 12–15.

Best, P. (2008) 'Interactive Reflections: Moving Between Modes of Expression as a Model for Supervision.' In H. Payne (ed.) *Supervision of Dance Movement Psychotherapy: A Practitioner's Handbook.* Hove: Routledge.

Best, P. (2010a) 'Creative Tension: Dance Therapists Shaping Laban's Ideas'. In V. Preston-Dunlop and L. Sayers (eds) *The Dynamic Body in Space: Developing Rudolf Laban's Ideas for the 21st Century.* London: Dance Books.

Best, P. (2010b) 'Observing Interactions Being Shaped: Multiple Perspectives within Supervision.' In S. Bender (ed.) *Movement Analysis of Interaction.* Berlin: Logos Verlag Berlin.

Corbett, A. (2009) 'Words as a Second Language: The Psychotherapeutic Challenge of Severe Intellectual Disability.' In T. Cottis (ed.) *Intellectual Disability, Trauma and Psychotherapy.* Hove: Routledge.

Corbett, A. (2014) *Disabling Perversions: Forensic Psychotherapy with People with Intellectual Disabilities*. London: Karnac.

Cottis, T. (2009) 'Love Hurts: The Emotional Impact of Intellectual Disability and Sexual Abuse on a Family.' In T. Cottis (ed.) *Intellectual Disability, Trauma and Psychotherapy*. Hove: Routledge.

Curen, R. (2009) '"Can they see in the door?" Issues in the Assessment and Treatment of Sex Offenders Who Have Intellectual Disabilities.' In T. Cottis (ed.) *Intellectual Disability, Trauma and Psychotherapy*. Hove: Routledge.

Department of Health (2001) *Valuing People: A New Strategy for Learning Disability for the 21st Century*. London: Department of Health.

Franklin, A., Raws, P. and Smeaton, E. (2015) *Unprotected, Overprotected: Meeting the Needs of Young People with Learning Disabilities Who Experience, or Are at Risk of, Sexual Exploitation*. London: The Children's Society.

Frizell, C. (2017) 'Entering the World: Dance Movement Psychotherapy and the Complexity of Beginnings with Learning Disabled Clients.' In G. Unkovich, C. Butte and J. Butler (eds) *Dance Movement Psychotherapy with People with Learning Disabilities*. Oxford: Routledge.

Ghani, N. (2016) *Now I Know It Was Wrong: Report of the Parliamentary Inquiry into Support and Sanctions for Children Who Display Harmful Sexual Behaviour*. Ilford: Barnardo's.

Ghendlin, E. (1996) *Focusing-oriented Psychotherapy: A Manual of the Experiential Method*. New York, NY: Guilford Press.

Hollins, H. and Sinason, V. (2000) 'Psychotherapy, learning disabilities and trauma: New perspectives.' *British Journal of Psychiatry 176, 37–41*.

Laban, R. (1992) *The Mastery of Movement* (Revised edn). Plymouth: Northcote House.

Loman, S. and Foley, L. (1996) 'Models for understanding the nonverbal process in relationships.' *The Arts in Psychotherapy 23, 341–350*.

Loman, S. and Merman, H. (1999) 'The KMP as a tool for dance/movement therapy.' *American Journal of Dance Therapy 18, 1, 29–52*.

Payne, H. (2008) 'Supervision in Dance Movement Psychotherapy: An Overview.' In H. Payne (ed.) *Supervision of Dance Movement Psychotherapy: A Practitioner's Handbook*. Hove: Routledge.

Sinason, V. (1992) *Mental Handicap and the Human Condition: New Approaches from the Tavistock*. London: Free Association Books.

Stern, D. (1985) *The Interpersonal World of the Infant: A View from Psychoanalysis and Developmental Psychology*. New York, NY: Basic Books.

Upton, J. (2009) 'When Words Are Not Enough: Creative Therapeutic Approaches.' In T. Cottis (ed.) *Intellectual Disability, Trauma and Psychotherapy*. Hove: Routledge.

Welldon, E.V. (1984) 'Application of Group Psychotherapy to Those with Sexual Perversions.' In T.E. Lear (ed.) *Spheres of Group Analysis*. London: Leinster Leader.

Winnicott, D.W. (1965) *The Maturational Process and the Facilitating Environment*. New York, NY: International Universities Press.

CHAPTER 15

Art Therapy with Long-Term Patients at Risk of Sexual Offending

LUCY GIBSON-HILL, ART PSYCHOTHERAPIST

Introduction

We often consider sex offenders to have committed abhorrent acts which repulse a society that struggles to understand how we can build a rapport to work with them. There are also men who have been incarcerated for decades for acts that society can tolerate – validated by the minimal prison sentence they are given – but who are considered too much of a risk to return to the community. In this chapter, I consider two such men who are a risk to others and themselves due to their impulsiveness and entrenched anger related to sexualized behaviour or threats.

Harry and Charles have almost polar opposite sexual experiences, but some very strong similarities in their upbringing and time in hospital. They reside in a low-secure hospital using a recovery model that supports working towards discharge and requiring active therapeutic engagement. They have engaged in art therapy for over three years. They attended groups separately and together, and having built a rapport, now attend a session together.

Working with sexual offending can be extremely challenging for both patients and professionals. It is particularly difficult when there is a damaged early attachment resulting in a perverse relationship to care and ambivalence towards discharge, as discussed by Ruszczynski (2010).

This chapter considers the benefit of art therapy at the point of reaching a low-secure hospital, following decades of incarceration in high- to medium-secure boarding schools, hospitals and prisons. At this point the work focuses on conscious and unconscious processing of repressed emotions related to entrenched institutional abuse and previous experiences of emotional deprivation or abusive family relationships. I will explore how treating the current presentation is paramount in addressing the index offence; and how the therapeutic relationship can address both.

I will focus on the importance of trust in the therapeutic relationship, and the difficulty of holding on to hope. The process of image-making has enabled the building of a relationship, in which the painful experiences leading up to the offences, and the offences themselves, can be discussed. We can also reflect on current incidents of acting out in relation to sexual offending – such as why threats to rape and boasting of sexual conquests are present when feelings become intolerable.

The system

For their sexual offences, Harry and Charles had each been given a prison sentence of under two years. But both men have now completed the equivalent of life sentences under the Mental Health Act 1983 (and as amended in 2007), with the rationale of preventing sexual offending. This can happen when someone is considered 'unfit to plead' in court and is given a sentence, but also placed on a hospital order that requires the Ministry of Justice or the consultant psychiatrist (depending on which section the order was made under) to revoke it. Another way it can happen is that people become unwell in prison and are sent to a forensic mental health unit until they are assessed as well enough to be discharged. Serious incidents whilst in a low-secure unit can lead to moving back to medium- or high-secure conditions, lengthening the process. In addition, behavioural issues often result from being locked up with other very unwell people, or from being known as a 'sex offender'; and decades of repressed emotions may emerge during the recovery process, leading to acting-out behaviour. All these factors may lead to the patient being considered too high a risk to be out in the community even on leave.

Such men are detained due to the prospective risk of escalated violent sexual offending in relation to the sexual assault already committed.

Risk is assessed in all aspects of the patients' daily lives. There is a risk meeting every six months to consider previous presentation and future management. The ultimate question is whether discharge is possible.

The men

Harry and Charles have not progressed to discharge, due to their aggressive presentation and previous inability to engage successfully in talking therapies. Both men have a personality disorder and share a history of traumatic childhood experiences. They both have suspected brain injury and are considered likely to be on the autism spectrum. They are developmentally stuck at the latency stage and have unprocessed anger at the institutional abuse they have experienced. This creates a barrier to reflective capacity and causes difficulty in taking responsibility, therefore not meeting what is required psychologically for working on risk.

They have both experienced being in care and having allegations made against them from a young age, which has implications for their current assessment. Charles is reported to have burned down the family home and Harry is reported to have threatened to rape his mother, both at primary school age. Although these events are unsubstantiated, they creep into current risk meetings and care plan meetings.

There have been violent reactive behaviours to being locked up, which have resulted in additional offences whilst incarcerated. Both men express anger at being locked up for so much of their lives, and sadness at the years that have been lost, entwined in ambivalence about discharge. There is uncertainty about how to function independently after being in services so long, paired with an unrealistic expectation that society has remained the same over the past 30 years. Neither man has had unescorted leave in the decades they have been locked up.

For me as a female therapist who is younger than both men, the work is a constant balancing act between their sexual transference and the real human relationship we have been able to achieve. The therapeutic alliance is key to being able to work on the uncomfortable feelings, and for the men to feel heard in sharing experiences. I am challenging whilst offering reasons behind my thought processes, helping them work through experiences and feelings around attachment and jealousy. I have been aware of the erotic transference of sharing an art therapist (Schaverien 1995, chapter 2). I have experienced this through statements such as 'If you were my wife' and the constant assertion of dominance and desire for attention within sessions.

Charles

Charles is a 60-year-old black British male of Caribbean descent; large in stature, standing at over six feet and weighing 22 stone. He intentionally uses his size to intimidate. He becomes aggressive when recalling past injustices and makes violent threats towards anyone he feels threatened by. He also openly makes grandiose sexualized comments to or about staff. Charles has a diagnosis of schizoaffective disorder and antisocial personality disorder. He described himself at school as 'backwards and a bit slower'. A neuropsychological assessment concluded that he has areas of deficit in processing speed, learning and retention, and comprehension, and generally performs below average compared to his peers.

Charles grew up witnessing domestic violence and was surrounded by sexual encounters from an early age, being taken to brothels and introduced to drugs by his father at the age of five. Charles's index offence was the rape of a 19-year-old autistic woman who was considered unable to give consent. The offence was 'rape by digital penetration' due to foreplay, rather than full sex. They met on her lunch break from college, reportedly engaged in consensual sexual activity, which he said he ended when she suggested she should 'ask her mum' if it was okay to continue. She went back to college and was asked where she had been, resulting in the police being called.

It has taken Charles three years of art therapy to consistently discuss responsibility for the offence, due to connotations of the word 'rape'. Charles is able to think within the art therapy setting but becomes extremely angry in a one-to-one verbal or formal setting such as a tribunal – where he feels accused, resulting in his aggressive and threatening presentation being recorded, which then prevents discharge or unescorted leave.

During his time in prison and Broadmoor (a high-secure mental health unit), Charles reports being sexually and physically abused by prison officers who inserted items inside him. He also stated that he was sexually abused at school, and remembers a neighbour encouraging him to suck on her breast when he was four, to distract him from the violence between his parents.

Charles uses the artmaking to get in touch with his inner child by drawing cartoon characters. He has struggled with the representation of a whole male body, moving from drawing disembodied heads to achieving full figures within the session. Figure 15.1 shows this achievement: drawings of whole bodies to depict Charles's different sides.

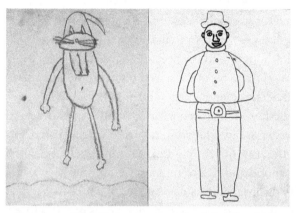

Figure 15.1: Whole bodies depicting Charles's different sides

Charles also writes spoken-word poetry to communicate his feelings to others. One of his poems, which we have spent time writing out together multiple times in groups, reads:

Good Morning Your Honour, how do you do?
I have been reciting these lyrics especially for you.
Now last week you sent me off to jail,
And didn't even consider giving me no bail.
Now lies were told in court to you,
And only God knows so he will see me through.
Yes your honour they claim I did a crime,
But if God was my judge I wouldn't get no time.
Peckham was a ghetto area you see,
And there was too much violence there for me.
In the past I have run you see.
They call me a coward which means nothing to me.
I had an illness some years ago,
But if it started re-occurring I'd let the doctors know.
They sent me to jail for a crime,
And it was there I learned to rhythm and rhyme.

Harry

Harry is a 42-year-old white British male. He also stands at over six foot and weighs 22 stone. He has scars on his head and body from falling/jumping out of a train when he was a child. Initially he said he was trying to kill himself in an attempt to escape from his mother, and more recently that the door was open, and he was trying to close it. When he was arrested for his index offence, he stated he had killed 'the woman on Wimbledon Common' (a well-known unsolved case). Although this was not true, both he and the police believed it. These stories have been the cause of Harry's reputation as a high-profile offender, despite his only actual offence being a bag-snatch.

Harry has been diagnosed with a personality disorder. His previous diagnosis of paranoid schizophrenia has been dismissed. He is the only person in the unit not on medication for a mental health condition. His erratic mood and risk of future offending are seen as related to the personality disorder and a suspected brain injury from when he fell (or jumped) from the train – which is what keeps him in a forensic setting.

Harry's index offence was attempting to rob and making threats to rape. He mugged an elderly lady and then disclosed thoughts about raping her to the police. In addition to his index offence, Harry says he has thoughts about raping old ladies and babies when he feels close to discharge or feels unstable. He has a history of absconding, and when he returns, he says he has had similar thoughts. Harry has reflected on this in groups as a way of eliciting feelings from others that replicate the feeling of disgust he feels towards himself.

Harry's early experiences of inconsistent care, attachment difficulties and abusive treatment from his father are understood to underlie his current difficulties, particularly those concerning emotion regulation and distress tolerance. He also has a strong fear of abandonment within interpersonal relationships. Harry also expresses anger that his mother placed him in care while keeping his brother at home. Harry's contact with his father and brother ended when his mother died five years ago, and now all his relationships are within the service.

Harry has been in secure settings for 32 of the 33 years since the train incident (after which he became violent and abusive), beginning with a secure children's home and reaching high-secure conditions due to his self-harm and stated murderous intent. He can become extremely angry and aggressive when he is not allowed leave. Harry is ambivalent towards recovery, constantly veering between wanting freedom and wanting to be looked after. After absconding, he adamantly demands either freedom or a return to medium-secure conditions. He attempts to get what he wants by openly using threats to staff and patients; the negative reaction he receives exacerbates his entrenched feelings of regret and shame.

Art has given Harry an outlet for his frustration and anger – he often writes his consultant messages, which he leaves in the room, or draws pictures of himself including his scars. He regularly produces many images and uses techniques he has observed from facilitators, and this has boosted his confidence. He says he misses the sessions when we have breaks, despite having often said he is never coming back. Harry often uses words in his artwork to make sense of and communicate his emotions, as in Figure 15.2.

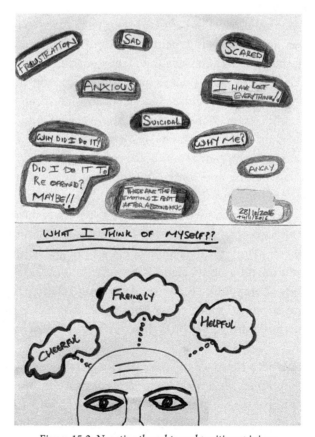

Figure 15.2: Negative thoughts and positive opinions

The approach

Professionals often consider art therapy a non-verbal treatment. However, my approach is very much a talking therapy with art as an additional member in the relationship, as described by Schaverien (1995, chapter 9). Art is also a means of 'cushioning' the conversation to prevent it from feeling too intrusive.

In my sessions, there are no restrictions on what can be discussed, which enables us to build trust and explore difficult feelings. However, I do challenge and question. I have found using measured self-disclosure whilst coming from a position of inquiry has allowed me into the dark and hidden place that these men have buried themselves in for decades. I constantly acknowledge how much they must have changed in order to get to low-secure conditions and that, despite their ambivalence and hopelessness, being in a recovery unit means that they are considered capable of discharge.

The artmaking process has allowed the men a place to hide when conversation and relational dynamics become difficult to tolerate. I make art in the sessions alongside the men, sometimes being the only one to make art. This allows me to have something non-intrusive to focus on when broaching difficult subjects and helps me to remain present when the projections or attacks are overwhelming. For men who have lived for years with shame, secrecy and low self-esteem, their artwork is often experimental and becomes a tangible representation of positive risk-taking and something they can be proud of. Circles are often part of my artwork (see Figure 15.3), which Harry invariably comments on, and which we think about as a symbol of the monotony of being locked up for years, as well as the cyclical nature of their presentation in being positive, ambivalent and negative. In working through the difficult emotions and tolerating the outbursts, we have built a strong therapeutic alliance and trusting relationship, which has become the only space these two men have to discuss their feelings openly. Figure 15.3 depicts the emotionally warm atmosphere in the room.

There have been times when I have felt hopeless and frustrated, and felt like giving up on both men. Their defences are so embedded that it has seemed that we take three steps forward and two back – which is still progress but can be frustrating. Looking back, I can recognize significant changes over the past three years in how the men feel about themselves and their ability to communicate and tolerate their emotions. I realize that it has taken years for trust to be established. Over time, I have been made to feel idealized, dismissed, attacked and depended on in the transference relationship. I have represented specific women and all women, as well as authority figures and caregivers. They have experienced a woman who has not abandoned them and who is prepared to be with them on their darkest days – also a woman who is not afraid to be on her own with them. I have remained constant and they have stayed with me, persevering with the process. We look forward to the sessions, which are no longer overwhelming, as there is now space to share, listen and reflect. It is no longer like giving two individual sessions at the same time. There is trust and respect.

Figure 15.3: Circles – artwork by art therapist

In terms of sexual-offending work, I have never identified their offences or used themes overtly related to sex. The foundation to being able to have those conversations has been to build a therapeutic relationship, which has taken dedication and perseverance on both sides through four years of clinical contact. It is only now that we can begin to do 'the work', where I can use the word 'rape' in the room in relation to the men, and talk reflectively and openly about past and present threats of violence, receiving an appropriate and measured response.

There is no one model for the work. I have adapted my psycho-dynamic training to incorporate other themes and models, such as the Compassionate Mind model used by psychologists in the hospital. As a psychodynamic model is considered inappropriate for personality disorder, I have employed the mentalization approach of Bateman and Fonagy (2004). For the ward group that both men attend, Barker's pre-therapy model (2015) is used in order to build a tolerance for human contact prior to treatment. Engaging with sessions on and off the ward serves as a useful means of comparison for the men, in considering themselves against the presentation of other members of the ward who are at a position of pre-therapy, whilst Charles and Harry have progressed to treatment.

Previously, I had co-facilitated two successful 30-week groups with a psychologist. These were Compassionate Mind and Brain Injury groups which used art therapy alongside mentalization. Themes were taken from Rothwell and Henagulph's (2018) work with individuals in a sex-offender treatment programme, in order to contain the sessions, given the complex presentations we were working with. Harry and Charles attended these groups, and as the work progressed they asked to choose their own themes within the groups. Later during their 2:1 sessions, they worked independently on what they were experiencing that day.

Using multiple interventions and their seeing me in different capacities has been a useful way of working. As they are both on the same ward now, I see the men twice a week – at the ward-based group and at an off-ward art therapy session. In the 2:1 session I began by offering three ten-session blocks, with the option of continuing after the first and second set. This replicated the Compassionate Mind and Brain Injury groups and in addition has served to promote autonomy, and work on attachment and endings, whilst maintaining momentum as a facilitator. For the first set of sessions with Harry and Charles separately, I added a break after each set of three sessions, due to the overwhelming content of the sessions as a single facilitator. We have now moved on to natural breaks for holidays or when I have training – this demonstrates to me the change that has taken place.

Charles and Harry attended a Recovery College web design course which became more of an art therapy intervention. It was the first time Charles had ever used the internet, and his first action was to type his name and offence into Google, so that his offence appeared at the top of the search results. His response to the result of 'rape' was to declare that he had consensual 'sex' with the victim. Harry was visibly surprised and seemed comforted at the honesty of Charles speaking openly about being labelled a rapist. Harry also saw that he was not alone in being held for decades under the Mental Health Act for an offence that was given a short prison sentence.

During the groups they attended together, Charles and Harry worked through feelings of shame and guilt, recounting painful experiences and acknowledging shared experiences of being in care, the way sex offenders are treated within institutions, and abuse within the system. They also discovered a shared experience of being humiliated in public by their first girlfriends and linked that experience to a lack of trust and feeling of dislike towards women – in addition to mothers who were unable to care for them properly. This shared therapeutic alliance built over many, many, hours and several interventions, has enabled us to focus more deeply on early childhood experiences and explore how they may have influenced feelings and opinions in later life, causing or being entwined in mental illness.

I have always provided the opportunity for artwork to be put on the walls inside the art therapy room. This has now progressed to framed pieces being hung in the corridors, tribunal suite and clinical rooms. The immense sense of pride that is achieved from having their work valued and seen by others has encouraged engagement and improved the therapeutic alliance with enhanced self-esteem. The feeling of being valued and not hiding the work away has helped the men to build confidence and repair their internal world. None of the work produced in art therapy has ever directly depicted the index offence or been of an explicitly sexual nature.

Some results
Charles
During the first session of one of the Compassionate Mind and Brain Injury groups, which had two other group members, I felt it was 'make-or-break' with Charles. The psychologist co-facilitating and I found his incessant talking completely overwhelming, and we spent several hours in supervision considering whether allowing him to talk enabled him to process years of repressed emotion and abuse, or whether it would never end and was counterproductive. Eventually there was a shift and he became more contained. I also noted that when concentrating on the artwork, he was silent and fully engrossed.

Charles can now listen to others and can tell a story without completely overwhelming the listener and getting a negative response. He has discovered how to use his artwork and lyrics to gain a genuinely interested response from staff and patients. He offers comfort and support to others, particularly Harry, without expecting anything back, often despite being abruptly dismissed by Harry, who struggles to accept compliments.

Charles recently expressed a desire to work on a timeline in order to structure the traumatic events of his life. He has presented as calmer and able to moderate his emotional responses. In the ward group he can tolerate accusations of being a rapist and correct these by explaining his offence, rather than become angry. He was also able to discuss explaining to his daughter during a visit, that men can be manipulative to women, in order to hurt them for sexual gain. He spoke about his father's death from alcohol for the first time, and how his father used 'crocodile tears' in court and never showed emotion at home, suggesting that Charles did not have a point of reference for his own emotional regulation. He was able to reflect on his offence and consider his victim, stating that at the time he had no idea what autism was, or that even if a vulnerable adult said they were interested in sex, it would be exploitation. He had gained a much better understanding of the ethical element in this situation, and of the signs that might indicate vulnerability.

Figure 15.4: Life in secure services as a theatre stage (see colour section)

Charles has experienced the past 24 years as having been done to him, as if he is being watched and judged, and is both observer and observed. He depicted this as a theatre stage (Figure 15.4). He is finally beginning to understand that he needs to participate in his recovery.

Harry

When I first met Harry, he scared most people, including me, due to his size and impulsiveness as well as the visible scars on his head. After 40 hours of sessions, the rapport between us was strongly established. The best way of working with him was to experience his tantrums and bad moods alongside him in the room, demonstrating that I could remain interested and not give up. He has consistently told me he is 'never coming back' to art therapy and not to collect him the following week. However, I have consistently invited and encouraged him, and he has never intentionally missed a session. He now shows disappointment if a session is cancelled.

Harry can now moderate his mood when he becomes angry, and although he has incidents of anger, he can bring himself back down to the humorous and friendly Harry that we have discovered underneath. When he is encouraged to stay in the room and engage in artwork, he begins to moderate his emotional responses, getting the feelings out on to paper. Then he feels better and appreciates that this is preferable to going back to the ward in a bad mood. When he asks to be taken back to the ward, I remind him that Charles is present, so I cannot escort him. I offer him the phone in the room to call ward staff to collect him. He has never made the call. He sulks and complains, then works through it, ending the session as 'happy Harry'.

He has progressed from being able to calm himself down in weeks to hours, and now within a session. He is able to tell people if he doesn't like something and go to his room to defuse a situation. He acknowledges that he makes sexual threats in order to remain in secure services, due to a fear of abandonment – he is ambivalent about discharge for fear of being alone.

Harry often replicates techniques he has observed from others, as in Figure 15.2, which he compared to his mental state.

Harry and Charles

The final session whilst writing this chapter was a real testament to the work that has been achieved. Harry was upset about his risk meeting, informing us that he had been asked if he was still at risk of absconding – he had said yes because it's always a possibility and he didn't want to lie. We discussed that *might* and *will* are different and that he hadn't done what he had threatened to do over the past 33 years (rape someone), and that we had also identified some of the triggers for absconding (feeling close to discharge). We also reflected on his negative experience of absconding, sleeping in a doorway and spending all his time on transport to be warm and not get caught. He became very distressed and fiercely defaced the artwork he had been making.

Charles commented that he didn't need to ruin his artwork, to which Harry replied, 'It's better than the alternative… to rape someone.' Charles questioned this and then asked whom he was going to rape, as there were only two other people in the room – and asked Harry to apologize to me. I said I hadn't heard a threat but more a choice not to do what could have been worse. There was an exchange in which an apology was offered by Harry, and finally accepted by Charles once it was confirmed that it was sincere.

Harry then burst into tears, sobbing that no one liked him, and staff hated him. This was the first time Harry had ever mentioned rape as his index offence in front of another patient, let alone current threats, and the first time he had openly cried. Charles had been making an image and he offered it to Harry saying, 'I like you,' and asked him to continue with it saying, 'I've done well with the porky bits… now you finish it and we can make a collaboration.' The 'porky bits' looked to me like pink hearts but also reminded Charles of pork fat. Harry took the image and began to expand it.

Charles continued talking about his experiences of accepting his illness, and when Harry offered the image back to show what he had done, Charles said, 'Well done, Harry, carry on.' I smiled at Charles and he winked at me in recognition. Harry developed the image into a series of hearts overlapping each other, with some broken-looking hearts laid over the top (Figure 15.5). There was no reaction to the completed picture itself but there was a recognition of the support that had been offered and the vulnerability that had been exposed and supported.

Figure 15.5: Collaborative picture

Conclusion

Working with male sex offenders as a female therapist has been an important part of building a therapeutic alliance with them and allowing the mother and victim transferences to be worked through. The current risk identified has been around the men instigating or attracting violence through threats, thus making themselves vulnerable.

When an offence is a threat (as with Harry) or was considered consensual and involved a finger rather than a penis (as with Charles), and happened over two or three decades ago whilst unwell and possibly psychotic, it is challenging to elicit empathy for a victim. It seems more useful to work in the present on considering potential victims, as well as their own vulnerability, and how to prevent an offence in the future. Prevention is the main focus of recovery work; cure is not something that is expected. The ability to reflect and mentalize, which has been promoted through art therapy, will hopefully lead to a point when unescorted leave or discharge to supported accommodation is possible. Age has played a role in increased reasoning and responsibility, which, alongside medication and continued therapeutic support, has allowed the unravelling and processing of complex histories and narratives. This has enabled the damage to their internal world to become part of the background, and positivity, hope, motivation and perseverance to be at the forefront.

Art therapy has achieved a relationship based on investment and continuity, where the men can talk in depth if they want to about what has happened. They can listen to each other and tolerate each other's trauma whilst sitting with their own. They can be proud of what they have achieved.

References

Barker, R. (2015) 'Using Pre-Therapy in Forensic Settings.' In A. Meaden and A. Fox (eds) *Innovations in Psychosocial Interventions for Psychosis: Working with the Hard to Reach.* London: Routledge.

Bateman, A. and Fonagy, P. (2004) *Psychotherapy for Borderline Personality Disorder: Mentalization-Based Treatment.* Oxford: Oxford Medical Publications.

Rothwell, K. and Henagulph, L. (2018) 'A Transdisciplinary Approach: Working with Individuals in a Sex Offender Treatment Programme.' In T. Colbert and C. Bent (eds) *Creative Collaborations: Working Across Modalities in the Arts Therapies.* London: Routledge.

Ruszczynski, S. (2010) 'Becoming neglected: A perverse relationship to care.' *British Journal of Psychotherapy 26*, 10, 22–32.

Schaverien, J. (1995) *Desire and the Female Therapist: Engendered Gazes in Psychotherapy and Art Therapy.* London: Routledge.

CHAPTER 16

Role-Play as a Therapeutic Tool

A Research Study of Sexual Offenders' Experiences of Victim Empathy Role-Play

MAXINE DANIELS, PSYCHODRAMA PSYCHOTHERAPIST

Introduction

In 1994, I was invited to deliver victim empathy role-play training to prison staff who would be conducting role-plays for the Core Sex Offender Treatment Program (SOTP), which was being rolled out across the prison establishment in the UK as a result of the 'What Works' literature on treatment (Andrews and Bonta 2003). Role-play was integrated into a standardized cognitive behavioural treatment approach, and I delivered this training for 23 years. During this time, I qualified as a psychodrama psychotherapist.

I recognized the importance of research in order to try to understand what the offenders experienced during the role-plays, to gain a deeper insight into the effect of treatment. Graduates of SOTP reported that the victim empathy role-plays were the most powerful part of the treatment programme. But what did this mean? I decided to embark on a clinical doctorate to explore this further. My research question was, 'What do sexual offenders experience when they reverse roles with their victims?' In this chapter, I present a slice of the research and highlight some of the main themes that emerged from it, including building on theory and linking it to the psychotherapeutic framework of the Assimilation of Problematic Experience (APE: Stiles *et al.* 1992).

I include a technique called 'victim offence chair work', which facilitators were trained to deliver in the program, as an example of the clinical work.

SOTP and victim empathy role-plays

Victim empathy role-plays were introduced to the prison service (in England and Wales) Core Sex Offender Treatment Programme in 1994 as a result of Hildebran and Pithers (1989) identifying victim empathy as an essential, non-cognitive component of relapse prevention. A study by McGrath *et al.* (2010) indicated that between 87 and 95 percent of American treatment programmes working with sex offenders included victim empathy. In the Core SOTP, 19 percent of time was dedicated to victim empathy (Barnett and Mann 2013). The purpose of delivering victim empathy treatment was to help offenders gain an understanding of the harm caused to their victims, and as a result reduce their re-offending (Wastell, Cairns and Haywood 2009).

One of the reasons for including victim empathy modules in treatment appears to be about political and public demand (Mann and Barnett 2013), yet when previous research studies recruited the views of offenders, it was deemed an important part of treatment (Levenson *et al.* 2009; Wakeling, Webster and Mann 2005). Although role-play has been a core component of victim empathy in SOTP, there is little literature about this work. There have been no qualitative studies that ask sexual offenders about their experiences of role-playing their victims. This study gives a voice to the offenders, whilst helping clinicians to work within a psychotherapeutic framework in order to use role-play as a therapeutic tool. Literature about empathy deficits in sexual offenders has been recorded (Hudson *et al.* 1995; Ward, Keenan and Judson 2000). Hanson and Morton-Bourgon (2005) conducted a meta-analysis of 82 recidivism studies and concluded that low victim empathy had no impact on sexual or non-sexual recidivism. However, the study included interventions such as letter writing to the victim and watching videos to record the impact of the offence on the victim – role-play was not included. Hence the reason for conducting this research, to hear from the perpetrators about their experiences of victim empathy role-plays.

The use of role-play in therapy

The term role-play is now a common feature in studies and clinical practices. However, it was not until after World War II that the use of 'role' and related terms were seen in titles of empirical studies (Thomas and Biddle 1966). There are three pioneers who used role-play as a therapeutic tool:

- Jacob L. Moreno (1934) in *Who Shall Survive?* describes an innovative methodology, known as psychodrama, which he introduced to his sanatorium, Beacon Hospital, New York, where he worked as a psychiatrist with patients with psychopathological disorders.

- George Kelly (1955), an American psychologist, was influential in terms of helping his clients to identify and enact a new role, in 'fixed-role therapy', which evolved from his personal construct theory.

- Joseph Wolpe (1958) introduced the idea of using role-play as a 'behaviour rehearsal' with clients suffering from anxiety disorder.

In offending behaviour programmes, role-play is used in various ways; however, it tends to focus on the behavioural model of practising 'skills'. These behavioural skills are practised in relation to assertiveness, social skills and life skills, which are generally included in cognitive behavioural treatment with offenders (Gredecki and Ireland 2011; Hall 1989; Marques *et al.* 2000).

The research: What do perpetrators think about their experience of victim empathy role-plays?
Research methodology

Interpretative phenomenological analysis (IPA) was used as the method to analyse the data (Smith 2004). It is a qualitative approach, and the term 'double hermeneutic' (Smith and Osborn 2008) is given to IPA because as the participants are trying to make sense of their world, the researcher is trying to make sense of the participants trying to make sense of their world. Eleven sex offenders were interviewed from three prison establishments who were graduates of the Core SOTP and had completed victim empathy role-plays. A semi-structured interview, an hour long, was conducted and the data transcribed. It is important to note that the 'phenomenological' quality of IPA is an attempt to clarify situations that are 'lived through' by people rather than reducing the phenomena to a set list of variables (Giorgi and Giorgi 2008). The study aimed to gain a deeper, richer understanding of the offenders' experiences of being in role as their victims.

Results and discussion

The analysis of the data used a psychological perspective and a psychotherapeutic template in order to collate the seven superordinate themes that emerged from the research, each one having a series of clusters in the domain:

1. Pre-role-plays

2. Objectifying self and victim

3. Embodiment of role

4. Walking in the victim's shoes – action insight

5. Understanding and integrating parts of self

6. Self-reflection and meaning-making

7. Moving on.

It was clear throughout the research that the data spoke about the offenders' 'aspects of self' even though the title is about role-reversing (role-playing) the victim. There was a sense of offenders moving forward with positive self-regard and how it manifests in terms of delivering treatment using a psychotherapeutic framework known as the APE scale (see above) (Stiles *et al.* 1992).

What emerged from the data was the sense of an 'objectified self' (offender) and an 'objectified other' (victim). These theories are based on the I-Thou and the I-It concepts (Buber 1958). The theory of 'multiple selves' (Cooper 2003; Sherif 1948; Sliker 1992) states that we are constructed of multiple internal centres of experience (Dimaggio and Stiles 2007) and that the *intrapersonal* 'I' positions are akin to 'sub-personalities' (Rowan 1990). Making sense of the offenders' experiences includes a cognitive recognition, an emotional understanding, a physiological response and the biological position (Gendlin 1997).

OBJECTIFICATION OF SELF
Alan (participant) describes his experience of the role-play where he was asked to take on the role of his victim and mark on a body diagram the feelings and pain associated with the rape. This role-play technique is called victim offence chair work (Daniels 2005).

> It was sort of like, oh no, I didn't want to do this, but then I got into the role of [victim] and found it easier to put down the actual marks and bruises that I gave her and stuff, cos I was sort of cut off myself, from my thinking. – Alan

The loss of self-relatedness is in part what Buber (1958) describes as the 'it-ifying' process in terms of an I-I (acceptance and relation to self) or an I-Me (objectifying self). The 'other' is experienced as a 'thing' an object, an 'it'. This can be both internal ('cut off' parts of self) and external (how people are viewed). The themes resonated with this theory.

> I think right, knowing now who I am, you know before I didn't kind of know, I lived an impostor's life. – Bobby

> It's like there's two of me, one here and one there you know I did it sitting here, but that person can't understand that I did it and yes you are opening those doors and sort of conflict starts as well. – Michael

In the three examples above, the participants did not 'connect' to the 'abuser' part of self, but rather saw themselves as distant from the offence until they engaged with the role-plays, which helped them to connect with this role.

OBJECTIFICATION OF VICTIM
The concept of 'it-ifying' the victim (Buber 1958) included the following statements:

> I didn't take into account the impact of the view on victims. – Simon

> Because you're thinking of self-gain, aren't you? You're thinking of yourself you're not thinking of your victim at the time you offend. – Ben

Everything you want, you just take. – Bobby

Role-play made me see her as much more of a victim. – Keith

I offended against [victim] and stuff like that but in me own mind, it wasn't that bad [rape of ex-partner]. – Alan

Didn't think about consequences to the victim, I never thought about anything other than myself. – Edward

I didn't see them as downloading images; I didn't see them as victims. – Steven

Clinical example: Victim offence chair work with Keith

Keith participated in victim offence chair work. He had been convicted of rape and defended his position by claiming that the victim did not say no during sex. The offence happened when the victim left the nightclub by herself after having an argument with her boyfriend. It was one o'clock in the morning. Keith followed her down the street and began talking to her. The victim told Keith she was upset and wanted to go home. At one point, Keith stopped and gave her a tissue, but as they approached an alleyway he pulled the victim into it. The victim began to resist, and Keith hit her across the face; the victim then went quiet and Keith demanded she lie on the cold ground and instructed her to take her underwear off. He then raped her. Keith believed that she must have wanted sex because she didn't tell him to stop at any point. The victim offence chair work allowed Keith to gain an experiential understanding of how the victim may have felt during this ordeal. It is important to let the reader know this is not a technique to be used in a punitive way. All treatment facilitators are coached in being non-judgemental and to contain the group and individual, and are trained in role-play techniques in order to direct the sessions safely.

Technique: Victim offence chair work and role-play rules

Four chairs are placed in a line next to each other. Pre-prepared and placed in front of the chairs on the floor are two sheets of flipchart paper sellotaped together with a diagram of an adult body outlined (see Figure 16.1). Keith is told that when he sits in the first chair he will be called by the victim's name (if the victim's name is not known, the perpetrator can use a name in order to personalize the victim rather than continuing to objectify and use the 'it' stance. The director (group facilitator) who is allocated to direct the role-play will narrate the scene. Before the action begins, the group is reminded of the role-play rules; these will have been flagged up before the role-play module. The rules include: No Touch, No Physical Violence, Time Out (if needed), No Props; and when the director says STOP, all action must stop. These rules, agreed with the group, help to keep the whole process safe. At an earlier point in treatment, group members would have given an active account of their offences, therefore at this stage the group and facilitators are aware of what happened at the time of the offence. This means the facilitator knows the action to narrate to the perpetrator.

First chair – getting into role and setting the scene

The situation with Keith is an example of how a facilitator would work with him.

Director: *Okay, Keith, when you take this first chair you will playing the role of your victim (Jan) and I will speak to you as Jan, your victim.*

It important to 'set the scene' by stating the time of day/night, where the action happens and who else might be around; this helps the perpetrator get in touch with the 'as if' of the scene. The action might include instructions such as:

Director: [Speaking to Keith 'as if' he is the victim Jan] *It's one o'clock in the morning, it's cold and you've just stepped outside the club. You are going home and feeling a bit upset because you've had an argument with your boyfriend.*

When Keith is sitting in the chair, the Director will proceed.

Director: *What are you wearing here this evening, Jan?* [to Keith in role as Jan the victim]

Keith begins to take on the role of the victim in the scene and responds as the victim.

Keith responds [in role as Jan]: *I'm wearing a gold necklace, a dress and high shoes because I've been to a nightclub.*

At this point, the Director punctuates the narrative with questions, for example:

Director: *How does it feel being here in the street at 1 a.m. by yourself? / How are you going to get home? / What do you think about this man following you?*

Keith is encouraged to develop a new perspective by thinking as the victim and also experiencing the situation of being alone at 1.a.m. with a strange man following her. The questions continue to help him gain a deeper understanding when setting the scene.

Second chair – developing the role and introducing Socratic questions

After the initial warm-up of Keith in role as the victim Jan, he is asked to move along to the second chair, when the action begins to change. Again, the Director will narrate the scene and ask questions that challenge Keith's version of events, such as:

Director: (to Keith in role as victim) *If you don't want help from this man in the street – who is around for you to call? / How do you know if you can trust this man?*

This is known as Socratic questioning, where we help the perpetrator to learn through role-taking, to think through and pose a seed of doubt in their usual response and learning. The responses are likely to be 'No one, there is no-one around' and 'I don't know if I can trust him, but I'm by myself and there is no one I can turn to'. Follow-up questions might include:

Director: *What do you think would happen if you tell him to go away and leave you alone? / What would happen if you tried to run away?*

These questions begin to challenge Keith's cognitive distortions about the offence. As Keith, he believes the victim is present through choice; however, in the role of victim (Jan), he gains insight into her world in which she is powerless to have free agency in this situation. These first two steps could take anything from 10 to 15 minutes, so there is time for questions and answers from the Director to Keith in role as victim Jan.

Third chair – working through the offence as victim

The third chair is used to highlight the offence and Keith (in role of victim) is asked to look at the diagram placed on the floor and to draw on the body of victim what is happening to her (as Jan) at the time of the offence. It is a representation of the victim's powerlessness during the offence.

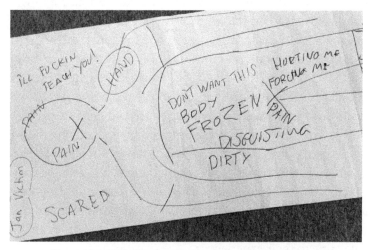

Figure 16.1: Body diagram for the victim offence chair work

Once again, the Director will use questions to challenge Keith's cognitive distortions, such as:

Director: *Jan, why don't you get up and walk away?*

In role, Keith as the victim will most likely come back with a statement such as:

Keith: [speaking as Jan] *I can't, I'm afraid of what he might do, he's already hit me, he might have a knife, he's told me 'I'll fucking teach you', which means he could kill me.*

The Director continues to challenge the distortions such as:

Director: *Why don't you say no? / Is this your idea of sex?*

Every time Keith responds to these questions with insight from the victim perspective, such as 'This is not my idea of sex' or 'I'm too frightened to say no', it demonstrates that he is 'taking on the role' and getting a cognitive, somatic and experiential understanding of the felt senses of the 'other' by not objectifying the victim – he is 'walking in the victim's shoes'. The victim becomes 'a person', the 'other', and not an 'it'. This is very powerful work for perpetrators and really helps them to shift their thinking and develop empathy for the victim.

I can imagine the reader beginning to feel uncomfortable with the description of the work, and it is certainly not something that I would advocate for professionals to undertake without training. It is unfair to ask staff to do this work with little or no understanding of psychodrama or dramatherapy. This is why the core creative therapies are so important and need to include training for those professionals who want to include role-play around sensitive issues. The prison service offered three full days training to deliver this work.

I can also imagine readers becoming concerned that the perpetrators are being re-traumatized. However, in my 23 years of doing this work, the perpetrators always described the victim empathy role-plays as one of the most valuable modules in the programme, hence the research to give them a voice to find out what they experienced. The research explores how they are able to separate out their own abuse and trauma from that of their victims and not 'objectify' themselves as an 'it' but give meaning to their experiences.

Last chair – de-roling and debriefing

Keith (still in role as victim Jan) moves to the last chair, which represents the de-roling and debriefing chair. The Director might say:

Director: *Could you please move to the last chair?*

The body diagram of the victim, with all its marks representing the physical and emotional abuse during the offence, will still be lying on the floor. This is a final opportunity to ask questions about the experience of the victim.

Director: *How do you feel, looking at your body left in this state, Jan? / Looking at your body on the ground, what images come to mind?*

At this point the perpetrator can see the marks, bruises and pain that have been caused by the offence from the victim perspective. The diagram is a stark reminder of the experience endured by the victim during this encounter. Finally, after questions at this stage, the Director de-roles and debriefs Keith, by saying:

Director: *Let's end the role-play here. You're going to leave Jan behind, and I would like you to sit back in the group. Take a moment, take a breath, and in your own time we'll ask you some debriefing questions.*

After reflection time, the facilitators (there are usually two in the group) will begin asking similar questions to the ones used in the role-play.

Director: *You initially told the group that Jan didn't say no or try to stop you, so you thought it was okay to have 'sex' as you called it. After doing this role-play, why do you think she didn't say no?*

Keith (now out of role) responds: *She couldn't say no, I had already hit her, and she didn't know what I would do. I could have killed her; she didn't know I wouldn't have done that.*

These statements challenge the beliefs that we encountered initially, whereby he said: 'She could have said no.' Hence the statement from Keith in the research: 'I knew my victim was a victim, but role-play made me see her as much more of a victim and it wasn't sex, it was rape.'

Assimilation of a problematic experience: Theory building

During the interviews for this research, the perpetrators spoke of different stages they encountered, and the data spoke to these themes. I wanted to build on the theory that explored the stages of working through the role-plays in the context of a psychotherapeutic framework. Stiles *et al.* (1990) developed a framework to use when working with clients who struggle to assimilate their 'problematic' experience, such as perpetrators who struggle to process their offending experiences. There are seven stages to the Assimilation of Problematic Experience (APE) scale that correlate with the role-play stages the perpetrators described in the research (see Table 16.1).

Table 16.1: Correlation of APE scale with research themes

Research Subordinate Themes	APE Scale (Psychotherapeutic Frame)
1. Pre-role-plays 2. Distancing self from sexual offence (shame and guilt)	Stage 1 Active Avoidance
1. Objectifying self and victim 2. Loss of self-relatedness	Stage 2 Vague Awareness
1. Embodiment of role 2. Getting into role	Stage 3 Acknowledgement/clarification
1. Walking in the victim's shoes – action insight 2. Feelings experienced as victim	Stage 4 Understanding/Insight
1. Understanding and integrating parts of self 2. Meeting their 'abuser' role 3. More understanding of self	Stage 5 Application/Working Through
1. Self-reflection and meaning-making 2. Self-reflection 3. Sense of wellbeing	Stage 6 Resourcefulness/Problem Solution
1. Moving on 2. Psychological strengths and new roles	Stage 7 Integration/Mastery

Using the APE scale to build on the data from the research, it became clear that the themes reflected the stages of the role-play process in relation to the problematic experience, namely the offence. The first stage, pre-role-play, was avoidance of the subject of victim, not thinking about them, as previously shown in the quotations from three participants. The second stage, of objectifying self and victim, meant that the offence stayed 'out of consciousness', in other words, as Michael, one of the participants, reported, 'There were two of me.' However, once the perpetrators took on the role of their victim, it appeared to move them into Stage 3 of the scale, whereby they acknowledged the victim and the offence. They were able to seek clarification about the 'problem' (the offence) and their part in it, whilst also understanding the harm to their victim. At this stage they were 'walking in the victim's shoes' by role-playing the victim in different scenarios and gaining 'understanding and insight' at Stage 4 of the APE scale.

Once the offenders had embodied the role of victim, met their internal 'abusing self', it helped them to integrate and gain more understanding of their own part in the offence and to have a cathartic experience (Moreno 1975), connecting with an emotional understanding of playing a role. This equates to Theme 5, Understanding and integrating parts of self, which also relates to Stage 5 of the APE scale, Application/Working Through.

In the final two stages of the APE scale, Stage 6: Resourcefulness/ Problem Solution and Stage 7: Integration/Mastery, the offenders reported:

> I think the role-play helped me to understand what I'd done, what harm I caused her. – Bobby

> If I didn't do role-play, a lot of understanding would be thrown away. – Gerry

The experience of believing they can move on in terms of their understanding of the offence, from both their own perspective and that of the victims, allows them to move forward in treatment.

> You've got to sieve out all the good and you've got to use what you learnt. – Ben

> I've got feelings, right, and I don't hide them now. I show them, and it's better to express how you feel, right, instead of hiding? – Bobby

Conclusion

It would appear from this study that offenders engaging in victim empathy role-plays are able to use it as a therapeutic tool in order to gain insight into their own 'abusing part of self', which they have previously objectified and avoided. The voices of the perpetrators from this study give an understanding of insight into their victims, as people and not 'it' objects. The APE scale is a psychotherapeutic framework that clinicians can use in conjunction with role-play techniques to target different stages of treatment. If the perpetrators are 'stuck' at any stage in the APE scale, then it is possible to develop techniques and interventions to be responsive to the therapeutic needs of the individuals. Clinicians need to develop their skills in order to respond effectively when using role-play as a therapeutic tool in therapy; the victim offence chair work is one example of a range of role-play techniques used in the Core SOTP. Research in arts therapies for sexual offenders is important in order to keep treatment relevant to their rehabilitation and to avoid creating more victims.

References
Andrews, D.A. and Bonta, J. (2003) *The Psychology of Criminal Conduct* (3rd edn). Cincinnati, OH: Anderson.

Barnett, G. and Mann, R.E. (2013) 'Empathy deficits and sexual offending: A model of obstacles to empathy.' *Journal of Aggression and Violent Behaviour 18*, 2, 228–239.

Buber, M. (1958) *I and Thou* (2nd edn, trans. R.G. Smith). London: Continuum.

Cooper, M. (2003) "I-I" and "ME": Transposing Buber's interpersonal attitudes to the intrapersonal plane.' *Journal of Constructivist Psychology 16*, 131–153.

Daniels, M. (2005) 'The Use of Role Play to Develop Victim Empathy and Relapse Prevention.' In B. Shwartz (ed.) *The Sex Offender: Issues in Assessment, Treatment, and Supervision of Adult and Juvenile Populations: Volume V*. Kingston, NJ: Civic Research Institute.

Dimaggio, G. and Stiles, W.B. (2007) 'Psychotherapy in light of internal multiplicity.' *Journal of Clinical Psychology 63*, 119–127.

Gendlin, E.T. (1997) *Experiencing and the Creation of Meaning*. Evanston, IL: Northwestern University Press.

Giorgi, A. and Giorgi, B. (2008) 'Phenomenology.' In J.A. Smith (ed.) *Qualitative Psychology: A Practical Guide to Research Methods* (2nd edn). London: Sage.

Gredecki, N. and Ireland, C.A. (2011) *Thinking Minds: Group Theory Treatment Package*. Merseycare NHS Trust, unpublished.

Hall, R.L. (1989) 'Relapse Rehearsal.' In R.D. Laws (ed.) *Relapse Prevention with Sex Offenders*. New York, NY: Guilford Press.

Hanson, R.K. and Morton-Bourgon, K.E. (2005) 'The characteristics of persistent sexual offenders: A meta-analysis of recidivism studies.' *Journal of Consulting and Clinical Psychology 73*, 6, 1154–1163.

Hildebran, D. and Pithers, W.D. (1989) 'Enhancing Offender Empathy for Sexual-Abuse Victims.' In R. Laws (ed.) *Relapse Prevention with Sex Offenders*. New York, NY: Guilford Press.

Hudson, S.M., Marshall, W.L., Ward, T., Johnston, P.W. and Jones, R.L. (1995) 'Kia Marama: A cognitive-behavioural program for incarcerated child molesters.' *Behaviour Change 12*, 69–80.

Kelly, G. (1955) *The Psychology of Personal Constructs: Vol. 1*. New York: W.W. Norton.

Levenson, J.S., Macgowan, M.J., Morin, J.W. and Cotter, L.P. (2009) 'Perceptions of sex offenders about treatment: Satisfaction and engagement in group therapy.' *Sexual Abuse: A Journal of Research and Treatment 21*, 35– 56.

Mann, R.E. and Barnett, G. (2013) 'Victim empathy intervention with sex offenders: Rehabilitation, punishment, or correctional quackery?' *Sex Abuse 25*, 3, 282-301.

Marques, M.J.K., Nelson, C., Alarcon J.M. and Day, D.M. (2000) 'Preventing Relapse in Sex Offenders: What We Learned from SOTEP's Experimental Program.' In D.R. Laws, S.M. Hudson and T. Ward (eds) *Remaking Relapse Prevention with Sex Offenders*. Thousand Oaks, CA: Sage.

McGrath, R.J., Cumming, G.F., Burchard, B.L., Zeoli, S. and Ellerby, L. (2010) *Current Practices and Emerging Trends in Sexual Abuser Management: The Safer Society 2009 North American Survey*. Brandon, VT: Safer Society Press.

Moreno, J.L. (1934) *Who Shall Survive? A New Approach to the Problem of Human Interrelations*. Washington, DC: Nervous and Mental Diseases Publishing.

Moreno, J.L. (1975) 'Mental catharsis and the psychodrama.' *Group Psychotherapy, Psychodrama and Sociometry 28*, 5–32.

Rowan, J. (1990) *Subpersonalities: The People Inside Us*. London: Routledge.

Sherif, M. (1948) *An Outline of Social Psychology*. New York, NY: Harper.

Sliker, G. (1992) 'Discovering Subpersonalities.' In G. Sliker (ed.) *Multiple Mind: Healing the Split in Psyche and World*. London: Shambhala.

Smith, J.A. (2004) 'Reflecting on the development of interpretative phenomenological analysis and its contribution to qualitative research in psychology.' *Qualitative Research in Psychology 1*, 39–54.

Smith, J.A. and Osborn, M. (2008) 'Interpretative Phenomenological Analysis.' In J.A. Smith (ed.) *Qualitative Psychology: A Practical Guide to Research Methods* (2nd edn). London: Sage.

Stiles, W.B., Elliot, R., Firth-Cozens, J.A., Llewlyn, S.P. *et al.* (1990) 'Assimilation of problematic experiences by clients in psychotherapy.' *Psychotherapy: Theory, Research, Practice, Training 27*, 3, 411–420.

Stiles, W.B., Meshot, C.M., Anderson, T.M. and Sloan Jr., W.W. (1992) 'Assimilation of problematic experiences: the case of John Jones.' *Psychotherapy Research 2*, 2, 81–101.

Thomas, E.J. and Biddle, B.J. (1966) 'The Nature and History of Role Theory.' In B.J. Biddle and E.J. Thomas (eds) *Role Theory: Concepts and Research*. New York, NY: John Wiley and Sons.

Wakeling, H.C., Webster, S.D. and Mann, R.E. (2005) 'Sexual offenders' treatment experience: A qualitative and quantitative investigation.' *Journal of Sexual Aggression 11*, 2, 171–186.

Ward, T., Keenan, T. and Judson, S.M. (2000) 'Understanding cognitive, affective and intimacy deficits in sex offenders: A developmental perspective.' *Aggression and Violent Behavior 5*, 41–62.

Wastell, C.A., Cairns, D. and Haywood, H. (2009) 'Empathy training, sex offenders and re-offending.' *Journal of Sexual Aggression 15*, 2, 149–159.

Wolpe, J. (1958) *Psychotherapy by Reciprocal Inhibition*. Stanford, CA: Stanford University Press.

Group and Individual Art Therapy with a Sexually Inappropriate Patient in an NHS Low-Secure Unit

ANNA GREEN, ART THERAPIST

Introduction

As part of the final year of my MA Art Therapy course at the University of Hertfordshire, I was on placement as a trainee art therapist two days a week, split between an NHS low-secure unit (LSU), the setting I describe in this chapter, and a community mental health team. From my experiences at the LSU, I compare the difference between the same patient in an open art therapy group and in individual art therapy sessions. My supervisor was an art therapist who previously worked at this setting but was not with me on the day of placement. This patient wasn't convicted of a sexual offence, but he remained an inpatient at the low-secure unit because of his sexually inappropriate behaviour. This chapter notes his complementary and flirtatious comments and how I responded to these in sessions. In the evaluation section I explore the changes in the patient's behaviour, his artwork and the therapeutic relationship, and compare these with how he was in the group and how he was in individual sessions. To conclude, I will argue which support seemed to have a greater effect on the patient.

Patient and setting

This NHS low-secure unit is a locked male ward within the grounds of a general hospital. There are 20 beds at the unit split between two wings. Much like the sun, patients arrive on the East wing and transition over to the West. It was hard to receive any phone service or stay connected to anyone during work hours. Because of this, I felt like I was entering a different world on this day. I always felt anxious about what I could be walking in to, having had no contact with the ward between each weekly placement day. I always questioned how much could happen during this period and what might have changed. Experiencing the secure environment in this way, and knowing I was able to leave at the end of the day, enabled me to see the value in the patient's Section 17 leave (MIND 2012). Section 17 leave is when the responsible clinician gives permission for the patient to have time outside the unit, alone or accompanied by staff. This is completed by a psychiatrist, and they consider the interest of the patient and the safety of others. This can be revoked depending on the patient's behaviour and mental state.

George is a 41-year-old male who is said to have had a happy, normal childhood with good physical and emotional development. George began using LSD, heroin and marijuana as a teenager, and at 19 he was admitted to a psychiatric hospital and diagnosed with paranoid schizophrenia. George had been detained under Section 3 of the Mental Health Act 1983, which meant that he was at the hospital to keep himself and others safe, and to receive appropriate treatment he wouldn't receive if he wasn't detained.

At the beginning of my placement George had both unescorted and escorted Section 17 leave; however, his leave was soon suspended because he smoked marijuana on leave. During unescorted leave the patients could possibly access substances and find ways of bringing them into the unit to use, to store or to share with others. George has smoked marijuana since he was 16 and, according to his psychiatrist, George didn't see any problem with this. My placement supervisor described George as being hedonistic. By saying this, she referred to his hippy-styled spirituality, drug use and relaxed attitude.

George hadn't been convicted of an offence but there were reported incidents of a sexual nature with vulnerable patients. There were also reports of inappropriate remarks made to staff, in the form of sexual advances, invitations and flirtatious behaviour. As reported by his psychiatrist, George was at the unit for his risk of being sexually inappropriate, violent and noncompliant with his medication, and for substance misuse.

Open art therapy group

My aim for the open art therapy group was to provide a supportive, non-judgemental space for patients to be playful, reflect on their feelings, and express themselves through artmaking. Marshall-Tierney (2014) says that an art therapist making art alongside patients can bring about an equal engagement. I agree with this, and I made art alongside the patients in the group so that I was less of an observing gaze.

I first met George when he expressed an interest in attending the open art therapy group I was facilitating. In the group, George was confident with the art materials, sociable, inquisitive, keen to collaborate and reflect on the sensory and aesthetic aspects of his and others' images. Frustrations regarding medication, substance misuse and Section 17 leave were regular conversation topics in the group.

In the group George would often compliment my jewellery, my nail varnish and my clothes. I hadn't anticipated this physical attention, expecting to be noticed for my role or personality instead. I felt unsure what to do or whether I needed to change my external appearance to avoid this – both my discomfort and the attention. Kavaler-Adler (2006) writes about a patient who constantly observed what she wore. She questioned whether, if she changed her appearance, the patient would think she dressed herself with them in mind? In supervision, we discussed how I didn't want to change the way I presented myself because of this patient. My supervisor had worked with George at this unit before, and she explained that, from her experience, he would find something to compliment if I continued to present myself in this way or not. This turned out to be true as he later discussed biological attributes, rather than accessories.

In session 14, George entered seeming particularly elated in mood. There was one other patient present in this session and, although he spoke at times, he was quieter than George and focused on his own images. In this session, George complimented my outfit, my hair, my attention to his feelings and my artwork. Near the beginning, George held up his image (Figure 17.1) and showed me 'two people hugging and kissing in the image'. I struggled to see any figures in the image although I had noticed a twisting of two cloth-like shapes, outlined in red at the centre of the image. These reminded me of Klimt's (1908) 'The Kiss' painting with the absence of heads. I found myself listening to George explain this and remained open-minded to what this image meant to him.

Figure 17.1: George's pastel image

In the same session, George compared me to the lead female in a sexual romantic film and drew out some similarities between us, such as our name, hair colour, profession and physique. Comments like George's bring the therapist's body and person into the session in an intimate way (Schaverien 1995). I noticed that when he made these comments in the group, I felt that the attention had shifted from the patients to myself and that I became embarrassed to be described in this way.

George would also ask questions about my family, my interests and my art. He sometimes seemed frustrated at my answers to his questions, as I tended to redirect them back, or answer with a question. George had said, 'I don't want to assume about you [*sic*], it's normal to ask questions and learn things about another person.' When I'm with patients, I try to be warm and supportive, but I do sometimes become a 'blank screen' upon which the patient could have their own internal representation of (Damarell 1998). Most patients didn't comment on my artworks in this group; however, George often discussed their energy, colour, shape and feeling. At times, I found this uncomfortable but easier to endure than comments about my physical appearance. Coming from art school,

I was familiar with my artwork being discussed and critiqued, rather than my personality or my appearance. This kind of attention was not something I had experienced before, hence I didn't really know how best to respond.

In supervision, we acknowledged my countertransference, exploring my feelings of wanting to avoid the attention and focus on something to hide my reaction, combined with the feeling of not knowing how to respond. Exploring these emotions also made us question the reaction and impact on the other patient present. The other patient did join in the conversation at times, but George's comments may have distracted me from this patient also.

In the same session, George explained how he was wary of me at first, and that now he was comfortable with me, but that I should tell him if I felt uncomfortable. I was feeling uncomfortable in this dialogue and surprised that George picked up on this. It made me question whether my external features weren't as subtle as I had hoped. In supervision at university, we questioned how others could respond to his comments and whether he expected me to be uncomfortable. I felt conflicted during this session and aware of how other staff could view George's comments as being inappropriate. I didn't want George to feel rejected or hurt if I told him he was being inappropriate, because I saw art therapy as a way for George to express or explore his sexuality in a more appropriate and contained way.

The therapist might feel a sense of shame where they feel unprepared to work with erotic transference material (Rodgers 2011). Although I had heard of erotic transference and suspected this occurring with George, I did not feel confident to call it this in supervision. I queried this as a narcissistic aspect of countertransference (Guttman 2006), where I was perhaps drawn to the aspects that were more flattering. When I discussed this in supervision and my supervisor named it erotic transference, I realized I wasn't alone in my thinking. I have understood erotic transference to be when feelings of love, desire or sexuality are present in the therapeutic relationship. Male patients are generally careful in expressing their sexual feelings so that they aren't considered dangerous (Guttman 2006). It seems George was wary of how I felt in response to his comments and needed confirmation that I was surviving his advances – advances in terms of comparisons to a current sexual character and continued compliments rather than a direct proposition. Rodgers (2011) mentions a study by Spilly (2008) which showed that when countertransference like this is present, the therapist can feel muddled, confused and doubt their competence. This was evidenced in supervision as we observed how I found ways of avoiding this discomforting content, but was aware that at some point it might need to be addressed.

Figure 17.2: Anna's collage

Maybe I was communicating my discomfort through my body language, my own artmaking or my attention to his image. I am uncertain whether my body language changed, and I feel this wasn't a controlled act; however, it seems likely that I shrunk into myself more in an effort to hide my body, to physically prevent him from seeing me. I also found myself creating an image using pre-cut shapes, as if I had lost the ability to think about what I was doing and needed a nostalgic technique of sticking to calm me – that maybe making anything else would have felt too personal or made me feel vulnerable in some way. Stott (2018) seems to think similarly in that she described not wanting to accidentally expose herself by accepting her patient's invitation to draw.

Erotic transference may also be contained in the artwork (Schaverien 1995). If this is so, then the therapist could be seduced and lured into an engagement with the image. Perhaps I was trying to block this being reciprocated through my own image-making by making something abstract where there was little room to assume any specific meaning from it. My own image (Figure 17.2) may have contained some of my countertransference feelings, but I was also drawn to George's image. My feelings in terms of my need for an 'easy' image-making task that I could be spontaneous with and that only needed me to decide where to place each item, rather than to construct from scratch.

Marshall-Tierney (2014) considers whether an art therapist making art alongside is a way of being helpful or a way for the art therapist to avoid something and distract themselves (Moon 2002). Morter (1997) asks whether the therapist's own artmaking could be intrusive or seductive. I questioned how much my artworks were revealing of me and whether the unknown mystery made them seductive. Perhaps the content of my artwork was irrelevant and simply the act of my engaging in artmaking may have felt too intimate. With George it seems that my artmaking, myself, the other group members and their images made him sociable and distracted from the opportunity of self-reflection.

After working with George for four months, non-recorded information came up from a conversation with his keyworker. It was brought to my attention that George's mother had been sexually abused by her father and that George's elder brother was a result of this abusive and incestuous relationship. According to staff, this history is known but not discussed within the family, nor clearly documented in his notes. George and his parents had attended family therapy in the past, but they were not ready to discuss this complex history.

In the group, George often invited others to add to his image or wanted to collaborate. His work in this space didn't feel solely his own or seem as if he had a strong sense of ownership over his art. At times George was distracted by others and, as he explained, 'feeds off others' creativity and their energy' in his images. I wasn't sure if this related to George's diagnosis, as patients with psychosis fail to develop a structure of the mind that enables relationships with self, others and the social world (Patterson *et al.* 2011). I then began to question the impact of his family history on this behaviour, and whether it emphasized George's lack of boundaries and understanding of self.

From what I had seen of George, he seemed to struggle to understand what was appropriate and what wasn't, who had the capacity to give consent and who didn't, and what was his and what wasn't. This new information made me query his behaviour in relation to his family. I wondered how George perceived his family history and dynamic.

Did he know from a young age, or was it discussed once and never acknowledged further? I questioned how confusing this could have been for him growing up or having found out as an adult.

I started to reflect on whether the group was helpful for George, or if it served a more social purpose, or a way to avoid self-reflection. This was when I began to consider individual therapy for George alongside the group sessions.

Individual art therapy

It was often reported on the ward round that George lacked insight, independence and motivation, therefore my aim for individual sessions with George was for him to gain greater independence and insight into his behaviours and feelings. I felt that individual sessions could be a way of helping George to be more independent, and I decided that I wouldn't make art alongside George in that hope that the focus would be on him and his making.

At first, George seemed hesitant and took a lot of time with artmaking decisions. He invited me to choose with him, but I would redirect this back, explaining how this time was for him to create and that I was interested in seeing what he was going to make. There was a bit of an adjustment period as George familiarized himself with the slightly changed format of the sessions.

Figure 17.3: George's felt-tip image (see colour section)

In George's third individual session he made Figure 17.3. This session came some days after the death of George's female friend. He seemed sombre as he discussed his feelings towards his friend's death, drugs and ways of loving: ways of loving in terms of different types of love and in various relationships; for example, with friends, family or more of a romantic love. George described the face in the image as being his friend moving up towards heaven. She was level with the cross and he saw her as being on a par with Christ. George described himself as being the pink curtained section underneath the cross. He described how he was down on Earth as she passed up to Heaven. The left section he named the 'mountain of life'. Near the end of the session George made the right section which he named the 'bookmark'. This consisted of colourful lines, which he then shaded over. Some of these lines are still evident in this image and he described them as 'exposed wires'. This was the first time I had seen George create a human figure in his images. When explaining the whole image George said, 'The death of my friend is a bookmark moment in my mountain of life.' This session had been the first time George connected his image to himself and his feelings and left sections untouched. This image felt like a tribute to his friend and a way for him to process his feelings. There was a sense of vulnerability as he 'exposed his wires' by sharing the meaning behind this image.

In this same session, George noticed the sound of a nurse outside the room, and this led on to a conversation about how George finds the staff attractive. George also said he was 'trying to be responsible'. In supervision, we acknowledged how George said this in a non-direct way and we understood his comment to mean that he will not overstep the mark. I tried to explore this with him, but he moved on to a conversation about love and different types of love. Kavaler-Adler (2006) describes her patient mourning for a friend as the beginning of their mourning in treatment. Her patient mourned parts of themselves as they mourned for their friend and it seemed to me that this was evidenced in George. As he acknowledged his behaviour with staff, this gain in insight seemed to be a way for him to say goodbye to his previous ways of behaving. The sadness of Kavaler-Adler's patient allowed them to open up to feelings towards their therapist, and again this seemed to resonate. George opened up to his feelings of love towards the staff, his family, his friend and perhaps towards me also.

Figure 17.4: George's second pastel image

In George's fifth session he created the image in Figure 17.4. When George used the chalk pastels, he was being cautious not to mark the surrounding page. At the beginning of making this image, George asked, 'Can you tell that I'm feeling sad?' George explained that when he was sad, he realized he got a lot closer to the paper and that his artmaking was more intimate. When he was happier or more energetic, he said that he was further from the page, faster and more spontaneous with his marks. George then reflected on the difference between the group sessions and individual sessions. He described how he got distracted in the group and sometimes sat watching others rather than making his own image. In the individual sessions he felt that he could focus more on his own images. I will refer to these comments whilst evaluating change shortly.

George continued to speak of his loss in this session. He said that his friend loved his family and that they loved her. George asked me whether I had met his family and explained that if his family and I met, we would both love each other. At the time, I felt quite uncomfortable as it sounded like he wanted me to meet his parents and that as they loved his friend, they would maybe love me too. This idea of meeting his parents didn't feel like he was suggesting a professional meeting, but it reminded me of a stage in a relationship where the next step is for the stranger (myself) to be brought into the other partner's circle for approval. I felt unsure whether he was comparing me to his friend who had met his family, or like in an earlier session, he was discussing different ways of loving. The love being referred to by George could have been a love of acceptance, a familial love when others begin to see the effect a person has on them, noticing a change in their mood as a result of the relationship, or loving a person for how they make another feel. It felt like George had accepted me, began to trust in our relationship and felt his family would accept me too. That they could accept or trust that George and I had a trusting relationship and that in turn, George saw they could be part of this too. Covington (2006) is a psychoanalyst who describes that for the analysis to work, a patient does have to fall in love with the analyst. She then explains that the analyst has to allow themselves to be loved by the patient and that they should respond with warmth and understanding. A love built from the trusting relationship encourages the patient to be open with the therapist.

Every so often, George would be complimentary towards me in these sessions; he commented on how proud my parents must be of me, on my eyes and my awareness of his feelings. The art therapist is a consistent and reliable presence, who shows continued interest (Brooker *et al.* 2007). In the individual sessions George always seems surprised and impressed when I'd help him name a feeling, link back to something he had said in a previous session, or acknowledge his feelings at all.

Evaluation

Supervision is a space to help self-reflect, contain and understand feelings and consider boundaries (Innes 1996). In supervision at university, and with my placement supervisor, I was encouraged to reflect on my countertransference and the therapeutic relationship. When erotic transference is present the therapist often has to confront their own attitudes and values relating to issues of sexuality (McKenzie, Chisholm and Murray 2000). I was able to reflect on my attitude towards sexuality and on my countertransference in personal therapy.

My supervisor's previous work with George enabled us to compare her experiences with mine and identify change. We noticed that through individual sessions George gained insight into his behaviour and feelings. His artmaking changed as he became more independent and confident. George was leaving parts of his images untouched and trying to keep the pages clean, seeming to have become more independent and confident in his art-making decisions. This varied from how George engaged in Figure 17.1. George's images often began as separate symbols that became joined and linked as the session progressed, normally filling the whole page. As George became more confident in his decision-making and more independent, he began to also link his images to himself.

My feelings of control as the art therapist changed positively as I moved from group to individual sessions with George. The therapist has more power than the patient, and when the patient shares their feelings and anxieties, this in turn empowers the therapist (Schaverien 1995). In the group, I often found George hard to contain and the multi-way of relating to group members, myself and everyone's images were a distraction away from George looking at himself. In Brooker's guidelines for art therapy with people who are prone to psychotic states, they suggest that art therapists focus on the process of artmaking as a joint physical and visual experience (Brooker *et al.* 2007). Following these guidelines with George could have evoked arousal and have been a distraction. Instead, by abstaining from artmaking in individual sessions I became more of a witness to George's artmaking. These sessions felt like a way of encouraging George to have a two-way relationship with his artwork (Schaverien 1995). Schaverien also explains two-way relating as a form of self-affirmation. This shift in my own experience also provided me with the confidence to redirect any discomforting remarks in response to erotic transference. By my declining George's invitations to help him with his images, he seemed to begin to establish a sense of self as an embodied person (Schaverien 1995). As I became more aware and secure in my role as the therapist, there was also a sense of him becoming more aware and confident with himself. This way of relating and parallel process felt useful for both of us.

In both the open art therapy group and individual art therapy sessions George discussed his desire for an affectionate relationship. George and I were in a therapeutic relationship in which the patient was encouraged to confide their thoughts and feelings to a woman who has a more accepting and nurturing role (Guttman 2006). A therapeutic relationship isn't an affectionate sexual relationship, but intimate relationships are part of an art therapist's work (Schaverien 1995). At first, the erotic transference felt like an expression of feelings of sexuality; however, this seems to have developed into feelings of love. As mentioned earlier, erotic transference may be embodied in George's images and artmaking, and art therapy provided him with an appropriate relationship and medium with which to explore these feelings. The NICE (National Institute for Health and Care Excellence) guidelines say art therapy helps a schizophrenic patient experience themselves differently and find new ways of relating to others (NICE 2009). The individual sessions gave George an experience of a relationship where he could 'be' and develop a sense of his own identity without it needing to be sexual.

Conclusion

In contrast to the recommendations in the literature by Brooker *et al.* (2007) and Marshall-Tierney (2014), this case study argues that individual art therapy without the art therapist making art alongside is best for this patient. The art therapist not making art provided George with a space to develop his sense of self. There have been notable changes in his behaviour, independence and confidence. These were noticed by how George started to make art more independently, link his artworks to his own feelings and reflect on these in sessions. As mentioned earlier, George said he became distracted in the group, watching others rather than making his own images. George also observed that in individual sessions he felt he could focus on his own images more. George began to identify these differences himself, which I feel confirms my conclusion. Individual art therapy enabled George to gain insight and reflect on difficult and intimate feelings. The therapeutic relationship and George's relationship with artmaking provided him with an appropriate platform to express feelings of sexuality and love.

References
Brooker, J., Gilroy, A. and Goldsmiths College (2007) *The Use of Work in Art Psychotherapy with People Who Are Prone to Psychotic States: An Evidence-Based Clinical Practice Guideline.* London: Goldsmiths, University of London.

Covington, C. (2006) 'Purposive Aspects of the Erotic Transference.' In J. Schaverien (ed.) *Gender, Countertransference and the Erotic Transference: Perspectives from Analytical Psychology and Psychoanalysis* (pp.90–103). Hove: Routledge.

Damarell, B. (1998) 'Grandma, what a big beard you have! An exploration of the patient's reaction to a change in the art therapist's appearance.' *Inscape 3*, 2, 63–72.

Guttman, H. A. (2006) 'Sexual Issues in the Transference and Countertransference Between Female Therapist and Male Patient.' In J. Schaverien (ed.) *Gender, Countertransference and the Erotic Transference: Perspectives from Analytical Psychology and Psychoanalysis* (pp.212–239). Hove: Routledge.

Innes, R. (1996) 'An Art Therapist's "Inside View".' In C. Cordess and M. Cox (eds) *Forensic Psychotherapy: Crime, Psychodynamics and the Offender Patient* (pp.547–553). London: Jessica Kingsley Publishers.

Kavaler-Adler, S. (2006) 'Mourning and Erotic Transference.' In J. Schaverien (ed.) *Gender, Countertransference and the Erotic Transference: Perspectives from Analytical Psychology and Psychoanalysis* (pp.104–122). Hove: Routledge.

Marshall-Tierney, A. (2014) 'Making art with and without patients in acute settings.' *International Journal of Art Therapy 19*, 3, 96–106.

McKenzie, K., Chisholm, D. and Murray, G. (2000) 'Working with sex offenders who have a learning disability.' *Inscape 5*, 2, 62–69.

MIND, National Association for Mental Health (2012) *Mind Rights Guide 6: Community Care and Aftercare.* Accessed on 20/4/2020 at www.mind.org.uk/media/46886/mind-guide-community-care-and-afterare_6_2012.pdf

Moon, C. (2002) *Studio Art Therapy: Cultivating the Artist Identity in the Art Therapist.* London: Jessica Kingsley Publishers.

Morter, S. (1997) 'Where Words Fail: A Meeting Place.' In K. Killick and J. Schaverien (eds) *Art, Psychotherapy and Psychosis* (pp.219–236). London: Routledge.

NICE (2009) *Schizophrenia: Core Interventions in the Treatment and Management of Schizophrenia in Adults in Primary and Secondary Care.* London: NICE.

Patterson, S., Crawford, M.J., Ainsworth, E. and Waller, D. (2011) 'Art therapy for people diagnosed with schizophrenia: Therapists' views about what changes, how and for whom.' *International Journal of Art Therapy 16*, 2, 70–80.

Rodgers, N.M. (2011) 'Intimate boundaries: Therapists' perception and experience of erotic transference within the therapeutic relationship.' *Counselling and Psychotherapy Research 11*, 4, 266–274.

Schaverien, J. (1995) *Desire and the Female Therapist: Engendered Gazes in Psychotherapy and Art Therapy.* London: Routledge.

Stott, S. (2018) 'Copying and attunement: The search for creativity in a secure setting.' *International Journal of Art Therapy 23*, 1–2, 45–51.

List of contributors

DAWN BATCUP

Dawn works clinically using dance movement psychotherapy with adults in mental health and forensic settings. She has worked on the Goldsmiths MA DMP and Foundation since their inception. Dawn completed her DMP training at the Laban in 1998 and was soon employed as a DMP in mental health. She has completed training in supervision and supervises DMPs, DMP trainees, NHS multi-disciplinary teams, counsellors and nurses on an individual and group basis. Dawn is also a mentalization-based therapy practitioner, an IGA group work practitioner and a dually qualified nurse with an undergraduate BSc in Anthropology/Sociology.

KATE BURN

Kate Burn is an HCPC registered art therapist specializing in work with children and young people who have been sexually abused. She qualified with an MA in Art Therapy from the University of Hertfordshire in 2011 and has recently been awarded an MA with distinction in 'working with children, young people and their families; a psychoanalytic, observational approach' with the Tavistock and Portman NHS Trust. Kate has recently become a scholar with the UK Centre of Expertise on Child Sexual Abuse, linking up with them on her clinical work.

EVA MARIE CHADWICK

Eva Marie Chadwick is a dramatherapist and clinical supervisor working in a forensic mental health hospital in the private sector. Eva Marie has a background as an actor and director and has developed applied theatre and film projects alongside therapeutic work. She has pioneered dramatherapy services within schools for young people with emotional and behavioural difficulties, Early Intervention in Psychosis service and offenders transitioning into the community. She is a Level 3 Lifespan Integration Therapist.

STEVE COBBETT
Steve Cobbett is the senior therapist (and a music therapist) at Beckmead Family of Schools in Croydon and manages the therapy team there. Beckmead is a specialist provision for young people with social, emotional and mental health difficulties who have not coped with mainstream education. Steve has worked in this field since 2004 and has worked with several boys who have been sexual offenders.

JESSICA COLLIER
Jessica Collier is an art psychotherapist and clinical supervisor working for the NHS in the criminal justice system with women in prison. Jessica is co-editor of the *International Journal of Forensic Psychotherapy* and sits on the executive board of the International Association for Forensic Psychotherapy. She lectures widely both nationally and internationally. Her published work focuses on forensic art psychotherapy in connection with gender, trauma, violence and unconscious re-enactments. Jessica has contributed to the training of art psychotherapists as visiting lecturer on the MA programme at the University of Hertfordshire and is a senior lecturer at the University of Roehampton. She is co-convenor of the Forensic Arts Therapies Advisory Group and has a private supervision practice.

MAXINE DANIELS
Dr Maxine Daniels is a UKCP-registered psychotherapist, supervisor and senior trainer. She holds a BSc (Hons) in psychology, a postgraduate Diploma in Psychodrama Psychotherapy and a Doctorate in Psychotherapy. She has over 25 years' experience working as an external consultant, trainer, supervisor and clinician with the prison service and in high-secure hospitals, including Broadmoor. She has worked in America, Finland and Hong Kong and has presented at many international conferences such as ATSA and IATSO. Maxine is an academic advisor at Metanoia for the Doctorate in Psychotherapy by Professional Studies and a senior trainer at the London Centre for Psychodrama.

THIJS DE MOOR
Thijs de Moor is a senior registered art psychotherapist holding a degree in Art Therapy (HAN CTO, 1997, Nijmegen), Professional Education (HAN

VO, 2005, Nijmegen) and an MSc Art Psychotherapy (Queen Margaret University, Edinburgh, 2015). For over 20 years he has worked in mental health care and forensic psychiatry offering art therapeutic treatment for patients suffering from schizophrenia and eating and personality disorders, both in the Netherlands and in Belgium. Since 2001, he has worked as a senior lecturer and international coordinator at the Institute of Arts Therapies and Applied Psychology, HAN University of Applied Sciences, Netherlands. On a frequent basis, he lectures as an invited lecturer in Art Psychotherapy at several art therapy education institutions throughout Europe and the USA. Thijs is a founding member of the European Federation of Art Therapy established in April 2018 in Brussels. Thijs is member of the Council and chairs the Conference Committee for the European Federation of Art Therapy.

LUCY GIBSON-HILL
Lucy Gibson-Hill qualified as an art psychotherapist from Goldsmiths in 2010. Having been in continuous employment as an art therapist mostly concentrating on mental health, offending and trauma, Lucy is now employed in two NHS roles – as art psychotherapist at a low-secure unit in North East London, and as manager and clinician of a neurodevelopmental pathway in a CAMHS in West Essex.

ANNA GREEN
After a year-long programme studying art at Bezalel Academy of Art and Design, Israel, and completing a degree in Fine Art from Nottingham Trent University in 2014, Anna went on to complete her Master's in Art Therapy at the University of Hertfordshire. Since graduating from the latter in 2016, Anna has been working as an art therapist with children and families in schools and hospices, whilst more recently working in adult mental health. From December 2018, Anna began working at an adult mental health rehabilitation inpatient unit, practising both art therapy and mentalization-based therapy. Alongside these positions, Anna is a practising artist and curator with an interest in an art therapist's use of artmaking alone and alongside patients. She has participated in exhibitions in the UK and abroad at galleries such as the Freud Museum, Tate Modern Turbine Hall and Pratt Institute, New York.

KATIE GREENWOOD
Katie Greenwood is a dramatherapist, clinical supervisor and reflective practice facilitator. She previously worked for Geese Theatre before qualifying as a dramatherapist. Since qualifying, Katie has specialized in working in forensic

settings, both in prison therapeutic communities and secure hospitals. This includes St Andrew's Healthcare, where the case study in this book was based. Katie has also worked with children and young people in education settings, as a guest lecturer and reflective practice facilitator for the Clinical and Forensic Psychology Doctorate course at the University of Birmingham, and as a senior therapist for a national charity that works with people affected by trauma. Katie currently works as a lead therapist in forensic mental health in the independent sector.

SIMON HASTILOW

Simon Hastilow has worked with offenders since 1995 in various settings. He currently works on the sex offender wing at HMP Grendon, a therapeutic community prison. He also works in an NHS medium-secure unit and is a senior lecturer at Roehampton University, teaching on the MA Art Psychotherapy.

MARIAN HUSTED

Marian Husted MScAT, CZT received her Master's in Art Therapy from Queen Margaret University in Edinburgh, Scotland in 2006. She worked in hospice care for all ages at the Marie Curie Hospice and the Royal Edinburgh Psychiatric Hospital with anorexic youth. Marian also worked with inner-city African American youth at Riverside Psychiatric Hospital in Washington, DC. She has been working at Coalinga State Hospital since 2007, a forensic-psychiatric facility in California that treats civilly committed sex offenders. She is a supervising rehabilitation therapist and Certified Zentangle Teacher.

THEMIS KYRIAKIDOU

Themis Kyriakidou BA, MA FA, MA ATh, MSc FPC is an art therapist who has worked with sexually harmful behaviour and sexual offending in a youth-offending team and with adults with learning disabilities in a low-secure unit. She has also furthered her studies with an MSc in Forensic Psychology and Criminology. Her approach on the treatment of sex offenders is based on her academic and clinical knowledge of working with both young people and adults.

RONALD P.M.H LAY

Ronald's extensive mental health career spans 23+ years in Canada, the US and Singapore. He is program leader of the first postgraduate art therapy training program in Southeast Asia, at LASALLE College of the Arts,

Singapore. He presents globally, maintaining a strong interconnected profile through leadership and consultation of innovative community arts projects, programme development and humanitarian collaborative engagement. His drive for sustained excellence in mental health has been recognized by the California State Legislature, and he maintains credentials and professional memberships with AATA, ANZACATA, ATAS and the ATCB.

MARIAN LIEBMANN

Marian Liebmann has worked in art therapy with offenders, with women's groups and community groups, and for 19 years in the Inner-City Support and Recovery Team (adult mental health), where she developed work on anger issues. She teaches and lectures on art therapy at several universities in the UK and Ireland. She has run art therapy workshops in several European countries, as well as the US and Africa. She also works in restorative justice, mediation and conflict resolution. She has written or edited 12 books, including *Art Therapy in Practice*; *Art Therapy with Offenders*; *Arts Approaches to Conflict*; *Restorative Justice: How It Works*; and *Art Therapy and Anger*. In 2013 she was awarded OBE for services to art therapy and mediation.

ALICE MYLES

Alice Myles is an art psychotherapist practising in forensic and adult mental healthcare. She also has a private practice in South London. She is studying Lacanian psychoanalysis at CFAR (Centre for Freudian Analysis and Research).

AMY PFENNING

Amy Pfenning MPS, ATR, CZT earned her Master's in Art Therapy from Pratt Institute in 1999. She works at Coalinga State Hospital in California, a treatment facility for sex offenders known as sexually violent predators. Amy has worked at the hospital since 2005 where she manages the hospital's Art Centre and provides art therapy supervision. She has presented at various conferences including the American Art Therapy Association conference, the California Coalition on Sexual Offending conference, the Institute on Violence, Abuse, and Trauma conference, and the Forensic Mental Health Association of California conference. She is a Certified Zentangle Teacher.

PREETHA RAMASUBRAMANIAN

Preetha Ramasubramanian MA DMT, MSc Psy, PG Dip (Spl. Ed) is a qualified dance movement psychotherapist, with a distinction in MA DMT from Goldsmiths, University of London. Preetha founded Kinesthetics – a centre for DMT in India that works with a varied population. She is an advisory board member for the Creative Movement Therapy Association of India and part of their core team that designs the curriculum, teaches and supervises in their diploma and certification courses. She is a visiting lecturer for the diploma programme in Expressive Arts Therapy, WCC, University of Madras, India.

KATE SMITH
Kate Smith has worked within forensic mental health as a dramatherapist and reflective practice lead for over a decade. She is a senior lecturer at the University of Derby and a Fellow of the Higher Education Academy. She is programme lead for the Dramatherapy MA programme and is an active participant of the BADth training subcommittee. Her most recent chapter is Smith, K. and Taylor, J. (2019) 'Tutor-led peer supervision groups within higher education.' In J. Taylor and C. Holmwood (eds) *Learning as a Creative and Developmental Process in Higher Education*. Oxford: Routledge.

KATE SNOWDEN
Kate has been practising as a dance movement psychotherapist for eight years. Kate currently works for a children's social care service supporting families and the parent–child relationship. Kate has provided dance movement psychotherapy in a number of settings, including working for a charity providing therapy and case management for individuals with learning disabilities and autism who have experienced abuse and trauma. Kate has worked in various mental health settings, including an adolescent therapeutic community, an adolescent assessment and treatment unit, CAMHS community services and with adults in a residential therapeutic setting. Kate is a registered clinical supervisor and private practitioner.

Index